the little PC book

Third Edition

by Lawrence J. Magid

Edited by Darcy DiNucci

Illustrated by John Grimes

Peachpit Press

The Little PC Book, Third Edition
by Lawrence J. Magid

Peachpit Press
1249 Eighth Street
Berkeley, CA 94710
800/283-9444
510/524-2178
510/524-2221 (fax)

Find us on the World Wide Web at:
http://www.peachpit.com

Peachpit Press is a division of Addison Wesley Longman.

Editor and packager: Darcy DiNucci
Project editor: Becky Morgan
Illustrator: John Grimes
Production coordinator: Mimi Heft
Copyeditor: Tema Goodwin
Compositor: David Van Ness
Cover design: TMA Ted Mader + Associates
Interior design: Chuck Routhier

ISBN 0-201-35366-0

9 8 7 6 5 4 3 2 1

Printed and bound in the United States of America

To my mother, Fae Magid.
She taught me the value of asking questions.

Acknowledgments

It would have been impossible for me to take on this or any other large task without the constant support and patience of my wife, Patti. My children, Katherine and William, deserve credit for helping with the Internet and children's software sections and for reminding me that there are things in life that are (a lot) more important than computers.

Nancy Ruenzel, publisher of Peachpit Press, and Peachpit's founder Ted Nace have been a tremendous help. I've worked with larger publishing companies, but never a better one. My editor, Darcy DiNucci, did an incredible job crafting, reshaping, and, at times, rewriting. Thanks also to John Grimes for his wonderful illustrations.

Don Sellers, author of the Peachpit books *Zap: 25 Ways Your Computer Can Hurt You and What You Can Do About It* and *25 Steps to Safe Computing*, reviewed the sections of this book having to do with computer safety. His extensive knowledge of the subject was a great help.

A special thanks to Susan Harrow of Harrow Communications for helping to spread the word.

Preface

The Little PC Book covers the absolute basics of using a personal computer that runs Windows 95 or Windows 98. It is meant to get you up and running with your PC, without bogging you down in technical details.

When you're done with this book, you should feel comfortable talking to a computer salesperson about how much "RAM" you need, using a new piece of software, or facing those strange icons on your computer screen. You'll learn what the jargon that surrounds computers really means, and you'll find out where to get help when you need it.

The Little PC Book is divided into five parts:

Part 1: Getting Oriented introduces you to the world of PCs. Here, you'll learn just what people mean when they say things like "Windows," "IBM compatible," and "applications."

Part 2: Putting Together a System describes the different parts that make up a PC, what each is for, and how to choose the one that's best for you.

Part 3: Working With Windows is an introduction to the rules of using Microsoft Windows, the software that controls how almost everything works on your PC. You'll learn how to give commands, open applications and files, and carry out the other basic tasks that will help you control your PC and get your work done.

Part 4: Exploring the Internet shows you how to use Internet Explorer, Outlook Express, and the other tools included in Windows 98 for exploring the Net. (If you have Windows 95, don't worry; you can explore the Net, too, by getting these applications separately.)

Part 5: Stocking Up on Software tells how to pick just the software you need. It sorts out the different categories of software and helps you choose exactly what's right for you.

The book is designed to make finding the information you need as easy as possible, and to make it easy to learn the jargon that clutters the world of computers. I've boldfaced new terms as they're introduced, and anytime you see a boldface term, you can look it up in the glossary that's at the end of the book.

Now, before you go any further, take note: This book covers Windows-based PCs, not Macintoshes. (If you want to know the difference, take a quick look at Chapter 3.) If you've gotten this book by accident and want to know about Macs instead, you can return the book to Peachpit Press or exchange it for a copy of *The Little Mac Book*. (Peachpit's address is on the copyright page.)

You should also know that I've assumed that the readers of this book will be using either Windows 95 or Windows 98. (If you don't know whether this means you, turn to Chapter 4.) That's the vast majority of PC users, though, so chances are good that this book covers your PC.

Ready? OK, let's get started.

Table of Contents

Getting Oriented

one

Why Learn About Computers?

You've gotten along so far without knowing much about computers. Why start now?

1. You've just bought a computer, and now you need to find out how to use it.

2. Your job depends on it.

OKAY, POP,
YOU TRY
IT NOW.

ME?

3. You've decided to buy a computer for your home so that you and your kids can have access to all the useful and fun stuff you've been hearing about. Now you need to know what to get, how to equip it, and what you can do with it once you've plugged it in.

4. You've heard about all the great things you can do on the World Wide Web and the Internet, and you've decided you want to get a computer that will let you into that world.

5. You're starting to feel like your life is a little bit out of control, and you've heard that a computer is a good way to get organized and get more done in less time.

6. You're using a computer at work and know your way around a program or two, but now you want to get to know a bit more about what the PC can do for you.

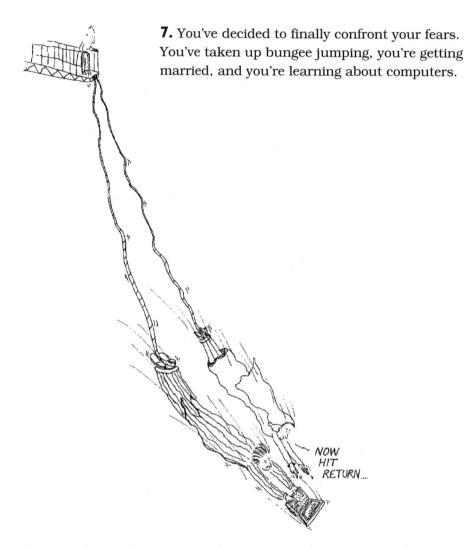

7. You've decided to finally confront your fears. You've taken up bungee jumping, you're getting married, and you're learning about computers.

NOW HIT RETURN....

There are lots of reasons to learn about computers. Yours may not be listed here, but it's probably a good one. The truth is, computers aren't going to go away. And they can, in fact, help you organize your finances, plug into everything that's happening on the Internet, and work more efficiently. More than that, they're getting a lot easier to use than they used to be, and these days, they're surprisingly affordable.

I think you've made the right choice.

How Is a Computer Like a CD Player?

Learning how to use a PC isn't as difficult as you might think.

2

The first thing to remember is that you don't need to know how a computer works; you just need to know how to use it. It's like a radio, TV, VCR, CD player, or any other piece of equipment. When you use a CD player, you don't think about laser beams, changer mechanisms, or music-sampling frequencies. You just want to play the music.

A PC is similar. With a VCR, you play videotapes. With a CD player, you play CDs. With a PC, you play **application programs** or **software**. Just as some folks compose their own music, some people write their own software. But being able to create programs from scratch is not at all necessary. Instead, you'll just buy the software you need, just as you buy the music you want to hear on your CD player. You don't need to know how a computer works; you just need to know how to use it.

With a computer, just as with a CD player, you'll need to know just enough about your system so that you can buy one, set it up, turn it on and off, and play the software. You'll also want to become familiar with the different kinds of software you can get and how to buy what you want. This book will tell you all those things—and no more, because that's everything you'll really need to know in order to buy and use a computer.

Of course, if you'd like to find out more, great. This book will give you a good start and provide basic reference information that you can come back to down the line.

The Two Kinds of Personal Computers

3

"MACs"
(APPLE MACINTOSH)

"PCs"
(WINDOWS)

When you go into a computer store, you'll see computers of all sizes and shapes, from many different manufacturers. You'll see desktop machines and laptop machines, from Toshiba, IBM, Compaq, Packard Bell, and countless other companies. Don't worry about it. There are really only two kinds of personal computers: computers designed to run Windows (or "PCs") and Macintosh computers (or "Macs").

Technically, both Macintoshes and Windows-compatible computers are PCs—personal computers. When most people say "PC," though, they're generally referring to a Windows machine (as I am in this book).

Let's get back to the CD player metaphor we used in Chapter 2. Computers, like CD players, are classified by the kind of software they play, not by who makes them. If you want to play standard CDs, you can get a CD player from Magnavox, Sony, Zenith, RCA—whichever has the features you want for the best price. If you want to play those old vinyl records, however, you'll need a different kind of device. It's the same with computers. All PCs play the same kind of software. Macintoshes run a different kind.

Most of today's personal computers are designed to run **Microsoft Windows** and Windows software. Unless the machine you're looking at has an Apple logo on it, it's probably a Windows machine.

Windows machines are called by many different names: IBM compatibles (because they run the same kind of software that personal computers from IBM run), **Wintel** machines (because they run Windows and use an Intel or Intel-compatible processor), or just PCs. And no matter what company they're made by—Toshiba, Compaq, Dell, Gateway, Hewlett-Packard—they work the same way and can run the same software.

In order to run the same software, all these computers have one important thing in common: They're all based on the same kind of **processor** (sometimes called the **central processing unit**, or **CPU**). (I'll talk more about processors in Chapter 10.) PCs are based on processors made by Intel or by other companies that have adopted Intel's technology. Most machines today have some version of Intel's **Pentium** processor or a chip from another company that's compatible with the Pentium. Older CPUs that you might hear about include the 486, the 386, and the 286.

The other personal computers on the market today are **Macintoshes**, made by Apple Computer. They use entirely different processors, called **PowerPC** processors, and require software made especially for them.

You might have heard about other types of computers, with names like Amiga, Atari, and Apple II, but you won't run into them in a computer store. They are older kinds of personal computers and are now largely obsolete. You also might hear people talk about **workstations**. Sometimes that term is used for a personal computer, but usually, it refers to very powerful desktop computers from companies like Sun Microsystems and Silicon Graphics, which are used primarily by people who work at NASA, do special effects for movies, or do other things that require a lot of extra processing power and speed.

Of course, the term "computer" is pretty generic, and it can also be used to describe other kinds of devices, including hand-held (or **palmtop**) systems like the Palm III from 3Com, or even the systems in cars that determine when to inflate the airbags. But here we're talking about desktop computers, where Windows rules.

Computers running Microsoft Windows are so common (more than 90 percent of all computers sold are Windows machines) that the U.S. Justice Department has filed an antitrust suit against Microsoft, charging it with monopolistic business practices. Personally, I agree that something should be done to protect consumers and the computer industry from being dominated by a single company. but that doesn't stop me from using, writing about, and recommending Windows PCs. The fact that there are so many of them out there means there's lots of software to run on them, and just as important, you'll have no trouble finding lots of information to help you use them.

Now, assuming you've settled on a Windows PC and not a Macintosh, let's get on with the book.

What Is Windows?

Microsoft Windows is a PC's operating system: the software **4**
that controls what you see when you turn your computer on each
time and how all other programs will work. Any PC you buy will
come with it already installed.

The newest computers will usually have the latest version of
Windows, called **Windows 98**, which looks like this:

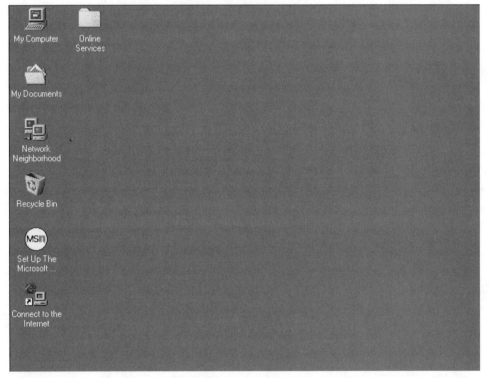

The Windows 98 desktop provides a graphical user interface for interacting with the files
and programs on your computer.

What you see is a **graphical user interface (GUI)**. It uses **icons**
(little pictures that represent the objects you'll be working with, such
as disks and files), which you choose and manipulate with a **mouse**.
(I'll get into just what these things are and how you work with them
later in the book.)

Windows 98 was released in June 1998, so if you're using a computer that's a bit older, you might be running **Windows 95**, which looks almost like Windows 98 but not quite.

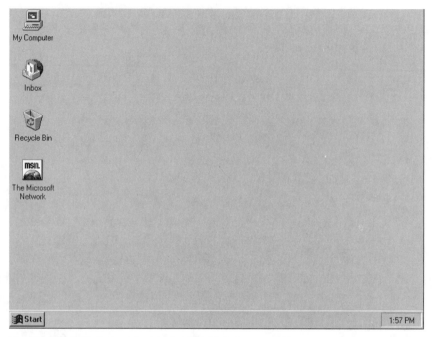

The Windows 95 desktop looks a lot like the Windows 98 desktop, and for the most part, the two operating systems work the same, too.

If you use a PC at work, you might be using yet another version of Windows called **Windows NT**, which looks and acts pretty much like Windows 95 or Windows 98 (depending on the version of NT you have) but is designed primarily for use in business environments. (It has special features for **networking**—connecting together computers in workgroups.)

The good news is that Windows 98 and Windows 95 are designed to use the same software so, for all practical purposes, they're really the same operating system. Windows NT runs most, but not all, of the same programs as Windows 95 and Windows 98. When I use the term "Windows" in this book, it will apply to all of those versions. (When there are any special considerations for different versions, I'll let you know.)

If you have an old computer (one that came out before August 1995 and was never upgraded), your computer might run an older version of Windows called **Windows 3.1** (or Windows for Workgroups), which looks a bit different.

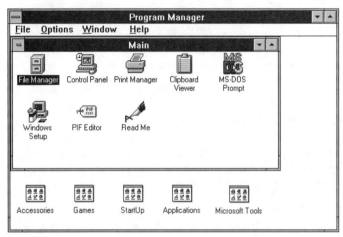

Windows 3.1 also uses icons, which you manipulate using a mouse, but it looks quite different from Windows 95.

And *really* old computers that don't even have *that* version of Windows, run under a basic system called **DOS** (pronounced "doss"). If you're running DOS you won't see any icons or windows on screen. Once your computer finishes starting up, the screen will be almost blank, looking something like this:

If you are only running DOS, you'll see an almost blank screen, showing only the DOS prompt, at which you type commands.

Should You Upgrade to Windows 98?

If you have Windows 95 you may wonder whether it's worth your while (and your $90 or so) to upgrade to Windows 98. Frankly, it's not that big a deal. As this book will show, there aren't all that many differences between Windows 95 and Windows 98.

One of the most important differences between Windows 95 and Windows 98 is that Windows 98 has some extra built-in features for using the Internet. But you can do pretty much the same things with Windows 95 and Microsoft's Internet browser (called Internet Explorer), which comes with it. (I'll talk about those features and Internet Explorer in Chapter 41.)

Windows and icons under Windows 98 also look a little different—I think better—than they do in Windows 95. And Windows 98 has some other differences that are "under the hood." Windows 98 is a bit less prone to **crash**, that is, stop working for no apparent reason. It loads faster on some machines and it shuts down faster when you turn off your computer. Programs, too, are likely to load a bit faster than they are with Windows 95.

All these advantages make Windows 98 better than Windows 95, but not remarkably better. It's an evolutionary—not revolutionary—improvement. I'll talk about the differences as we go on. You might decide that the added features are important to you, but I don't think you need to rush out to upgrade if you don't already have Windows 98.

If your computer is running Windows 3.1 or DOS, it's really time to think about upgrading your computer and getting Windows 98. (You can get it for around $90 at any of the software sources I talk about in Chapter 48.) Most new software requires Windows to run, and an increasing number of new programs require Windows 95 or Windows 98. Besides, these versions of Windows are a lot easier to use than Windows 3.1 or DOS.

Sometimes, you'll hear of another version of Windows, called **Windows CE**. That's a special compact edition of Windows, made to run on hand-held and other special-purpose computers. Windows CE looks and works a lot like Windows 95 and Windows 98, but it does not run the same software. Programs that run on Windows CE must be made specially by the software company to work on CE systems.

Other operating systems that you might encounter at work or in other places include **Unix**, **Linux**, and IBM's **OS/2**. These operating systems are mostly likely to be used in corporations, government agencies, and universities.

Those are all the possibilities, but as I said at the beginning of this chapter, if you're using a PC, chances are you're using Windows, and Windows (98, 95, and NT), is what I'll be talking about when I describe how a PC works in the rest of this book.

OK. Now you know what people are talking about when they say "a Windows PC," a "Wintel machine" or an "IBM-compatible computer running Windows," and you know that that's what the rest of this book will be covering. Before we move on to how to buy and assemble such a system, though, let's find out about how to get help with your computer any time you need it.

Good Places to Get Help Learning About Your PC

5

The first thing you should know when you set out to learn about computers is that you're not on your own. There is something called the "computer community" out there, ready to give you help when you need it. Don't worry; it's a very informal group, and you don't need to sign up anywhere.

The computer community consists of all those people who, just like you, have learned about—or are just now learning about—computers, so they will understand your questions. This community has created a lot of publications and a lot of ways to get in touch with others who can help you. Here's a list of resources you can turn to at any time.

The Manual and the Help Command

Most pieces of hardware or software come with a manual, or user's guide, which is designed to be your first resource when you need to find out something about your computer or a piece of software. Some programs now come with a very small guide or no guide at all, but they have onscreen instructions.

Onscreen help is usually available quickly and easily in most Windows programs. Usually you can press the F1 key or pull down the Help menu to get instant help. Help with Windows itself is always available from a special menu, called the **Start menu**, on the desktop.

Help for Windows is available from the Windows Start menu.

A Quick Guide to Software Manuals

Over time, most manuals have evolved into a standard format that has been proven to work. Assuming the software you buy has a manual, look for these sections:

System requirements The minimum hardware and software you'll need in order to use the program are listed right up front in the user's guide, often in the installation instructions. Sometimes this information is also on the outside of the box.

Installation instructions These are usually near the front of the user's guide, or in a separate booklet, and lead you step by step through installing the software.

Tutorial Also generally near the front of the user's guide, the tutorial leads you through a practice session with the software. Sometimes the tutorial is on the CD-ROM so you view it on screen rather than read it in the manual.

Reference guide An alphabetical listing of commands. Use this when you want to know how a particular command works.

Troubleshooting A list of problems you might run up against and how to solve them. Of course, no troubleshooting section lists every possible problem, but it's the first place to look when you hit a snag.

Quick-reference card A card that summarizes the commands you're most likely to need.

Friends, Relations, and Gurus

You know who I'm talking about. That person down the hall who seems to know everything there is to know about computing. Your niece, your dad, your brother-in-law. Whoever it is, they're your best resource for

 helping you solve any little problem that's gotten you stuck. Most people are glad to help. They're honored—flattered even—to be asked to show off their knowledge, even if their level of accomplishment is only a month or two beyond your own.

The Internet

If you have a modem and access to the Internet you can probably get online help from the product's manufacturer or from fellow users online. Most software and hardware companies have Internet sites that offer help as well as information about new products and, in many cases, free updates and bug fixes.

Help can come from many sources on the Internet. In addition to manufacturers' sites, you'll find answers from sites published by computer magazines (described below) and from other users in online **forums**—places where Internet users congregate to ask questions and supply information to others. I'll talk about how to get to all those resources in Part 4.

Tech Support Lines

In addition to the tech support they post on the Internet (the best place to look first, if you can), most hardware and software manufacturers have a telephone support line you can call when you need help with their product. Some have toll-free lines, but others require you to make a long-distance call. A few, though not many, have installed 900 lines that charge you a fee for the call or require that you give them a credit card number so they can charge you for help. Most companies that sell PCs (as opposed to software) offer free support only during the warranty period. Some offer free support for as long as you need it.

When you call a software company's tech support, make sure you know the version number of the program you have, as well as exactly what hardware you're using it on, especially how much **memory** your computer has and what **expansion boards,** if any, you have installed. (You can usually tell the version number and the amount of memory installed by selecting the About command from the Help menu in any folder window. Some technical support people will require that you tell them the serial number of the program as a way to prevent "pirates"

A Bunch of Tech Support Numbers

Listed below are phone numbers and website addresses for popular hardware (computer) and software (application) companies. If the number you need isn't listed here, check the user's guide for the product you need help with or, if you have access to the Internet, visit www.larrysworld.com/resource.htm.

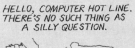

HELLO, COMPUTER HOT LINE. THERE'S NO SUCH THING AS A SILLY QUESTION.

SORRY, SIR — THAT'S A NEW ONE....

Software

Company	Phone Number	Website Address
Adobe Systems	408-536-6000	www.adobe.com
Broderbund Software	415-382-4700	www.broderbund.com
FileMaker Corp.	408-727-9004	www.filemaker.com
Corel	800-772-6735	www.corel.com
Disney Interactive	800-228-0988	www.disney.com/DisneyInteractive
Intuit	650-944-6000	www.intuit.com
The Learning Company	617-494-1200	www.learningco.com
Lotus	978-988-2500	www.lotus.com
Microsoft	425-882-8080	www.microsoft.com
Mindscape	415-897-9900	www.mindscape.com
Symantec, Norton Computing	800-441-7234	www.symantec.com

Hardware

Company	Phone Number	Website Address
Acer America	800-637-7000	www.acer.com
Compaq	800-652-6672	www.compaq.com
Dell	800-624-9896	www.dell.com
Epson America	800-922-8911	www.epson.com/northamerica.html
Gateway	800-846-2301	www.gateway.com
IBM	800-237-5511	www.ibm.com
Quantex	800-809-0349	www.quantex.com
NEC/Packard Bell	800-733-4411	www.packardbell.com
Micron	800-209-9686	www.micronpc.com
Toshiba	800-999-4273	www.csd.toshiba.com

(people who didn't buy the program) from using the service. You can sometimes find the serial number or product ID in the About command in the application's Help menu, and you'll almost always find it in the manual, on the box, or on the registration card. If you don't know the serial number, call anyway. Most tech support people are very understanding.

The tech support provider will often try to walk you through a solution over the phone, so make sure you're sitting at your computer with it turned on when you call.

And have a good book handy. Help support lines will often keep you on hold for a while. Some calling times are better than others, so once you get through the first time, ask the person to advise you about the best times to call should you need more help.

User Groups

User groups are organizations formed by users of a particular kind of computer or software. They come in all shapes and sizes, from those

that meet in large auditoriums to tiny groups that focus on a particular type of software. There's bound to be a PC user group in your town or nearby.

Most larger user groups have meetings and "special interest groups" (sometimes called "SIGs") aimed at novices. The typical group meets once or twice a month, giving users a chance to meet, ask each other questions, and see new products demonstrated by their makers.

Some have a newsletter and perhaps a site on the Internet. Typically, user groups don't charge for their help, but if you want to get the newsletter, you might be asked to pay a small fee to join.

Many user groups offer a library of free or low-cost software. Often, belonging to the group gives you access to special discounts on software, books, and other products. Many groups publish the phone numbers of people who can be called with questions about a particular software product.

Perhaps the best part about being involved in a user group is the informal opportunity it provides to ask the sorts of questions that you just can't ask anywhere else, such as: "I've taken my broken PC back to the local Fix-a-Computer three times, and they just can't seem to get it right. Is there another shop someone can recommend?"

As in most volunteer groups, a handful of stalwart souls ends up doing most of the work. If you have the time to pitch in for some of the chores, your efforts will be heartily appreciated. (You volunteer to bring refreshments one week, and the next week you find out you've been nominated for a two-year term as group secretary.) Pitching in is more than courteous, though. If you get involved, you'll find you're on the inside track for all kinds of information. Whatever you do, make friends with the newsletter editor. He or she can always use more help and may be able to get you free software—as long as you're willing to test it and write a review.

You can find a local user group by calling the User Group Locator hotline at 914-876-6678. (Call from a touch-tone phone.) You can also find them online at www.apcug.org.

Your Local Computer Store

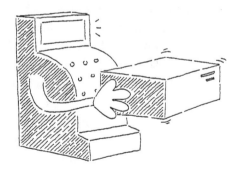

Chances are you live within driving distance of a computer store. One would hope that computer stores would be staffed by people who know a lot about computers and are willing to share that knowledge.

Maybe yes, maybe no. While some computer and software salespeople are very knowledgeable, others just act as if they are. People who sell computers certainly know more than the average novice, but they just can't know everything there is to know about what they sell.

With these caveats in mind, it's still a good idea to become friends with the folks who work at the computer store. Once you've latched on to one or two of these people, milk them for all they're worth. Call them up with questions, ask their advice, flatter their ego. And, when you need some hardware or software, make sure you buy stuff from them, too. I'm encouraging you to use these people—not exploit them.

Magazines and Newsletters

There are lots of magazines devoted to personal computing, and many of them can be understood by beginners. All of these publications carry software reviews that are written by professional computer journalists who give educated opinions. The magazines are a good place to start when you want to find out about a particular program. They are all available at any good newsstand and by subscription.

Family PC offers excellent sources of information for newcomers who plan to use their computers at home.

Another group of magazines specializes in product information. They're the place to turn to find out about hardware and software you might consider buying. *PC Magazine* is a great place to turn for encyclopedic data on any product. Its product reviews cover all the bases and then some. Another resource to check out is *Windows* magazine.

Computer Shopper is mostly a compendium of advertisements for computer hardware and software. It's a good place to find bargains. It's also a good way to build up your muscles—it's huge.

Some communities have free computer newspapers like *Computer Currents* (which has editions in San Francisco, Boston, Dallas, Chicago, Atlanta, and other cities). These papers often have some very good articles, including reviews and tips. They often bring you a local angle, and they're a good place for notices of user group meetings, training classes, and other local resources. Lest you think I'm totally objective, I must disclose that I write for *Computer Currents*, but that, of course, doesn't blind me to its true worth.

Several software companies also publish newsletters and, in some cases magazines, devoted to providing tips and current information on their software. To find them, check the company sites listed in the

Resources

Computer Currents
800-365-7773, 510-547-6800
www.currents.net
....
Computer Shopper
800-274-6384
www.zdnet.com/cshopper/
....
Family PC
800-413-9749
www.familypc.com
....
PC Magazine
800-289-0429
www.pcmag.com
....
Windows magazine
800-829-9150
www.winmag.com

box on page 19, or just search for them on the Internet. (I'll be telling you how to do that in Part 4.)

Books

Computer books can be a great aid for learning about computers in general or about a particular piece of software. If you're confused by the array of computer books at the bookstore, just ask the clerk or your friends for a recommendation.

A Pocket Guide to Computer Books

Any trip to the computer section of a bookstore will overwhelm you with choices. The books will range from beginning through advanced information, and from general topics to very specific. You can narrow your search with these guidelines.

Beginner books These are generally slimmer, under-$20 volumes with titles like *ABCs of …*, *Introduction to …*, … *Made Easy*, … *For Dummies*, *The Little* …, and so on. (You're reading one now.)

Quick-reference books These generally cost less than $10 and provide very brief explanations of the various commands or menu options of a program. They're better for looking up an occasional piece of information than for learning a program.

Tutorials These books walk you through exercises classroom-style.

Interactive tutorials These books come with a disk that leads you through lessons on your own computer.

Advanced books Titles such as *Tips & Tricks* or *Supercharging* make it clear that these books are for those who already know a program and want to get better at it.

Reference books These tend to be the super-fat books, sold by the pound. Once you know the basics of a program, they're useful for looking up features.

Dictionaries If you really want to be able to talk the talk, look for a nice, easy dictionary of common computer terms. The glossary at the back of this book is a good start. If you're interested, you can get dictionaries (thick ones) that have nothing but computer terms. Armed with a few terms like "gigabyte," "coprocessor," and "asynchronous communications," you too can be wowing the masses around the water cooler, at cocktail parties, and at your next family reunion.

Courses

Of course, for personalized help, there's no substitute for a live instructor. Computer courses are available everywhere. Start by checking out the course offerings at a local community college. There are also many private companies that offer computer training. Check your local Yellow Pages under "training" or "computer training."

Experiment

Last but not least, don't be afraid to experiment. You should know that no matter what you do on a computer, it's very difficult, if not impossible, to actually damage the hardware (unless you directly assault the machine or try to use it in the bathtub). The worst you can do is lose some data and waste some time. Pull down the menus and see what's there. In any program, try out any commands you don't know about. Watch what happens and you'll learn your software in no time.

Part 1 introduced you to your new partner, a personal computer, or "PC," running Windows. Now that you know you want one, and you're convinced you can get any help you need to use it, you're ready for one of your own.

Part 2 will show you all the parts that go into a complete system and help you put together one of your own.

Putting Together a System

What Do You Call That Thing Anyway?

6 The **monitor** (sometimes called the **display**, the screen, or the **CRT**) is the main way your computer communicates with you. This is where the computer shows you what your system is doing and what your files contain. See Chapter 15 for more on monitors.

The speakers let you hear sounds coming from your PC. These can include music (you can even play an audio CD from your CD-ROM drive), voices, and all sorts of beeps, whirrs, and other sounds that might come from your software or from Internet websites. Speakers can be next to the machine, attached to the monitor, or built into the monitor or system unit. The speakers plug directly into the **sound card** at the back of the PC. For more on sound cards and speakers, see Chapter 9.

The **expansion slots** and **ports**, at the back of the system unit, are where you can plug in extra equipment and expansion boards that enhance what the machine can do. Expansion boards can add features such as TV tuners, a faster modem, and other kinds of capabilities. For more on ports and expansion slots, see Chapter 14.

A **modem** connects your PC to the Internet, online services, or other computers over a phone line. A modem can be external to the computer or it can be inside the main system unit. Modems can also be used to send and receive faxes. For more about modems, see Chapter 18.

This box, called the **system unit**, contains the guts of your computer. It holds the **central processing unit** (**CPU**), the memory (**RAM**, or **random access memory**) chips, disk drives, and all the other electronic components that make your computer do what it does. For more about CPUs and memory, see Chapters 10 and 11.

The **hard disk** (which is inside the system unit) stores most of your data. Most of today's hard disks store two or more **gigabytes** of data (1 gigabyte equals 1,000 megabytes or just over a billion characters). For more about hard disks, see Chapter 12.

The **floppy disk drive** holds disks on which you can store programs and data that you want to get into or out of your computer. For more about floppy drives, see Chapter 13.

The **speaker**

The **modem**

The **monitor** ("THE SCREEN")

The **system unit**

The **keyboard**

Almost all computers now have a **CD-ROM** or **DVD drive**. You'll use that drive to install software and run games, encyclopedias, and other kinds of software that require lots of storage. For more on CD-ROM and DVD drives, see Chapter 13.

A *desktop PC system is made up of many parts. When you buy a PC, you can buy just the system unit, or you can buy a system that includes everything you need: a keyboard, a monitor, a mouse, a modem, and even basic software. Most of the time when you see a machine advertised, it includes everything except the monitor and printer, and in many cases, the monitor is also included in the price.*

Buying a complete system makes your choices easier, of course, but buying separate components makes it possible to get exactly what you want. If you see a complete system advertised, don't be afraid to ask if you can make changes. The worst they can do is say no. In any case, here are the basic pieces that make up a full PC system. Each one is explained in detail in the chapters that follow.

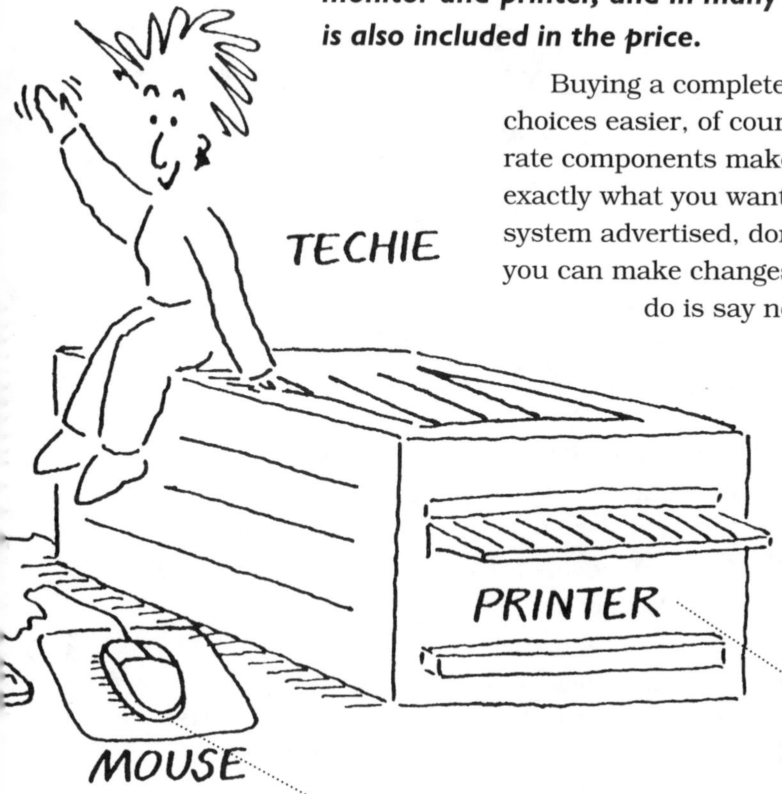

TECHIE

PRINTER

The **printer** puts the documents you create onto paper. For more on printers, see Chapter 19.

MOUSE

The **mouse** is used to move a **pointer** around your monitor's screen. The pointer lets you to show the program where you want your next action to occur. For more on mice, see Chapter 17.

The **keyboard** is one way you communicate with the computer. Its layout is similar to that of a standard typewriter keyboard. See Chapter 16 for more on keyboards.

LAPTOP POSITIONING

Laptop, or notebook, PCs combine all of a system's components into a single, portable unit. They look different, but they have essentially the same kind of components as desktop machines have—just smaller.

Notebook PCs can usually run either from a wall socket or from batteries, allowing you to take them on business trips or anywhere else you might need your computer. (I'll talk about the pluses and minuses of laptops and notebooks in Chapter 8.)

Where to Buy a PC

Used to be you bought a computer at a computer store. You still can, but now you can also buy computers at department stores like Sears and Walmart, at warehouse stores like Price Costco or Sams Club, at home electronics stores like Circuit City, or via the phone or the Internet. I haven't seen them for sale at 7-Elevens yet, but that day may come. I'll describe the advantages and drawbacks of each option here.

7

Computer Stores

Computer specialty stores tend to be the most expensive option, but the advantage is that the good stores offer a great deal of customer support. If you buy from one of those stores, you can ask their service people to preinstall your software and check to see that everything works together before you take it home. You can even ask them to deliver the computer and set it up for you, and many such stores offer extensive technical support, so you have the right to expect someone to answer all your questions. Some computer specialty stores offer their own "house brand" machine, which, in some cases, is built right there at the store. Those systems are generally cheaper than brand-name systems and can be just as reliable.

Discount Stores and Department Stores

If you know exactly what you want, and if you have such stores in your area, you can get a great deal by buying your computer at buyers' clubs like Price Costco or computer super-stores like *Micro Center* or *CompUSA*. You'll even find PCs at department stores like Sears and Montgomery Ward. You're not going to get any hand-holding at those places, but you can always call the manufacturer's technical support department if you have a problem.

Resources

CompUSA
800-366-7872
www.compusa.com

Micro Center
800-743-7537
www.microcenter.com

Stereo and Home Electronics Stores

An increasing number of stereo and home electronics stores are carrying computers right along with CD players, TV sets, and boom boxes. You take potluck when it comes to help on the sales floor. The guy or gal who knows all about hi-fidelity may not be all that helpful if you have a technical question about a computer. You may find a good deal at one of those stores, but if you decide to buy from a stereo store, make sure you get a brand name from a company that offers a national warranty and a toll-free technical support line.

Catalogs and Websites

Buying computers by mail order used to rank on the spectrum of foolishness somewhere up there with buying desert real estate by phone. But in the last few years, ordering computers from catalogs or from Internet sites has become quite popular. You can find ads for mail-order computer sellers in the major computer magazines. (Some of the best-known computer-by-mail companies are listed in the box on the next page.) These companies will build a machine to your specifications and send it via UPS or another express service, generally within a few days. Some companies offer next-day delivery for a surprisingly small extra fee.

Configuring and ordering a PC via the Web can sometimes be frustrating, but it can also be very enlightening. A number of leading PC companies, including Dell, Micron, Compaq, and Gateway have websites that let you "build your own" PC. You select every component and the website prices the system accordingly. It's a great way to comparison shop and find out what your options are. You can also play "what if" games with various components or specifications that you are considering. When you're done you can either order it directly from the website (have your credit card handy) or call the company's 800 number and order it by phone.

The best way to be sure you're dealing with a reputable company is by word of mouth. Ask other people where they bought their computer and whether they were satisfied.

One disadvantage of mail order is that you can't walk in to return items, get repairs, or ask questions. Some catalog companies offer attractive service contracts with 24-hour on-site repairs, or free pickup

Ordering a Computer Online

All of these companies let you buy a PC on the Web.

Company	Website	Phone
Compaq Computer	www.compaq.com	800-345-1518
CompUSA	www.compusa.com	800-266-7872
Computability	www.computability.com	800-554-2186
CDW	www.cdw.com	800-998-4239
Dell Computer	www.dell.com	800-545-1567
Gateway	www.gateway.com	800-846-2000
IBM	www.ibm.com	800-426-2968
J&R Computer World	www.jandr.com	800-221-8180
Micron Electronics	www.micronpc.com	800-388-6334
Packard Bell	www.packardbell.com	800-733-5858
PC Mall	www.pcmall.com	800-523-2292
Toshiba America	www.csd.toshiba.com	800-457-7777
USA Flex	www.usaflex.com	800-766-1940

and delivery for repairs off site. Most of the major mail-order firms at least offer toll-free telephone technical support. This is critical. Test them before you buy. Your first call shouldn't be to the sales department but to the technical support group. Ask some questions and see how responsive they are. Did you get through on the first call? Were you kept on hold? If they had to call you back, did they get back to you quickly? Are the people patient and friendly? Also, check the technical support section of their website. It should have plenty of information as well as places where you can download the latest software for their equipment.

If you do buy mail order, it's a good idea to use a credit card. That way, if you have a beef with the PC vendor, you can request a refund by calling or sending a detailed letter to the credit card company describing your problem. The credit card company will suspend the bill while it investigates. That won't protect you against buyer's remorse, but in some cases it can protect you against fraud.

New, Used, or Refurbished

Most people buy new computers, but if you're looking for a bargain, consider buying a used one. Unlike a car, a PC isn't likely to break down just because it's old. Two years from now, the PC you buy today should be just as good as the day you bought it. In fact, there are still thousands of original, vintage 1981 IBM PCs in use.

Older machines are reliable, but they're also less powerful than newer ones. If a machine is too old, it won't be able to run Windows or today's software unless you upgrade it. (See the box on page 44 for the minimum specs you should look for.) You can always upgrade an older PC with new parts, but before you plan to do that, you should figure out what the upgrade will cost and compare that to the price of a newer machine. Prices for computers are always coming down, and if you can afford it, it's often cheaper to just buy a new one.

How do you decide what you should pay for a used PC? The best way is to watch the ads in your local paper: You'll find that the market sets pretty standard prices. You can also check out the websites of companies, like **American Computer Exchange**, that match buyers and sellers of used PCs. American Computer Exchange even publishes an index of used computer prices (updated weekly) on its site. And note: Prices change quickly, sometimes going down by $50 to $100 a month, so I wouldn't rely on any price list that's more than a few weeks old.

Some PC companies sell refurbished equipment, which, generally, is as good as new. Usually these are machines that were sold and returned for one reason or another and then checked to make sure they're up to factory specifications. Compaq has a whole division for this purpose called **Compaq Works**.

One last thing: If you're buying a used machine that has software on it, make sure you're getting legal copies that you can register in your own name. Insist on the original manuals and the original disks that the software came on.

Resources

American Computer Exchange
800-786-0717
www.amcoex.com

Compaq Works
888-215-8864
www.compaqworks.com

When to Buy: Now or Later?

One frequently asked question is, "Should I buy a PC now, or should I wait till the prices come down or the technology improves?" It doesn't matter when you ask the question, the answer is always the same. If you need or really want a computer now, buy it now, assuming you can afford what you want. And, yes, if you wait, you'll get a better and faster machine for less money.

In fact, Intel cofounder Gordon Moore once observed that the power of PC chips doubled every 18 months. That observation, known as "Moore's law," has been pretty much constant over the years. That law also seems to apply when you compare performance per dollar. What that means is that things will continue to get faster over time, so no matter when you buy a machine, a year or so later you can get one that's half as fast and twice as cheap. If you worry about that, though, you'll never buy a system. Since Moore's law is constant, now is as good a time as any.

So go ahead. Take the plunge.

Should You Get a Notebook Computer?

8 *The first decision you'll need to make when considering a PC is whether to get a notebook (sometimes called laptop) or a desktop machine. Before you decide, consider your needs carefully. Notebooks are great—for some people.*

Notebook vs. Desktop

Lots of people like the idea of a notebook computer because they can have it with them wherever they go. You can carry it between your office and your home, you can take it on trips, and you can even use it on planes and commuter trains. People who work by themselves look forward to working at the beach, in the park, or in the neighborhood cafe. And yes, all that is possible. Even though I wrote most of this book on my desktop PC, I worked on parts of it on planes, in hotel rooms, and from a local coffee shop, thanks to my notebook PC.

Given all those benefits, why get a desktop PC? Well, desktop PCs can't really be hauled around, but they do have some advantages over notebooks. For one, they are generally a lot cheaper. Feature for feature, a notebook PC could cost you about half as much again as a comparable desktop machine, so if you've got certain amount of money to spend on a computer, you can generally get a much better one—faster and more loaded with options—if you get a desktop machine.

Another possible disadvantage to a portable computer is that you're pretty much stuck with what you get. With a desktop machine, you can swap out the keyboard or monitor if it breaks or you decide you need something better; not so with a notebook. Notebook computers are also less "expandable" than desktop machines. Even the most common ways of upgrading an older machine—adding memory or upgrading to a larger disk drive—can be difficult and expensive on a portable, because the parts aren't as interchangeable as they are on desktop machines. And if you want to add features like CD-quality sound or the ability to plug in a video camera, you might have to ask for it up front; adding such capabilities later often means adding expensive and somewhat clumsy attachments.

The Best of Both Worlds

If money isn't tight, there is a way to get the best of both worlds. Most portable computers let you plug in external monitors, keyboards, mice, and other **peripherals** so that you can get all the comfort of working at a desktop machine while you're at your desk, and then you can just unplug the peripherals when you want to take your computer on the road.

DON'T WAIT UP.

Some notebook machines make this easier (if more expensive) by offering a **docking station**. The docking station holds the ports for the external keyboard, mouse, monitor, printer, and other devices. You can keep all the devices plugged in to the docking station, and then just slide the notebook PC from the docking station when you're ready to hit the road.

Perhaps most important, if you're usually going to be working at a desk anyway, a desktop machine can be a lot more pleasant to work with. The keyboards are larger and generally more comfortable to use. The monitor can be set at the height that works best for your chair and desk. Lots of people find mice a lot easier to use than electronic touch-pads or the other pointing devices used on notebook PCs.

If you expect to do a lot of traveling on business, where you'll need your computer, a notebook may really be the best option for you, and it could be worth the extra money and other trade-offs to get a notebook machine. If you don't travel a lot, though, it's easy to overestimate just how much you're going to use your computer away from your desk.

If you decide to get a notebook PC, make sure you take a critical look at all the components described in the next section. Unlike desktop systems, notebook computers are difficult to upgrade once you've bought the machine.

If You're Buying a Notebook Computer

If you decide to get a notebook PC, you'll face the same decisions about its components as you would buying a desktop machine—plus a few more. In this section, I'll run down a few special considerations for notebooks. If some of them don't make sense to you yet, read what I say about each item in the other chapters in this section, and then come back here when you're actually considering a purchase. And remember, these issues are more critical for notebooks because, unlike desktop PCs, you can't upgrade the components of a notebook after you've bought the machine.

Keyboard. Some notebook machines (especially the subnotebook and ultra-light models) save on size and weight by reducing the size of the keys or the distance between the keys. Be sure you're comfortable with the keyboard, especially if you're a touch typist.

Screen. There two basic kinds of notebook screens. **Passive matrix screens** (also known as dual-scan screens) are less expensive. **Active matrix screens** (sometimes called thin film transistor, or **TFT**, screens) cost more than passive matrix but produce gorgeous color, arguably better than the color offered by monitors for desktop machines. Active matrix screens can be viewed from almost any angle, but you can only see the images on a passive matrix screen if you're directly in front of it. That's not to say you should absolutely get an active matrix screen, even if you can afford it. Most new color passive matrix screens are quite good (look for a dual-scan type), so it may not be worth the extra $400 or so for an active matrix screen. Just be sure you consider the options before you buy.

Weight and size. Unless you're into body building, get the lightest notebook PC that suits your needs. If you just plan to haul it in your car between work and home, then it's not a big deal. But if, like me, you

like to carry it with you as you go about your
business, then you should look at a **subnotebook** or an ultra-light. There are lots of nice
subnotebooks from **IBM**, **Hewlett-Packard**,
Toshiba, and other companies. When considering weight, be sure to add in the weight of the
external power supply cube and the external
floppy drive, since you'll probably be carrying
them around, too. And be careful of trading
weight for features you really need. In some
cases it might be worth it to carry a bigger
machine if you can't live with, say, the small
keyboard of a subnotebook.

Resources

IBM
800-426-2968
www.ibm.com

Hewlett-Packard
800-752-0900
www.hp.com

Toshiba America
800-457-7777
www.csd.toshiba.com

Peripherals and expandability. Any portable computer you buy should
have at least one **PC card** slot (a slot that lets you plug in credit-card-
size expansion boards), and two is even better. Also, be sure there's a
place to plug in an external monitor, printer, modem, keyboard, and
mouse, either directly into the notebook or via a docking station (see
the box "The Best of Both Worlds" on page 37). An external monitor
port is especially important if you plan to use your portable computer
to give presentations—you may want to connect it to an overhead pro-
jector that plugs into that port.

Battery life. A notebook PC won't do you any good if the battery dies
halfway between Chicago and Cleveland. Look for a notebook PC with a
nickel–metal-hydride battery or (even better) a lithium battery. The
machine should be able to run from two to three hours between battery
charges. (If you plan to use it on long trips, you'll still want to buy an
extra battery for backup.)

Disk drives and memory. Today's notebook PCs can be configured with
almost as much memory and disk space as top-of-the-line desktop systems, but they don't always come that way. Be sure you get a system
that has ample hard disk space and memory. The machine may be
smaller than a desktop model, but the software you'll run on it is just as
big, so get at least 32 megabytes of RAM and plenty of hard disk space.

Also, note that some subnotebook computers don't have floppy drives. I don't like that, but it's how manufacturers reduce the size and shave an extra pound off the weight. You can get an external floppy disk to plug in to the PC card slot, but that adds more bulk and inconvenience than a built-in drive. (See Chapter 13 for more on floppy drives.)

Pointing device. You can plug a mouse into any notebook PC, but you don't really want to have to carry one everywhere you go. All portable machines have a built-in pointing device, but the type of pointing device varies. Many have an electronic **touchpad**, which senses the movement of your fingers. You move your finger around the pad just as you would move a mouse around a mousepad. Some people love touch-pads while others (including yours truly) find them hard to use. It's really a matter of personal preference.

My favorite pointing device, found on machines from IBM, Toshiba, and some other companies, looks like the tip of a pencil eraser that sticks up between the G, H, and B keys. You don't have to take your hands off the keyboard to position the cursor. A few companies still use a **trackball**, which is like an upside-down mouse that you roll around with your fingers. Whatever kind of pointing device you use, try it before you buy to make sure it works for you.

How to Choose the Right Computer

Once you've made the distinction between desktop and notebook, **9** *you still have a few decisions to make, but they're pretty easy ones. There are three major things that make one PC different from another. The first is the machine's central processing unit (CPU). The second is the hard disk. And the third is the amount of memory it has.*

Once you've figured out what you need in those three areas, your selection will still be wide. That's when you start thinking about the "extras," such as a DVD drive (see Chapter 13), the number of expansion slots the system has, the kind of keyboard and mouse and the quality of the components. Other considerations might be the quality of the case and whether the controls and switches are in a convenient location. Does it fit into your work environment? Will it fit on (or under) your desk? Is it quiet? (Some PCs have very noisy fans.) You get the idea. (For extra considerations that apply to notebooks, see Chapter 8.)

You Don't Need a Brand Name

Does the brand name make a difference? There was a time when I would have told you to stay away from "no-name brands," but those days are over. It's now possible for a neighborhood PC dealer to assemble a quality computer that stands up against the likes of those from IBM, Dell, Gateway, Compaq, or other big-name companies. And who knows: One of today's no-name companies could be in tomorrow's Fortune 500. I remember when Michael Dell, whose Dell Computer is now one of the biggest computer companies anywhere, sold PCs out of the back of his car.

The advantages of dealing with well-established companies *usually* include a nationwide guarantee, telephone support, and the peace of mind of that comes from knowing that you're dealing with a stable company. But although the big-name companies generally deliver quality systems, they sometimes cut corners by limiting the number of available expansion slots or by going with less memory, smaller disk capacity, or slower CPUs than comparably priced systems from less-well-known companies. My advice is not to get too hung up on the name but to

Brand-Name Buys

Lots of companies make PCs, but a few manufacturers account for the lion's share of sales and are considered the field's "brand names." Buying from any of these companies will pretty much ensure a quality product, but no-name PCs can be just as good.

Company	Phone	Website
Acer	408-432-6200	www.acer.com
Compaq Computer	800-345-1518	www.compaq.com
Dell Computer	800-545-1567	www.dell.com
Gateway	800-846-2000	www.gateway.com
Hewlett-Packard	800-752-0900	www.hp.com
IBM	800-426-2968	www.ibm.com
Micron Electronics	800-388-6334	www.micronpc.com
NEC/Packard Bell	800-733-5858	www.packardbell.com
Sony	408-432-1600	www.sel.sony.com
Toshiba	800-457-7777	www.csd.toshiba.com

judge each computer by its qualities and by how well its manufacturer backs it up.

One thing I like to do when evaluating a PC company is divide the price by the warranty to determine the "worst case" cost of ownership. If you spend $1,500 for a PC from a reputable company that offers a three-year warranty, in the unlikely event it fell apart the day after the warranty expired, your total cost of ownership would be about $1.37 a day. Still not a bad deal.

It's the Components That Count

Although the name of the company that makes your PC might not make all that much difference, the companies that make the components do. I wouldn't worry about components if you buy a name brand, but if you buy from a lesser-known maker, be sure the PC is built from quality components. You don't have to worry too much about the stuff inside the box—just about all disk drives, memory chips, and other components made today are up to snuff. What you mainly have to worry about is the monitor, the keyboard, the mouse, the modem, and other accessories. Manufacturers sometimes skimp by using slower modems or low-quality sound cards, for example. (I tell you what to look for in each of these pieces of equipment in later chapters.)

A PC for Multimedia

If you buy a brand-name machine, you're almost certain to get one designed for multimedia—games, reference works, and other software that uses animation, video, and sound. (I'll talk about some of those applications in Part 5.) That means it has a CD-ROM drive, a sound card, and speakers, as well as enough memory and computing power to handle today's multimedia software. A multimedia PC is especially important if children will be using your machine because most children's games and learning programs are designed for multimedia PCs.

The Buyer's Guide to the Perfect PC on the next page lists specs for the multimedia equipment you'll need. For the CD-ROM drive, you should make sure it's at least 12X speed. (That means that the drive is 12 times faster than the first CD-ROM drives that came out. A 20X CD-ROM drive is 20 times faster, and so on.) Anything 12X and over is more than fast enough to run multimedia software.

Sound cards come with all computers right now, and the one in your computer will probably do the job for you unless you're a hard-core gamer looking to blow the roof off with your sound effects. If you fit that description, you'll be looking at something like Creative Labs' *SoundBlaster PC164*, which has "3-D sound," 16 channels, and 10 drum kits for about $100.

Resources

SoundBlaster PC164
Creative Labs
800-998-5227
www.soundblaster.com

Most PCs also include speakers, but the built-in models vary in quality from barely audible to blow-your-socks-off. You can always go out and buy better speakers, but before you do, think about how you use your PC's audio system. If I'm going to relax and listen to a piece of music, I'd rather use my living room stereo than my PC's CD-ROM drive. The sounds that emanate from games, websites, and other PC programs typically sound OK (though not terrific) on just about any set of speakers. However, if there is a gamer in your family, then you might want to treat that person to a higher-end set of speakers so that he or she can almost feel, as well as hear, the roar of the

A Buyer's Guide to the Perfect PC

It's not necessary to buy the latest, greatest, and fastest PC around but it's not a good idea to buy the oldest and slowest either. My rule of thumb is to go for a machine whose specifications were state of the art maybe three to six months ago. That will still be plenty good enough for almost anything you plan to do for the next two or three years but a lot cheaper than today's top of the line. The specifications listed here were about right when this book was published. If you're reading this after about the middle of 1999, though, you may need to check out the latest specs. Things change fast. If you don't know what all these terms mean, read on. I'll explain them all in the next chapters.

CPU: At least a 200-MHz Pentium with MMX (see Chapter 10).

RAM: Windows 95 and Windows 98 require at least 16 megabytes of RAM; 32 megabytes is better (see Chapter 11).

Hard disk: At least 4 gigabytes, and more is better. Most machines now come with two or more (see Chapter 12).

CD-ROM or DVD drive: Any CD-ROM drive rated 12X or higher should be fine. A DVD drive is even better (see Chapter 13).

Expansion slots: At least two empty slots for a desktop PC (see Chapter 14). At least one PC card slot for a notebook computer (see Chapter 8).

Monitor: Super VGA with .28 (or lower) dot pitch, comfortable for you (see Chapter 15).

Keyboard: Anything that's comfortable. It's handy if it has the Windows key on it (Chapter 16).

Technical support: Free technical support by phone.

Warranty: At least a one-year written warranty and quick turnaround time via a local repair shop or courier service if repairs are needed.

planes, the thunder of the ammunition, and the squeal of the tires. All the major speaker companies produce self-powered speaker systems designed for PCs, but any self-powered speaker system for "walkman"-type stereo systems will also work. I have the *PCWorks* speaker system from Cambridge Sound Works, which includes a subwoofer and two amplified speakers for around $70—a great deal for such a good set of speakers.

Resources

PCWorks
Cambridge Sound Works
800-367-4434
www.hifi.com

The CPU:
How Fast Is Fast?

10

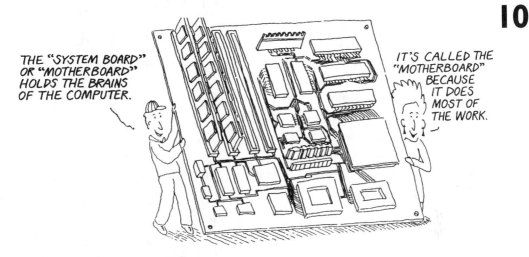

THE "SYSTEM BOARD" OR "MOTHERBOARD" HOLDS THE BRAINS OF THE COMPUTER.

IT'S CALLED THE "MOTHERBOARD" BECAUSE IT DOES MOST OF THE WORK.

The central processing unit, or CPU, is the part of the computer that does the main computing work. It sits on the computer's "system board" (sometimes called the "motherboard"), along with other chips. It's not very big, but when you talk about the computer, that's what you're talking about. The rest of the PC is just a way of getting data to and from that chip.

As I explained in Chapter 3, having a processor based on Intel's technology is what makes a computer IBM compatible. The processors in the earliest IBM PCs were called 8088 chips. Later, more powerful, versions were called, in order, the "8086", the "80286," the "80386," and the "80486"—later shortened to just "386 and "486."

After that, though, Intel figured out that if it gave its chips names instead of numbers, it could trademark the names. The next chip after the 486 was called the **Pentium**. The one after that is called the **Pentium II**, and by the time you read this, who knows?—Intel may have introduced another Pentium model. Intel also makes a CPU called the **Celeron**, which is similar to a Pentium II but a bit slower. Since those names are trademarked, chips from other makers that use the same kind of technology have different names. Cyrix's equivalent to the Pentium II is called the Cyrix M II; AMD's is called the AMD K6-2.

Sometimes you'll hear about Pentium chips with **MMX** technology. MMX refers to extra circuitry that makes the chip run faster with certain kinds of graphic and multimedia applications. For most applications, though, it makes a very small difference in performance. I've used both standard and MMX machines and they seem pretty much the same. The Pentium II is a Pentium MMX machine on steroids: It contains all the circuits of the Pentium with MMX chip, plus more that make it even faster.

When I wrote this it was still possible to get machines with Pentium, Pentium with MMX, and Celeron chips (and the compatible chips from other manufacturers), but most new computers came with Pentium II processors.

"Intel Inside": Is It Important?

Intel has been conducting an expensive marketing campaign to convince consumers that it's important to have a PC with "Intel Inside." The ads suggest that Intel's chips are the ones you'll need to be fully compatible with today's software. It's clever marketing, but that's really all it is. Fact is, the other major chip makers create CPUs that are, for all practical purposes, 100 percent compatible with Intel chips. If you buy a machine from a major PC maker such as Compaq, IBM, AST, or Dell, then you really don't need to worry about whether your CPU was made by Intel, Cyrix, IBM, or AMD. Major PC companies put their machines through a great deal of testing and stake their reputations on the fact that their machines can run Windows and all Windows programs.

Clock Speeds

Not all chips with the same names are created equal. After the name of a chip, you'll usually see a **clock speed** rating in **megahertz** (MHz). For example, when I wrote this some standard speeds for Pentium II processors were 300 MHz, 350 MHz, and 400 MHz. When you read this, you may be able to get chips rated at 500 MHz and even more. The chart on the next page shows that different megahertz speeds can make a big difference in how fast a chip can process data. You should also notice that the megahertz rating only tells part of the story; different chips with the same megahertz rating run at very different speeds. A Pentium II running at 266 MHz is half again as fast as a Celeron running at the same speed.

Relative Processor Speeds

This chart shows the relative speeds of several current Intel processors when running the same set of tasks. You can see that the fastest processor (a Pentium II running at 400 MHz) is more than twice as fast as the slowest chip (the Pentium running at 233 MHz). But any of these chips is fast enough to run any software you're likely to be using for the next several years.

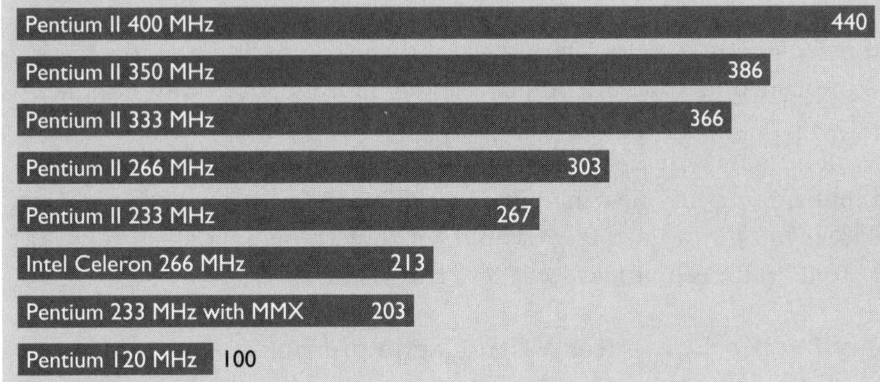

Processor	Relative Speed
Pentium II 400 MHz	440
Pentium II 350 MHz	386
Pentium II 333 MHz	366
Pentium II 266 MHz	303
Pentium II 233 MHz	267
Intel Celeron 266 MHz	213
Pentium 233 MHz with MMX	203
Pentium 120 MHz	100

Source: Intel

What Speed Do You Need?

The speed of a CPU is, in many ways, like the horsepower in your car. In the 1950s people were nuts about horsepower, and car manufacturers bragged about cars with bigger and faster engines. By the '70s, though, consumers and car manufacturers started wising up. Any car is more than fast enough for the average driver on public roads, so instead of worrying about horsepower, car buyers started to concentrate on more important features like economy, safety, and comfort.

The same thing is becoming true with computing. Back in the '80s and early '90s, people had to wait for their PC to perform tasks, so the industry kept coming up with faster and faster processors. The industry is still coming out with faster CPUs, but the highest speeds aren't needed for running typical applications. Today, most CPUs from Intel and its competitors are more than fast enough to run typical home and office applications. Faster chips are being developed for two reasons: first, because there are people who are willing to buy them, and second, because they make it possible for software developers to come up with new and even more complex programs. But, for mainstream use, you don't need a superfast processor.

The data in the chart on the previous page shows the relative speed of several Intel CPUs that were on the market when this book was written. By the time you read it, though, the chart will be out of date: Intel and its competitors will have come up with even faster processors. But that doesn't mean that the CPUs will be out of date. The CPUs that Intel and its competitors were offering when the second edition of this book was published in 1996 are still fast enough for most of today's applications, and even the bottom of Intel's line at the time this book was written will be fast enough for most applications through at least the end of the millennium. Any new machine you buy will be fast enough for your needs. If you buy a used PC, I would get something with a Pentium 200 or better. (You need at least a 486 to run Windows 98.)

Speeding the Computer With Cache Memory

Lots of other things besides the processor affect how fast your CPU does its work. One important factor is **cache memory**. A cache is a bank of high-speed memory on the system board that runs up to five times as fast as the computer's regular memory (described in Chapter 11). Cache memory speeds up the operation of some programs by storing the most recently used information (which generally will be needed again soon) in this faster bank of memory.

All chips since the 486 have had at least some cache memory built in. All Pentium CPUs have at least 16 kilobytes (K) of cache. (See the box "Units of Measurement: Bits and Bytes," on the next page, for what terms like *kilobyte* mean.) The Pentium with MMX and the Celeron have at least

Two Kinds of Cache

Don't confuse cache memory with **disk cache**. The concept is similar, but cache memory requires special hardware, whereas you can always create your own disk caching using software that comes with Windows. A disk cache uses your computer's regular RAM to speed up hard disk performance by copying recently used data from the disk to a portion of your RAM. Since RAM is faster than a disk, the data in the cache can be accessed more quickly than can the data on the disk.

Units of Measurement: Bits and Bytes

Computer data is measured in special units called **bits** and **bytes**. These terms (and the variations on them described here) are used to describe the size of files, memory, hard disks, and the speed with which data is transferred—any measurement of computer data. Here's what the terms mean.

A **bit,** the smallest unit: an "on" or "off" signal in the computer.

A **byte,** the next unit up on the ladder, is made up of 8 bits. It takes 8 bits to store a single alphanumeric character, such as the numeral *1* or the letter *J*. The word *the* is 3 bytes long, for example.

A **kilobyte** (KB) is approximately 1,000 bytes (1,024 to be exact). It's equivalent to about a page of double-spaced text.

A **megabyte** (MB) is just over one million bytes (OK, 1,048,576)—about as much text as in the average novel, or maybe a scanned 3-by-5 photo.

A **gigabyte** (GB) is just over a billion bytes (1,073,741,824 to be exact) or 1,024 megabytes. Most hard disks can store a gigabyte or more of data.

A **terabyte**, just in case you're curious, is about a trillion (1,099,511,627,776) bytes, but you won't see that measurement used for a PC. The last time I saw it, it was referring to the amount of data published on the Internet since it began.

32K of cache, and some chips have even larger external caches to supplement the built-in one. Cache memory that is internal to the CPU is called the L1 (level one) cache. Cache memory that is external to the CPU (on the motherboard) is called L2 (level two). Cache memory is different from the computer's main memory, or RAM, which I cover in the next chapter.

Many computer companies increase the memory cache by adding "external high-speed cache memory." It's not uncommon to see ads for 128K, 256K, or even 512K of L2 cache memory. A larger cache does improve performance, but there's a point of diminishing returns. There is only a slight difference in performance between 256K and 512K of cache. The extra L2 cache will have the biggest impact if you work a lot with graphics, but all things being equal, at least 256K of L2 cache is nice to have.

A Faster Bus

Another hardware specification that affects a computer's speed is its **bus**. Think of a computer's bus as carrying not passengers, but data between points in your computer. The bus is basically the collection of circuits or tiny wires through which data travels within the computer.

Bus speed is measured, like chip speed, in MHz. Common speeds are 66 MHz and 100 MHz. The 100-MHz bus can handle a third more data than the 66-MHz bus can.

Don't get too hung up on this one specification—like all other specifications it's only part of the story. But if you hear about a bus, just remember that, all other things being equal, the faster the bus, the faster the computer.

The speed of the CPU, the amount of cache memory, and the speed of the bus all affect how fast your computer processes information, but that's really only part of the story when you talk about a computer's overall speed. The kind of video card in your computer, the amount of memory, the speed of the disk drive, the software you're using, the speed of the modem and the printer, and even how fast you type affect how fast you get your work done. Considering all that, you can be pretty comfortable with any fairly modern CPU.

Memory: The Electronic Workspace

The computer's RAM (random access memory) is where it keeps any programs and data you have open. The more memory you have, the more programs and files you can keep open at once.

11

More memory also makes your computer run faster. Many programs can work with a limited amount of RAM by keeping only the most often used parts of the program in memory. When you want to use a less often used part, it needs to stop and load that data from the hard disk, which takes a bit of time. If you have more memory, the computer can load more of the data at one time so that it's right there when you need it.

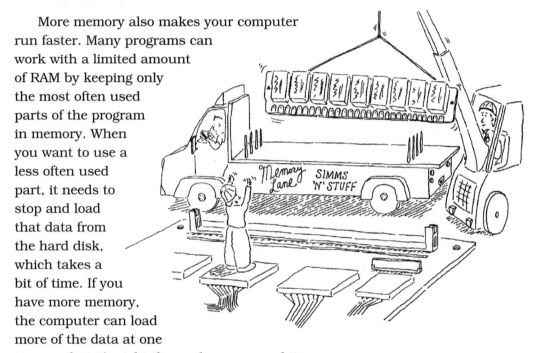

Don't even think about using a computer with less than 16 megabytes of RAM. And if you want reasonable performance with Windows 95 or Windows 98, you'll want 32 megabytes. Having 64 megabytes of RAM might make your PC run a little faster but, unless you're running special types of programs, the difference will be negligible.

Memory comes in units called **SIMMs** or **DIMMs** (The S stands for "single," the D stands for "dual," and the IMM stands "in-line memory module.") SIMMs and DIMMs are small bars with preinstalled memory chips that plug into your computer's system board. To add memory to your computer, you plug in one or more of these modules.

When you buy a computer, the salesperson will say something like, "It has 32 MB, expandable to 128 MB." That probably means that it

Types of Memory

DRAM:Fast. Found in most basic Pentium machines.

EDO RAM: Faster. Found in Pentium II systems.

SDRAM: Really Fast. Found in some high-end machines.

has four memory slots, one of which has a 32-MB SIMM plugged into it, with three empty slots, to which you can add 96 MB more (three more 32-MB SIMMs).

You'll also hear about different kinds of memory, such as **DRAM**, **EDO RAM**, and **SDRAM**. DRAM (dynamic RAM) is the most common type of memory. (It's what people are referring to when they just say "RAM.") EDO (extended data out) RAM is faster, and SDRAM (synchronous dynamic RAM) is the fastest yet. Most computers work with only one of these kinds of memory, so you'll need to know what type you have if you ever want to add more.

The price of memory chips changes all the time, so check with local computer dealers, in the ads in computer magazines, or on the Internet for the latest prices. Last time I checked you could get a 32-megabyte SIMM for about $80, but, trust me, the price will be different by the time you read this and different again a few weeks later. In any case, memory is easy to install and relatively affordable. Ask your dealer to preinstall as much memory as you think you'll need to start with. Later, if you find you need more memory, you can easily buy more SIMMs or DIMMs.

If you decide to add new memory, you'll need to know exactly what type of SIMM or DIMM to buy. Ask your dealer or PC company to tell you details about the memory, including its speed (in nanoseconds for DRAM or EDO RAM, in MHz for SDRAM), the number of pins on each SIMM or DIMM, and how many SIMMs or DIMMs you need to install (some must be installed in groups of two). You also need to know whether your memory modules have tin or gold connectors. It doesn't make much difference which you have, but you shouldn't mix them. If you can't find this information in your manual, most companies that sell memory can look it up for you. You can also buy memory on the Internet. Some Internet-based dealers, such as *BuyinGuide*, let you look up the type of memory you need for your PC model on its website.

Resources

BuyinGuide
www.buyinguide.com

The Hard Disk: The Computer's Filing Cabinet

12

Disk storage is your computer's filing cabinet, where it keeps all the programs you use and the files you create. Unlike RAM, disks hold their information even when the computer is turned off; the information is physically recorded on the disk's magnetic surface.

You probably won't ever see your hard disk; it's buried in the system unit of your computer. You'll only see a blinking light on the front of the system unit that indicates when the hard disk is in use.

How much hard disk storage do you need? The rule of thumb is simple. Estimate what you think you'll need, double it, then go for the next higher size. Hard disks are like closets. You think you have plenty of room until you've lived with it for awhile.

Today's machines typically come with a hard disk that stores anywhere from 2 to 12 gigabytes of information. You might find one with less, and you can easily find a machine that stores more. Windows take up a lot of space, as do many of the programs you'll want to run.

I recommend that you get at least 4 gigabytes (GB), which is the low end these days. The extra cost for the larger hard drive isn't all that much, and it's a lot better to have too much room than too little.

Some terms you might hear when you're looking for a hard disk are **IDE** and **SCSI** (pronounced "scuzzy"). They describe different ways that the hard disk connects to your computer (sometimes called a **hardware interface**). For PC hard drives, an IDE (integrated drive electronics) interface is the most popular method because it is the least expensive. You can have up to two IDE hard drives on a single machine without having to buy a new interface card. The biggest advantage to SCSI is that it's possible to connect several devices (hard drives, CD-ROM drives, scanners, and so on) to a single controller board. Unfortunately, it doesn't always work as it should because not all companies that make SCSI devices follow the same technology standards. There's nothing wrong with SCSI, but unless you really need it (if, for example, a device you really want to add only comes with a SCSI connection), there's no reason to pay more for it. Besides, you can always add a SCSI card if you need one, and some scanners and other devices that require a SCSI interface even come with SCSI cards in the package.

If you run out of room on your internal hard disk, you can replace it with a larger-capacity disk or—more conveniently—you can add another hard drive. You can get external hard drives, which come in a separate case and attach to the IDE or SCSI expansion slots, or internal drives, which replace your old drive or fill an additional slot, called a **drive bay**, inside the system unit. Another option is to connect a high-capacity removable disk drive. (I talk about those in the next chapter.)

Why Does My Computer Say I'm Out of Memory When I Have Plenty of Space on My Hard Disk?

A lot of people have trouble keeping the difference between memory (RAM) and storage (the hard disk) straight, probably because they're both usually measured in bytes.

THINK OF "STORAGE" AS A FILING CABINET FOR LONG-TERM INFORMATION....

....WHILE "RAM" IS LIKE THE DESK WHERE YOU KEEP JUST THE STUFF YOU'RE WORKING ON.

Maybe it will help to remember it this way. Storage (the hard disk) is your computer's filing cabinet, where you keep everything you may ever need to use again; memory (RAM) is like a desktop, where you keep just the programs and documents you're working on at the time.

Information stays in RAM (the electronic desktop) as long as the computer stays on, but once you turn off the power, that information is erased. In order to hang on to that data when the computer is off, you need to store that information on disk, where it is physically written to magnetic platters that keep the information intact until it's needed again.

If your computer tells you you're out of disk space, you've got to delete some files from it—closing some of the programs you have open won't help. If you're out of memory, you don't need to delete any files; you just need to close some programs you have open.

Removable Disk Drives:
The Computer's Front Door

13

THIS PC HAS
ONE FLOPPY AND
ONE CD-ROM DRIVE.

WHICH
ONE
MAKES
TOAST?

3½"
FLOPPY   CD-ROM

On the front of your computer's system unit, you'll usually find two or more slots into which you insert removable disks: floppy disks, CD-ROMs, DVDs, or Zip disks. These are the doors through which you get files and programs into your computer—files and programs that are stored, of course, on floppy disks, CD-ROMs, or DVDs.

Like hard disks, these removable disks store information even after the computer is turned off. Unlike hard drives, though, removable storage devices separate the storage medium (the disk itself) from the drive (the mechanism that reads the data). That way, you can buy as much of the inexpensive storage medium as you need, without also investing in the expensive drive mechanism.

You'll use removable disks in a lot of different ways:

- When you buy a new piece of software, it usually comes on a CD. If someone gives you a data file, it's often on a floppy disk.
- When you want to share files with someone else, you can give them the files on a floppy.
- When you want to remove files from your hard disk but keep an archive copy elsewhere, or when you just want to have extra, backup copies of files, you can usually save them on removable disks.

You can open files and save them on a floppy disk in your floppy drive just as you would use them if they were on your hard disk.

Floppies

Floppy disks, which typically store 1.44 MB of data, are 3.5 inches square, with a rigid plastic case. Why do they call them "floppies"? The answer lies inside the case, which contains a round, thin piece of flexible mylar that does, indeed, flop around. Floppies are cheap— typically less than 50 cents each—providing an inexpensive way to share individual files with friends and co-workers. You can record on them, erase them, and record on them again and again. The only problem with floppy disks is that you can't store much data. The 1.44 MB they hold might be enough for a few word processing files but not enough for some files that contain photos, audio, or any other multimedia information.

When you go shopping for disks, your choices will be trickier than you might expect. The 3.5-inch disks come in two varieties, double-density and high-density. My advice is, stick with the high-density. Although your computer can use the double-density disks, they hold a lot less data (about 720K, or half as much as high-density disks) and still cost about the same amount of money.

When you buy disks, you'll notice that you can buy them either **formatted** or unformatted. Formatted disks usually cost more, and their only advantage is that it saves you about a minute per disk because you don't have to run the Format command before you use them (see the box "Formatting Disks," on the next page, for more on that). If you buy formatted disks, be sure they are formatted for

Formatting Disks

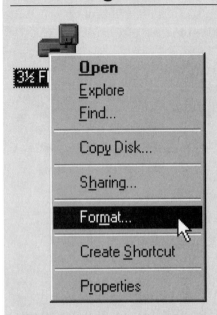

To format a disk, open the My Computer window, then right-click on the icon of the disk you want to format and choose Format from the menu that appears.

In order to save information on a disk, the disk needs to be formatted—magnetically encoded with information that helps Windows store and then find information you save on it. Some disks you buy, including your hard drive, some floppy drives, Zip drives, and other removable disks, may already be formatted when you buy them. If the disk isn't formatted or becomes unreadable for any reason, you may need to format it. Windows includes a reformatting utility for floppies and hard drives (right-click on a disk drive icon in the My Computer window to use it). Other removable drives usually come with any software you need for formatting them.

Formatting a disk erases all the data on the disk. Sometimes that's what you want, and sometimes it isn't.

If you don't need whatever it is you've saved on a floppy, formatting the disk is a good way to get rid of all the files and get the disk ready for reuse. Because Windows does some housekeeping chores on the disk as it formats, formatting can create more room on a disk than simply erasing it or recycling all the files.

Once in awhile, though, you'll insert a disk that contains important files, and your computer will tell you that the disk isn't formatted. That usually means the disk is damaged. But it could also mean that there's something wrong with the disk drive. Before you click Yes to reformat or give up on the disk entirely, try removing it, turning off your PC, and trying again. If that doesn't work, try putting it into a different computer (if possible), or using a disk utility that specializes in saving damaged disks. (I describe some in Chapter 58.)

Windows or MS-DOS. If you do buy unformatted disks or disks formatted for Macintoshes, don't worry: You can always reformat them.

You might also see Windows-formatted disks that are bigger than the ones you're used to—disks that are $5^1/4$ inches square and really do flop around (they don't have a rigid case). Those are for older PCs.

CD-ROM, CD-R, and DVD

CD-ROM stands for "compact disc, read-only memory." CD-ROMs look just like audio CDs. They store a lot more data than floppies—about 690 MB—and so are used to distribute software that takes up a lot of room on disk, such as complicated application software, games, and electronic encyclopedias. However, standard CD-ROM drives can not record or erase a CD. That's why they call it "read-only" memory. (And don't get confused by the term "memory." It's really disk storage.)

CD-ROM drives are standard on most computers, but you can also buy a special kind of CD drive called a CD-Recordable, or **CD-R**, drive, which can you can use to create your own CDs. These devices are still a bit pricy ($300 or more) but recordable CDs are relatively cheap— about $3 each. You can record to a CD-R disc only once: After you record to it, you're stuck with what's there. Of course, that's an advantage if you're using it to back up information for safe storage. (I talk about how and why to back up information in Chapter 35.)

An even newer type of disc, which looks just like a CD-ROM, is called **DVD**, short for "digital versatile disc." A single DVD stores between 4.7 and 17 gigabytes of data—enough for a full-length movie with stereo sound or very sophisticated computer games that require a lot of graphics, video, animation, and sound. Some machines now come with DVD instead of CD-ROM drives. DVDs hold a lot of data, and a DVD drive can also read a CD-ROM disc, so the advantages are obvious. The only disadvantage is that they cost a bit more than CD-ROM drives. Like everything else with PCs, though, the price of DVDs is coming down rapidly. I could be wrong (if I were always right, I'd be a full-time investor instead of a writer), but I suspect that DVD will quickly take over. If I were buying a PC today, I'd seriously consider getting one with a DVD drive instead of a CD-ROM drive. If you get a CD-ROM drive now, though, don't worry: You can always add a DVD drive later.

Zip, Jaz, and SparQ Drives

A couple of years ago, a brand new kind of removable storage appeared and became incredibly popular right away. That was Iomega's *Zip drive*, which can hold 100 MB on a disk that's just a little bigger than a regular floppy. The Zip drive costs about $140 (at least when I wrote this) with one removable disk, and extra disks sell for about $15 each.

100 MB is a lot of storage for $15. If you're buying a new PC, you can often order it with a built-in Zip drive, and Zip drives come standard on some models. If you already have a PC you can add a Zip drive yourself. You can have your dealer install an internal Zip drive, or you can buy an external Zip drive that plugs into your PC.

Iomega also makes a drive, called the *Jaz drive*, that stores even more—1 or 2 GB per disk, depending on what version you get. A 2-gigabyte Jaz drive costs about $600 and an extra 2-GB disk is about $120.

Other companies have quickly come to market with similar products. One popular competitor is Syquest, with its **SparQ drive**. Prices, product specifications, and the products themselves are changing quickly, so check with some computer dealers or computer magazines before you buy to find out the latest on these drives.

Resources

Jaz drive, Zip drive
Iomega
800-778-1000
www.iomega.com

SparQ drive
Syquest
510-226-4000
www.syquest.com

Just for Backup: Tape Drives

The cheapest form of removable storage is a tape backup drive and cartridge. The cartridges look like giant cassette tapes, and, in fact, work in pretty much the same way. As with audio and VCR tapes, the disadvantage of tape cartridges is that you can't go directly to just the track you need; you've got to go through the whole tape until you get to the part you want. This makes them too slow to use for the files you work with every day, but they're great for backups and archives, because the tapes are so inexpensive—about $20 for a 2-GB cartridge. (For more on backing up, see Chapter 35.)

Expansion Slots and Ports: Ways to Add More Stuff

14

If you think your hardware buying spree is over once you buy a computer, then you haven't heard about peripherals. Peripherals are those wonderful things, such as modems and video boards, that can increase the performance of your machine or add new capabilities. So in order to make sure you can add peripherals down the line, you've got to make sure you've got places to plug them in on your PC, and that's where expansion slots and ports come in.

Parallel Ports and Serial Ports

Every PC comes with one **parallel port** and either one or two **serial ports**. The parallel port is mainly used for a printer, but other devices, such as scanners and digital cameras (described in Chapter 20), may also plug in there.

Serial ports are used for all sorts of devices, including modems, digital cameras, and hand-held computers. If you have an internal modem, then one serial port is probably sufficient, because the modem won't need a serial port. If you have an external modem, though, it's nice to have two serial ports. (If you only have one and need to switch between a modem and another device, you can buy an inexpensive switch board for about $20 from an electronics store.)

Expansion Slots

Expansion slots are openings at the back of your computer into which you can plug **expansion cards** (sometimes also called **boards** or **adapters**). These cards hold circuits that are needed to run peripherals or add additional capabilities to your system. Anything you plug into an expansion slot plugs right into the computer's system board.

Some PCs come with as many as eight slots, and others have as few as three. More to the point, some computers use up most of their slots with the basic functions. Sometimes computer makers plug the controllers that handle the hard disk and monitor into the expansion slots. Some are taken up by an internal modem or other device. The real question, then, is how many slots the computer has free once it's set up with the basics. All things being equal, of course, the more slots you have, the better.

The next thing to remember is that not all expansion slots are the same. Most PCs these days have two kids of slots: **ISA** (for "Industry Standard Architecture") and **PCI** ("Personal Component Interconnect"). Some have a third type of slot called **AGP** ("accelerated graphics port"). And as I mentioned in Chapter 8, notebook computers use another kind of expansion slot, for PC cards. Video cards and SCSI cards typically require a PCI slot, while other peripherals, such as internal modems, typically plug into an ISA slot. (These aren't hard and fast rules; you'll also find some PCI modems, for example.) Network cards for connecting your PC to a local area network are designed for both types of slots. When you're ready to expand your PC, you'll need to know what type of slots you have available.

AGP slots are used for high-speed graphic adapters that come with some newer PCs. (I'll talk about that in the next chapter.) If you have a PC with an AGP slot, you probably also have an AGP graphics adapter plugged into that slot.

Plugging cards into ISA or PCI expansion slots can be a little intimidating, because you've got to open the computer's box to do it. I'll tell you how to do it in Chapter 22, where you'll learn how to put together all the pieces of your system.

USB Ports

In addition to parallel ports, serial ports, and expansion slots, most new PCs now also have a **USB port**. (USB stands for "Universal Serial Bus.") Unlike expansion slots, plugging peripherals into the USB port doesn't demand that you open up your computer—you just plug the device into the port. A single USB port can be used to connect up to 127 devices; you "daisy chain" the devices by plugging one into another. You can use USB ports for mice, printers, modems, digital cameras, scanners, and lots of other kinds of peripherals.

Windows 98 is the first version of Windows that fully supports USB. (There are some add-on programs that allow you to use USB devices with Windows 95, but they're not all that reliable.) There also aren't too many devices yet that connect to USB ports. When there are, though, USB ports are so easy to use and so versatile that they're likely to replace the serial port, parallel port, and expansion slots altogether.

Firewire Ports

Lately some computer makers have started adding an even faster connection option to their high-end computers: a **Firewire**, or 1394, port. (1394 is the number of the industry standard that describes Firewire's workings.)

A Firewire connection can transfer data at up to 400 megabits per second and can support up to 63 devices on a single port, but when I wrote this, Firewire was pretty rare, and it was pretty hard to find devices that used it. If you're not working with video, you probably won't use it, but getting a PC with a Firewire port means that you will be among the first to be able to quickly move video in and out of the PC when Firewire-compatible devices appear.

Monitors: The Face of the Computer

15 *A computer's display system actually has two parts: the monitor itself (also called the "display," "CRT," or "screen"), and the display adapter it plugs into, which generates the picture information for the monitor. Together, they control the number of colors, the speed, the sharpness, and the quality of the image you'll be looking at whenever you work or play on your PC.*

When you buy a system, the display adapter (also called the "video adapter," "video board," "graphics adapter," or "graphics board") is already installed. (It either plugs into one of your computer's expansion slots or is built into the motherboard.) Often, though, you'll need to buy your own monitor, and down the road, you may want to upgrade your graphics adapter to get more speed or more colors, run a bigger

THE "DISPLAY ADAPTER"
(ALSO CALLED "VIDEO CARD")
WORKS IN TANDEM WITH
A COLOR MONITOR.

monitor, or get 3-D effects. Getting a good match—and all the features you'll want—requires understanding how each component affects the image, and how they work together.

When considering an adapter, you'll look at how much video memory it has, what resolution and how many colors it supports, and its refresh rate. For monitors, you'll need to choose a size, then look for factors that affect image quality such as dot pitch and interlacing. I'll talk about each of those features here.

Video Memory

Every graphics adapter comes with built-in video memory (**VRAM**)—a special stash of memory, separate from your system's main memory, used specifically for processing image data. How much VRAM you need on your adapter depends on how many colors you want to display, what resolution you want on your screen, and what size monitor you're using. I'll go into resolution, colors, and monitor size next; for now, you just have to remember that the larger the monitor, the more VRAM you'll need to support a given resolution or number of colors. If you're working with text and simple graphics, 1 or 2 MB of VRAM is probably sufficient. However, if you plan to play a lot of speedy, color-rich games, you might want 2, 4, or even 6 MB of video RAM on your graphics card.

Resolution

Resolution refers to the number of dots of light, or **pixels** (picture elements), you see on screen. The resolution of an adapter is usually referred to as **VGA** (for "Video Graphics Array"), which displays 640 pixels horizontally across the screen and 480 pixels vertically down the screen, or (more commonly these days) **SVGA** (Super VGA), which can also display resolutions of 800-by-600 pixels, 1,024-by-768 pixels, or even higher.

The higher your resolution, the more you can see on screen at once—at a resolution of 1,024-by-768 pixels you can see almost twice as much on screen as you can at 640 by 480. The trade-off is that as the resolution gets higher, the

AGP

Many new computers now come with an Advanced Graphics Port (AGP), which is essentially a high-speed SVGA video adapter. It's nice to have, but it's only important if you use games and other graphics-rich applications a lot.

Graphics Adapters for 3-D

People who play a lot of games on their computers might find themselves frustrated by the slowness of their system's graphic response, because games often use 3-D graphics. Such graphics don't actually seem to pop from the screen, and you don't need 3-D glasses to view them, but they do use special rendering techniques that are much more sophisticated than everyday 2-D graphics. If you have AGP on your PC, you won't have any problem with 3-D effects, but 3-D rendering can tax the abilities of everyday video adapters.

If you don't have AGP and graphics are important to you, you can upgrade your video system with boards from makers such as ATI, Matrix, and others that are designed especially to render 3-D graphics speedily. (To really make your system zip, you'll also need a graphics-optimized CPU—a Pentium with MMX or Pentium II, which you can read more about in Chapter 10.) Unless you're a heavy gamer, though—or if you just got a job offer at Pixar, Silicon Graphics, NASA or some other organization that does really way-out special effects—a regular old 2-D adapter will probably be all you need.

image gets smaller. On smaller monitors, though, the tighter-packed pixels may make text sizes too small to read. With SVGA, you can set your resolution to the setting that suits your eyesight and your monitor size. (See Chapter 36 for information on how to change your screen resolution.)

Most monitors today are **multiscan monitors**, which means they are able to work with different kinds of display adapters at different resolutions.

Number of Colors

Your video card also determines how many colors or shades of gray your monitor can display. (This is also sometimes called "bit depth," as described in the box at right). Mostly, this is a factor of the amount of video RAM you've got.

Bit Depth and Number of Colors

How many colors your monitor can display depends on its **bit depth**—how many bits of information the graphics adapter uses to describe each color. If you work mostly with text and business applications, 8-bit color (256 colors) is probably enough. For games and graphics work, you'll want more.

Bit depth	Number of colors
8-bit	256
16-bit	65,536
32-bit	16.8 million

Refresh Rate and Interlacing

Graphics adapters also control the number of times per second the image on the monitor is repainted from top to bottom, called its **vertical refresh rate**. The higher the number the better. A refresh rate of about 60 passes per second (referred to as 60 Hertz, or 60 Hz) is OK for text but can cause annoying flicker in Windows and other graphics applications. For Super VGA, 72 Hz is considered good.

Interlaced monitors refresh every other line of the picture with each pass, and therefore require two complete passes of the electron beam to refresh the display. (Televisions use this method.) A **noninterlaced** monitor updates the entire display in a single pass and is less likely to flicker, so if possible, you should choose one that's noninterlaced.

Monitor Size

Most new PCs that come with monitors these days come with 17-inch models (measured diagonally, like a television set). That is a good size for most people, but if space is at a premium or if you want to save a $100 or so on your monitor, you can opt for a smaller, 14- or 15-inch monitor, which will do the job just fine. And if you want a bigger display, you can get a 20- or 21-inch monitor. Those are useful for desktop publishers who need to see two pages side by side or for people who work on very large spreadsheets, but they generally cost substantially more, and they take up a lot of desk space. They can also be too bright for many people. Personally, I don't like staring at a very large monitor. If you really want to go wild, you could get something like the **Gateway Destination PC**, which comes with a 35-inch monitor that's also a TV set.

Resources

Destination PC
Gateway
800-846-2000
www.gateway.com

Dot Pitch

Each pixel on a monitor's screen is actually made up of three dots, one red, one green, and one blue—the primary colors that blend to create a wide spectrum of colors. The tighter these three dots are packed, the sharper the image. That's what **dot pitch** refers to. The lower the dot pitch, the better the image. Make sure you get a monitor with a dot pitch of .28 or lower.

Whatever you do, don't fall for any "bargain basement" monitor that has a higher dot pitch; it really makes a difference. If you are considering a PC that comes with a monitor that isn't .28 or lower, tell the dealer to substitute a better monitor.

Personal Preferences

Finally, and perhaps most important, is what looks good to you. It's hard to define, but you'll know it when you see it. I love the look of Sony and NEC monitors. But though they look great, they also cost a lot more than other brands, and whether it's worth it is really a matter of preference and priorities. My advice when buying monitors is to go with your gut feeling. I'd gladly order a computer from a catalog or a website, but I wouldn't buy a monitor that I've never seen working. Ask the dealer to show the monitor displaying both text and graphics in real-life applications such as a word processor, a spreadsheet, a graphics program, and a multimedia CD-ROM or game that includes a moving video. Viewing small black type against a white background is an excellent way to judge overall resolution and quality.

Flat-Panel LCD Monitors

So far, we've talked about standard CRT (cathode ray tube) monitors—the kind that look like a TV set. These days, though, you can also get "flat-panel" **LCD** (liquid crystal display) monitors. They use the same technology used for notebook computer screens, creating a monitor that takes up a lot less disk space. They're expensive, but if you can afford one, they're wonderful.

Unlike a standard CRT monitor, LCD screens have no gun that scans up and down or left and right, so you don't have the flicker effect you get with a CRT. (You can't usually detect that flicker, but some experts say that it contributes to eyestrain and fatigue.) Another advantage to LCD screens is that they give off fewer electromagnetic emissions, which can interfere with other equipment or, according to some people, have an effect on health.

Some flat-panel displays are now designed to plug into a special port called a **digital flat panel** (DFP) interface. Flat-panel displays that use this kind of interface can be a lot faster than flat-panel displays that plug into regular video cards; the digital interface bypasses the complicated digital-to-analog, then analog-to-digital translation required to run LCDs with a regular video card.

Are Two Monitors Better Than One?

With Windows 98 it's now possible to have two monitors on one PC. I know that seems strange, but it does have its advantages. You can have one program running on one monitor and another on the other monitor. Mac users, especially those involved with desktop publishing, have been doing it for years. To make this happen you not only need two monitors but also two display adapters.

The Bottom Line

Confused yet? I'll make it simple. If you want a quality display system without having to sweat the details, get a noninterlaced Super VGA display adapter and a multiscan monitor with a dot pitch of .28 or below. If your PC comes with an AGP port, so much the better. It might not do you any good but there's no harm in it and, hey, maybe you'll discover a cool 3-D game or two.

The Keyboard: Not Exactly a Typewriter

16 *A computer keyboard is, to a large extent, like a typewriter keyboard. But there are some important differences. Surrounding the alphabetic keys are a lot of keys you won't see on an old Smith-Corona.*

The keys labeled F1 through F12 are called the **function keys**. These keys can be programmed by a piece of application software to carry out special, often-used functions. Usually, F1 means "give me some help." Most programs have pre-assigned functions for each key.

You might think that the Backspace key would move you back one character, but that's what the backward-pointing arrow on the cursor pad is for. The Backspace key deletes the character to the left of the cursor.

The Esc (Escape) key can often be used to get out of trouble. It backs you out of whatever situation you're in.

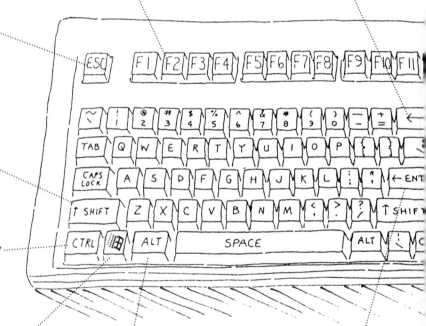

The Shift and CapsLock keys work just like they do on a typewriter. On a computer, though, pressing CapsLock has no effect on number keys.

You usually hold the Ctrl (Control) key down while you press some other key to perform a special command. With most word processing programs, for example, you press Ctrl and Home to go to the top of your document.

The key that has the Windows logo on it pops up the Start menu.

As with the Ctrl key, you hold the Alt (Alternate) key down while pressing some other key to perform a special command. In Windows, the Alt key activates the menu bar. To activate the File Menu, for example, you type Alt-F.

When you're typing, you use the Enter (or Return) key to start a new paragraph. (You don't have to press it to start a new line; word processing programs automatically do that for you.)

Keyboards vary a lot in their layout, but the one shown here is a pretty standard one.

The Print Screen key copies an image of the entire screen to the Windows Clipboard. You can then paste that image into a word processing or graphics program. (Pressing Alt plus Print Screen copies the image of the active window.)

When you're working in DOS, the Pause/Break key causes the screen to freeze, until you press it again. Pressing Shift and Pause at the same time activates the Break key, which interrupts and discontinues some programs. In most Windows programs it doesn't do anything.

In most programs the Scroll Lock key doesn't do anything.

In many programs, when Ins (Insert) is on (that's usually the default), the cursor pushes characters to the right as you type. When it's off, you type over (erase) existing characters as you type.

Pressing the NumLock (Number Lock) key changes the numerical keypad so that the numbers are active. Pressing it again makes the numbers inactive and the arrow keys, Home, End, PgUp, and PgDn active.

C'MON UP HERE. IT'S TIME YOU LEARNED TO TYPE.

The numeric keypad has two uses; you toggle between the two with the Num Lock key. When Num Lock is on, you can use this keypad to enter numbers, as with a 10-key calculator. When Num Lock is off, you can use this keypad to navigate around your document. The numbers become inactive, and the arrow keys, Home, End, PgUp (Page Up), and PgDn (Page Down) become active.

SORRY— OLD DOG, NEW TRICK

Some keyboards have extra buttons, designed to launch often-used programs or execute common commands.

The arrow keys, also known as **cursor keys**, move the cursor around the screen.

The Del (Delete) key, generally, deletes characters. Depending on the program, it may also delete entire words, lines, or even files.

Choosing a Keyboard

Keyboards vary in feel as well as layout. Some are virtually silent. Others click every time you press a key. Some keyboards are mushy; others provide a slight amount of resistance. You'll have to experiment to see which kind is best for you.

Preferences for keyboard layout are also subjective. The illustration on the preceding pages shows just one possible configuration for a PC keyboard. Another keyboard might have the function keys on the left, or at both the left and the top. Some keyboards have no separate cursor keypad, since the numeric keypad does double duty as a cursor keypad. I always look for a large Backspace key (the one I use to correct mistakes as I type).

You don't have to blindly accept whatever keyboard your system comes with (unless it's a notebook computer, of course). Make sure you try a keyboard out before you buy it. After all, if you're a touch typist, you probably enter two or three thousand keystrokes per hour. A poorly designed keyboard can slow you down, increase your mistakes, and cause wrist strain. You should be a fanatic about getting a keyboard that's right for you.

Most PC keyboards work with just about any PC, so a mismatch isn't likely. There are, however, two types of keyboard plugs. Keyboards used on PCs sold in the last few years usually have little round plugs, which are sometimes called "PS/2 connectors" because they were originally designed for IBM PS/2 machines. Older PCs and some store brands or no-name brands may still use the larger round ones. If your keyboard and keyboard plug don't match up, you can buy an adapter for about $5. It's also theoretically possible to use a USB port (described in Chapter 14) to connect a keyboard, but when I wrote this, no such keyboards were available yet.

Ergonomic Keyboards

There are now several keyboards available, from *Microsoft, Key Tronic*, and other companies, that are specially designed to reduce some of the wrist and finger strain generally associated with typing for long periods on standard keyboards. These keyboards, generally referred to

Resources

Key Tronic
509-928-8000
www.keytronic.com

....

Microsoft
800-426-9400
www.microsoft.com/
products/hardware.htm

as **ergonomic keyboards**, typically have a break in the middle that sets the two halves of the keyboard at different angles, letting you keep your wrists in a more natural position. I've tried a couple of ergonomic keyboards, and I find them hard to get used to, but—as with so

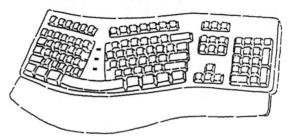

On ergonomic keyboards, the keys are angled outward and raised slightly toward the center so that the wrists stay in a more natural position. Studies have shown that such keyboards can reduce the risk of repetitive stress injuries such as Carpal Tunnel Syndrome.

much about computers—it's really a matter of personal choice. Tests have shown that these keyboards can actually help reduce wrist injuries, but so can taking a few precautions, like using a wrist rest and setting up your workspace correctly. In Chapter 23 I talk about safe ways to use your PC. If you don't take any other advice in this book, please take that seriously, so that you can continue to enjoy your PC—and the use of your hands—for many years to come.

Mice and Other Pointing Devices: Making Quick Moves

17

Windows and Windows programs are designed to be used with a mouse—a device you move around your desk to manipulate a pointer on screen. When the pointer is pointing to the item you want to use, you click one of the buttons on the mouse to select the item, open it, move it, or otherwise bend it to your will.

Practically all PCs come with a mouse; if yours didn't, or if the mouse you have breaks down, you can get one for about $20.

As soon as you see a mouse, you immediately understand how it got its name: It's about the size of a little rodent, and its cord resembles a tail. A small ball on the bottom of the mouse tracks the mouse's movement on the desktop and communicates that information to the computer, which then moves the on-screen pointer in the same direction. In most cases, the kind of sweeping movements you can make with a mouse are much quicker than what you can accomplish using the keyboard's arrow keys, which is the alternate method for moving around the screen. Most programs allow you to carry out almost every action with the mouse except actually typing text.

Mice connect to the computer in one of four ways. Most brand-name PCs have a built-in socket, called a **mouse port** (sometimes called a "PS/2 mouse port" because it was first used on IBM PS/2 machines), that you plug the mouse into. That's the most trouble-free method. Some mice, called "serial mice," plug into a serial port on your computer. Others, referred to as "bus mice," come with an adapter board, which plugs into an expansion slot in your PC, and some newer mice connect via the USB port. (See Chapter 14 for more on all these methods of connecting peripherals.)

Special Features

Windows requires a mouse that has at least two buttons. (I'll explain how they're used in Part 3 of this book.) Some mice have three buttons or four; they can be programmed to provide extra features using software that comes with the mouse.

Microsoft, IBM, and other companies are now offering mice that have wheels or other devices that help you scroll through a document or carry out other actions. Microsoft's *IntelliMouse* looks and acts like a regular two-button mouse but has a wheel in the middle that lets you scroll up and down if your software supports it. (Microsoft Office products and a growing number of other applications do, and they work great when you're surfing the Web.) Logitech offers a similar mouse

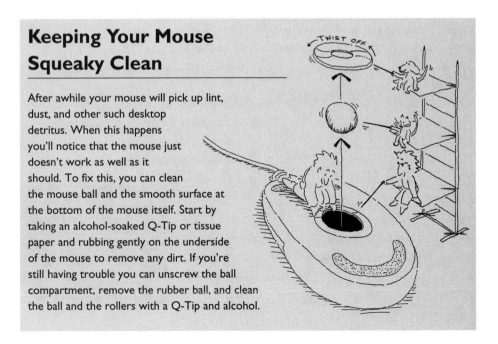

Keeping Your Mouse Squeaky Clean

After awhile your mouse will pick up lint, dust, and other such desktop detritus. When this happens you'll notice that the mouse just doesn't work as well as it should. To fix this, you can clean the mouse ball and the smooth surface at the bottom of the mouse itself. Start by taking an alcohol-soaked Q-Tip or tissue paper and rubbing gently on the underside of the mouse to remove any dirt. If you're still having trouble you can unscrew the ball compartment, remove the rubber ball, and clean the ball and the rollers with a Q-Tip and alcohol.

called the **MouseMan +**. IBM also has an innovative mouse, which scrolls both vertically and horizontally. The IBM **ScrollPoint Mouse** has a small stick (like the TrackPoint device on IBM and some other notebook PCs) that lets you move the pointer in any direction.

Other Types of Pointing Devices

Mice aren't the only way to move your pointer around the screen. Another device, called a **trackball**, does the same thing as a mouse, but in a slightly different way. A trackball is sort of an upside-down mouse, with the ball on top. You move the on-screen cursor by rolling the ball with your hand. Some people find trackballs easier to use than mice, and because they stay in one place, trackballs work well where desk space is limited. You can get a trackball at any computer store for about $50 to $75, and they work with any program that works with a mouse.

For games, you might want to use a **joystick**. Microsoft makes a really cool one called the **Sidewinder Force Feedback Pro**, which breaks new ground in game play by introducing the sense of touch, or force. Armchair pilots can now feel the "stick" shake as they enter a spin or fire a rocket at an enemy plane. Notebook computers have a whole different set of pointing devices (covered in Chapter 8).

Resources

ScrollPoint Mouse
IBM
800-426-2968, 914-765-1900
www.ibm.com

MouseMan +
Logitech
800-231-7717
www.logitech.com

IntelliMouse
Microsoft
800-426-9400
www.microsoft.com

Resources

Sidewinder Force Feedback Pro
Microsoft
800-426-9400
www.microsoft.com/products/
    hardware.htm

DON'T TRY THIS AT HOME.

TRACKBALL

Modems:
Dialing for Data

18

You don't need a modem to operate a PC, but having one gives you access to a lot of information and services you can't get to without one. A modem is a sort of digital operator—a device that connects your call to another modem. It makes sure the information you're transferring makes it safely across the telephone lines and cables that make up the information highway.

By far the most important use for a modem is that it lets you hook into the Internet and online services so that you can surf the World Wide Web, exchange e-mail, meet new people in chat rooms, download free software, and get information at any time of day or night. I'll talk more about how to get access to these services in Chapter 40. Here, we'll just talk about the basic hardware you'll need to get online.

When people refer to modems, they're usually referring to analog modems. An analog modem translates your digital data into analog sounds that can be transmitted over phone lines, and it translates the analog sounds it receives into digital data for your computer. (The word "modem" comes from this process, called *mo*dulation and *dem*odulation.) In the last couple of years, though, several new technologies have appeared that provide lightning-fast connections using completely digital transmission. I'll talk about standard modems first, then describe some of the options for faster, all-digital communication.

If you bought your PC in the last couple of years, it probably came with an internal modem. If you're not sure, check the back your system and look for a telephone jack. If you find one, it's probably connected to a modem. If you don't have a modem, now is as good a time as any to get one.

Leading modem makers include **Hayes**, **3Com**, and **Diamond/Supra**. **Megahertz** (which is owned by 3Com) makes popular PC card modems for notebook computers. There are also some bargain brands that are quite reliable. In the next few sections, I'll go through the features you should look for when buying a modem from any maker.

Resources

Diamond/Supra
408-325-7000
www.diamondmm .com

....

Hayes Microcomputer Products
770/840-9200
www.hayes.com

....

3Com/Megahertz
408-326-5000
www.3com.com

Speed

Modems are rated by speed and, these days, most modems operate at 56K, which means that they transmit and receive data at 56,000 bits per second (bps). Some older or less expensive modems operate at 33,300 bps or even 28,800 bps. (You may see those speeds referred to as 33.3 or 28.8.)

It's always best to get the fastest modem you can, because the speed of the modem is a major factor in determining how long it takes to view Web pages, get and send e-mail, and transfer files from the Internet to your computer. Even with a 56K modem, you'll still find yourself waiting for Web pages to display on your screen.

When 56K modems first came out there were two competing standards, X2 and 56Kflex, which caused major confusion for consumers, modem makers, and Internet service providers (ISPs). Fortunately, the warring sides in the modem war came together and, in early 1998, ratified a standard called **V.90**. If you're going to buy a 56K modem, you should definitely get one that conforms to the V.90 standard.

When you try out your 56K modem, you may notice that it doesn't really operate at 56K. To begin with, it's only 56K in one direction. Data flows at up to 56K from the ISP to your PC, but it flows at only 33.3K from your PC to the ISP. In other words, you receive data faster than you send it out. That turns out not to be a big issue, because most of the time you're just sending out short e-mail messages or even shorter commands from your World Wide Web browser, while the real traffic jam is created by the graphics and other media that comes to you from the Internet.

In reality, you'll never really get the full 56K even in one direction. For one thing the maximum actual speed is 53K due to government regulations in the United States and Canada. For another thing, maximum speed on any modem assumes that you have an extremely clear phone line. I've tested several 56K modems on a variety of different lines and generally experience download speeds of between 40K and 45K. Finally, as you'll discover once you start using the Internet, there are factors other than the speed of your modem that determine how fast information flows your way. The "information highway," like the ones we drive on, can get pretty congested at times. When lots of people are trying to access the Web at the same time, you can count on extra delays. Nevertheless, you're still better off with a faster modem.

Internal or External

Modems come in either internal or external models. An internal modem is a board that plugs into one of the PC's expansion slots or is built onto the PC's motherboard. For a notebook computer, it's either built in or it slides into the PC card slot. An external modem sits on your desk and is connected by a cable to a serial port on your computer.

The advantages of internal modems are that they are generally cheaper, they don't take up any desk space, and they don't require any cables. However, I prefer external modems for a number of reasons. You don't have to take the PC apart to install them, they don't take up an expansion slot, and you can easily move them from machine to machine. What's more, most external modems have lights or displays that provide a visual indication of what they're doing. If

Sharing Your Phone With a PC

Before you buy a modem, consider its effect on your phone service. If you're using your computer and modem a lot, you may need at least one extra line. This is especially true if you're using your modem to receive faxes.

If you plan to use your modem for short periods of time, you can probably get away with a single line. Remember, however, that when you're online, your phone is busy. If you have a call-waiting feature on your phone line and someone calls when you're online, your connection will be interrupted. (In most areas, you can turn off call waiting for the duration of outgoing calls; check with your local phone company for instructions.)

If you plan to use your modem often, or if you use your modem for incoming fax messages, you'll probably want another phone line. Depending on where you live, they cost as little as $8 per month, after the initial installation charge. In most situations you won't even need any toll-call service, since most ISPs can be accessed by a local call from most areas.

your PC already has an internal modem, though, relax and enjoy it. It will do the job just fine.

Unless it already has a built-in modem, a PC card modem is definitely the way to go for a notebook computer. They're so small and light that you won't even know you have it with you until you need it.

Fax

Most modems also include fax capability. With good fax software, sending a fax with your modem is as easy as printing; you give the Fax command, and voilà, your fax has gone to its destination. Faxing from the computer saves you the step of printing out the file and sticking the document into a separate fax machine. When you receive a fax, it is stored on your disk, waiting for you to print it out or view it on screen. Some people like the fact that, since you print the faxes on your regular printer, the faxes are printed on plain paper, which won't fade and curl like normal fax paper. (In fact, that's a feature you would pay a lot extra for on a stand-alone fax machine.)

If you're thinking of using your modem for faxing instead of using a stand-alone fax machine, though, you should also consider some of the disadvantages. First, you can't receive a fax unless your PC is turned on and the fax software is running. If you want to send a copy of a brochure, newspaper article, or other document that's not in your computer, you'll have to get a scanner (described in Chapter 20), which turns hard-copy information into graphics information for the computer. That means adding one more piece of equipment and one more step.

Personally, I like using a fax modem to send documents (they come out clearer on the other end because they don't have to go through the fax machine's scanner), but I prefer receiving them on a standard fax machine. However, if you receive faxes only occasionally, it might make sense to use your PC as your fax machine rather than go out and buy a separate unit.

Surfing in the Fast Lane

Thanks to the popularity of the Internet, local phone companies and cable services have given a lot of attention to how to provide home and business computer users with fast connections. These special services are not available everywhere yet, but at least some may be available in your area. Call your phone and cable companies and ISPs to find out.

ISDN Integrated Services Digital Network (ISDN) services use the same twisted-pair wire used for regular phone lines. A single ISDN line actually offers two 64,000 bps (64Kbps) phone lines (called channels), which can be used for both voice and data. Using a single line gives you just a bit more speed than a 56K analog modem provides, but using both channels for data doubles your speed to 128Kbps. (It's up to you whether you use one or two channels; if there is a per-minute usage cost, using both channels doubles the cost as well as the speed.) Even single-line ISDN is usually faster than an analog connection because the digital transmission is free of line noise, which can slow analog modem speeds. ISDN is available in many areas of the United States, but most phone companies charge for each minute of usage, which makes it too expensive for most consumers.

If you decide to use ISDN, you'll need a special ISDN modem like the *3Com Impact*. Actually "modem" is a mis-nomer for the device used for ISDN or other digital transmissions, because a modem, by definition, is an analog-to-digital converter (modulator/demodulator). But I'm being technical. While "ISDN adapter" is the correct term, most people just call them ISDN modems.

Resources

3Com Impact
3Com
408-764-5000
www.3com.com

Cable modems Cable companies send TV signals into your home via coaxial cables that are also capable of carrying computer data. However, to carry computer data in both directions (to you and from you), the cable company has to adapt its equipment and some of its wiring. As of this writing, cable modems were available to only about 350,000 people in the United States, but lots of cable companies around the country were in the process of updating their lines. (Some cable companies are only able to offer one-way service. The data flows to your computer through the cable at high speeds but you send commands and e-mail to the service through a regular phone line and modem.) A cable modem typically operates at anywhere from 500Kbps to as high as 5,000Kbps (that's 5 megabits per second, or 5 Mbps). Even 500Kbps is about 10 times the speed of a 56K modem, and 5 Mbps is about 100 times the speed of a 56K modem. I have a cable modem where I live, and I love it.

In addition to being faster, most cable modems have the added convenience of giving you a full-time connection to the Internet; your PC is connected to the Internet whenever it is turned on, and you don't have to dial up and make a new connection when you're ready to use it, as you need to do with regular modems and ISDN.

The cable modem itself is generally supplied by your cable service, but to use it, you will usually need a **network interface card** (also called an **Ethernet** card) in your PC. Those typically cost between about $30 and $50.

DSL Digital Subscriber Line (DSL) service is typically offered by phone companies. This kind of service runs over standard telephone lines and can support extra-high-speed transmission—up to 9 Mbps, depending on your service. DSL, like cable, requires a special modem (often provided by the phone company for an extra charge) and, in some cases, a network interface card. As a new technology, DSL is just now being rolled out across the country, and prices are still usually too high for home users.

Internet connection services are changing rapidly. Before you choose a service, your best bet is to call your phone company, your cable company, and any experts you know to find out what's currently available in your area.

Printers: Putting Your Work on Paper

19

Almost everyone needs some kind of printer, and this is one piece of equipment that you'll probably love to buy. Prices have come way down and quality has gone way up in the last couple of years.

There are a number of different kinds of printers on the market, but the vast majority of users opt for either an **ink jet printer** or a **laser printer**. One other kind you might hear about, **dot matrix printers**, used to be popular but now are used mostly for special purpose printing—jobs like printing receipts from cash registers in stores. In this chapter, I'll describe the benefits of ink jet and laser printers and talk about some features you might look for in each kind.

Ink Jet Printers

An ink jet printer works by spraying ink onto the page through tiny nozzles. Ink jet printers are virtually silent, use almost no electricity when they're not in use, don't take up much space, and are light-weight, easy to move, highly reliable, and inexpensive (starting under $100). Best of all, they can print great-looking images either in color or black and white. For home offices and even small businesses, they're a great option. The leading ink jet printer companies are **Hewlett-Packard**, **Epson**, **Canon**, and **Lexmark**.

The output from an ink jet printer isn't usually quite as sharp as that of a laser printer (the wet ink can blot a little when it hits the page), but the difference can be almost indecipherable. Ink jet printers are sometimes slower than laser printers, though that's starting to change. The $799 **Hewlett-Packard 2000C**, for example, prints at up to 10 pages per minute, which is actually faster than most laser printers. Even if the printer does have a slower page per minute rate, it probably doesn't matter. For short jobs the total time it takes to print may be pretty close.

Today's color ink jet printers not only do a good job with general printing but can also print photos that look almost as if they came from a darkroom (see the box "Printing Photos" on the next page).

Ink jet printer manufacturers historically measured quality by reporting the printer's resolution in dots per inch (dpi). Common measurements are 720-by-720 or 1440-by-720 dpi, where higher numbers mean better resolution. This is a good general benchmark, but, as with other numbers, they can be deceiving because there are so many other factors that determine quality (such as the size of the pixels and how they are placed on the page). Hewlett-Packard has actually stopped reporting its printers' resolution because the company feels (with some justification) that the numbers are misleading. HP's 890 series, for example, doesn't have a dpi rating, but the quality is similar to what you get from Epson's 1440-dpi printers.

Resources

Canon
800-848-4123
www.ccsi.canon.com

Epson
800-463-7766
www.epson.com

Hewlett-Packard
800-752-0900
www.hp.com

Lexmark
800-358-5835
www.lexmark.com

Printing Photos

The key to printing good quality color photos is the paper you use. Most color printers will do an OK job printing photos on plain white paper, but if you want the best quality, you'll have to buy special glossy paper that costs about $1 for an $8^1/2$-by-11-inch sheet. That's pretty steep for paper, but it's cheaper than having an 8-by-10 print made at a photo lab. And when you print at the highest quality (and slowest speed), the results can be pretty amazing. Epson's Color Stylus printers do a phenomenal job of printing color photos. Hewlett-Packard and Canon also produce some printers that do a great job with color photography.

Most of these companies also offer printers especially designed for color photos. These printers will do a better job at color photos than a general-purpose printer can, but that's all they can do. My recommendation is that you get a good general-purpose color ink jet printer that is capable of high-quality photo printing and use it as your one and only printer.

To get the photos into your computer, ready for printing, you'll need a digital camera or a scanner. I talk about those in the next chapter.

The best way to determine if a printer is right for you is word of mouth, reviews, and your own observations. Don't be fooled by demos that a dealer may show you. Chances are they're printed on very expensive paper at the slowest (and best) speed the printer runs on. Also, dealers typically show very colorful graphics, which can fool your eyes. Run your own tests using color, black, and all sorts of type sizes, including the small type you'll be using to print most of your documents.

Other factors to consider are speed and the cost per page for both color and black-and-white printing (including the cost of the ink cartridges and the cost for any special paper you might need). Look for a model that can handle at least 100 sheets of paper at a time, and make sure the printer makes it easy to insert envelopes and other special kinds of paper.

It is especially important to get a printer that has a black ink cartridge you can replace separately from the color cartridges (which use red, green, and blue, or cyan, magenta, and yellow ink to generate a full spectrum of colors). Some of the cheaper color ink jets require you to either change your cartridges each time you switch between black-and-white and color printing, or they create black by mixing colored inks. Changing cartridges is inconvenient, and mixing inks produces

Getting an Ink Jet Printer, Fax, and Copier All in One

Several companies offer multifunction devices that combine a color ink jet printer, a fax machine, and a copier in a single piece of equipment. Until recently, I didn't recommend them because the manufacturers generally made too many compromises with at least one of the functions. That's still a danger, but as the market for these has grown, the products have gotten better. Today, Canon, Hewlett-Packard, Brother, Sharp, Panasonic, Toshiba, and other companies make multifunction devices that work reasonably well in each category.

Still, there are some tough decisions to make. With any device, you have to decide what features you need, what level of performance you require, and what you're willing to pay. If you buy a multifunction machine, you can't pick and choose among features for each function—you're stuck with the entire package. One machine, for example, might have a great printer but a not-so-great scanner. Another issue to consider is what happens if something goes wrong. If your stand-alone scanner or fax machine breaks, you can still print. But if any component goes down on a multifunction machine, you have to do without the whole system until it gets fixed. Another issue is that you can't generally use more than one function at a time. If one person is using a machine to print, others will have to wait if they need to send a fax, make a copy, or do some scanning.

Still, the fact that multipurpose devices are cheaper than buying the components separately would be, and that all-in-one devices save so much desk space, can make them a compelling choice for homes and home offices.

lousy-looking black-and-white documents. And if you need to replace all the cartridges whenever your black runs out, you're going to spend a lot of extra money, since you're bound to use more black (for text) than any of the other colors.

Laser Printers

Laser printers, which are popular in offices, are generally faster than ink jet printers and produce very crisp black-and-white pages. A document printed on a laser printer can look almost as if it were professionally typeset.

There are only two reasons to get a laser printer instead of an ink jet printer. The first is if you print a lot of long documents, which laser printers can handle faster than ink jet printers can. The output from laser printers is also of a bit higher quality, so if you're printing final output for publishing or business documents, a laser printer is for you. However, if you want color, you'll have to either spend a lot for a laser printer or go with an ink jet.

If you decide to go for a laser printer, you'll need to first decide whether you want a personal or office model, and then base your choice on how fast it is, its resolution, how it handles paper, and what language it speaks.

Personal or Office. Laser printers are often categorized as "personal" or "office" models. The office models are built to handle printing for several computers linked together over an office network. They generally have faster print speeds, larger paper trays, and tougher components—and are a lot more expensive—than personal models.

Speed. Laser printers vary in speed from 4 pages per minute for the less expensive, personal models, to 8, 9, or even 40 pages per minute for high-end office models. The speed rating is based on the maximum speed that the printer can operate. Your actual speed will be a bit slower, and documents that have a lot of graphics will take longer than those with only text.

Resolution. A laser printer's print quality is primarily a function of its resolution: The higher the resolution, the better the text and graphics will look. Most laser printers print at a resolution of 600 dpi, which looks good enough for any kind of correspondence or business graphics. Some of the more expensive ones, such as the $2,500 **Hewlett-Packard 5000**, operate at 1200 dpi, which, of course, is even better.

Resources

Hewlett-Packard 5000
Hewlett-Packard
800-752-0900
www.hp.com

Paper handling. Laser printers vary in terms of how many sheets of paper they can hold at a time and how they handle envelopes, single sheets of paper, and special stock such as cardboard and transparencies. Office printers generally store between 250 and 850 sheets of paper, while personal laser printers usually store about 100, though some handle up to 250. Some printers can handle two types of stock at once (for example, legal and letter size, or letter size and envelopes, and many allow you to insert one envelope at a time without having to remove the paper. Some printers offer extra paper-handling options for an extra cost; check with your dealer for your options.

PostScript and PCL. If you shop for a laser printer, you're going to hear the terms "PostScript" and "PCL." These terms refer to the language that's built into the printer. Don't worry. You don't have to learn these languages. Your software knows how to "speak" to both PostScript and PCL printers.

PCL stands for "Printer Command Language," and it's built into most brands of laser printers.

PostScript provides more power for working with graphics, color, and fonts than PCL offers. PostScript also works with professional typesetting systems, so a PostScript laser printer is an excellent proofing device for people who, ultimately, plan to output their documents on a typesetting system. But PostScript printers cost quite a bit more than those that don't support PostScript, so there's no reason to get it unless you're a professional graphic artist.

Brand names. Hewlett-Packard's *LaserJet* printers are the most popular and are of excellent quality. Other companies that make good laser printers include *Lexmark*, *Xerox*, *Panasonic*, *Epson*, *Brother*, and *Canon*.

Hewlett-Packard's *LaserJet 6L* is currently one of the hottest on the market. At a street price of about $800, it's more expensive than some other personal laser printers, but it operates at 8 pages per minute, has excellent resolution (600 dpi) and paper handling (250 sheets of paper), and lets you connect to the PC via a wireless infrared adapter as well as via the parallel port. Pretty slick.

Color. Until a few years ago, you could only get monochrome laser printers. Then, when color laser printers appeared, they were incredibly expensive. Now that's no longer true. The *QMS Magicolor 2*, a highly regarded color laser printer, sold for $2,499 when I wrote this. Chances are that there will be even cheaper ones by the time you read this book.

Scanners and Digital Cameras: Adding In Art

One of the great things about personal computers is their ability to work with graphics. You can include photos in your letters or e-mail to relatives, make your own greeting cards, or create a newsletter for your organization that includes snapshots of members and events. In this chapter, I'll describe the hardware you need to get graphics into your computer: scanners and digital cameras.

20

Scanners are useful when you want to bring in art and text that is already on paper and for which you don't have a computer file. Digital cameras are the easiest way to get photos directly into your computer. They save the photos you take as electronic image files rather than on film.

Scanners

Scanners are essentially photocopiers. But instead of producing a paper copy, they create computer image files that can be edited with graphics software, printed out, or posted online. You can use a scanner to capture photos, drawings, and other images. You can also scan in text from hard copies, and using **OCR** (optical character recognition) software you can convert it to a form that can be edited by any word processing program.

There are basically two kinds of scanners on the market—sheet-fed and flat-bed. A sheet-fed scanner works sort of like a standard fax machine. It lets you insert a photo or other document into a roller that sucks it into the scanner and spits it back out after the scan is made. A flat-bed scanner looks like a standard copy machine. It has a glass plate (bed) on which you lay your document. A lens inside the scanner moves back and forth to capture the image.

The advantage of sheet-fed scanners is that they take up less desk space and, in some cases, are cheaper (by about $50) than flat-bed scanners. The advantage of flat-bed scanners is that they can be used for bound material, such as books, and not just for single sheets. Also, some people feel more secure placing precious photos on a flat bed scanner because there is no chance that they can be damaged by the scanner itself (not that there is much risk of a photo being damaged by a sheet-fed scanner). I've used both types and generally prefer a flat-bed because of its versatility.

There are also specialized kinds of sheet-fed scanners. Some, such as the **Easy Photo Reader** from Storm Technologies ($50), are smaller and cheaper than others and are designed specially to scan snapshots (up to 5 by 7). Another type of sheet-fed scanner is designed primarily to handle documents, such as letters, newspaper articles, and receipts, for which image quality isn't really an issue, but speed is. The **PaperPort Strobe** from Visioneer (about $200) is perfect for such quick-and-dirty filing purposes, and it also serves as a general-purpose color scanner.

Resources

Easy Photo Reader
Storm Technologies
800-787-2983
www.stormtech.com

PaperPort Strobe
Visioneer
800-787-7007
www.visioneer.com

Using OCR Software

The files created by scanners are bit-mapped image files (usually in the JPEG, TIF, or some special format), which describe the scanned page as a collection of colored dots. (I talk more about bit-mapped files in Chapter 56.) That means that any text included on a scanned page is described only as an array of different-colored pixels, not as separate letters. In order to use the text in a word processing program—to edit it or change its type style, for instance—you need to convert the description of the page from a bit-mapped description into a text file that records the actual letters in the document. That's the role of OCR software.

OCR software works by analyzing the shapes stored in the image file and matching them to known letter shapes, then creating a text file that includes those letters. It's an inexact science, and results depend on the colors, crispness, paper quality, and typefaces of the original as well as the quality of the OCR software. If the original text is in a very strange typeface, or if the type in the original doesn't contrast well with the background, the OCR software will have problems deciphering it. You always need to do proofreading and cleanup on any file you get from an OCR program.

Law offices are major OCR users because the software makes it easier to edit contracts and other documents that arrive on paper. Some people use OCR software to digitize scanned newspaper or magazine articles or pages from books, but most people won't have a lot of use for it.

When buying a scanner, look at resolution (typically 300 dots per inch, 300-by-600 dpi, or 600-by-1200 dpi) as well as bit depth (typically 24, 30, or 36 bits). In each case, the higher the number the better. The resolution indicates the maximum number of pixels in the scanned image. The bit depth indicates how many colors or shades of gray the scanner can detect.

All scanners come with some kind of scanning software or photo-editing software that you use to control the scanner. Usually, the software has an automatic mode that makes it easy to get a pretty good scan, as well as features that let you tweak the image. Going from pretty good to excellent, however, requires knowing how to use the software to adjust the sharpness, tone, color saturation, and other variables—skills that you can learn from books or classes if you want to become an expert.

Digital Cameras

If all his customers were like me, the guy who runs my local camera shop would be pretty lonely by now. Thanks to my digital camera, I hardly ever stop in to buy or develop film. The photos I shoot are saved as digital files rather than on film. And instead of taking my pictures to the photo shop to be developed, I just transfer the images to my PC, touch them up on screen, and print them out on my ink jet printer.

Digital cameras essentially cut out the developing and scanning processes that usually stand between the taking of a photo and getting it into your computer. And once they're in your computer, you can make all sorts of changes—airbrushing out skin blemishes, fixing crooked teeth, or even shedding a few pounds by stretching out an image so people look thinner. You can "crop" photos (delete portions of them)—which can be great if you've got a terrific looking picture of you and "what's his name" and you want to keep your photo but get rid of his.

Like today's regular film cameras, digital cameras generally offer "point and shoot" operation, with automatic focus and exposure controls. Also like film cameras, digital cameras come in different shapes, sizes, and levels of quality.

No digital camera that sells for under $20,000 can give you the picture quality that you get with even a cheap point-and-shoot film camera, but the photos you take with them are fine for most purposes. The quality of a digital photo mostly depends on its resolution—the number of pixels of information saved per image. Today's low-end cameras typically capture 640-by-480 pixels per image (a total of 307,200 pixels), which is OK if you plan to print very small prints (like 3 by 5) or look at your photos on a computer or TV screen. If you're willing to spend about $600, you can get a digital camera that can turn out 5- by 7-inch prints that look very good on paper and on websites. So-called megapixel cameras capture a million or more bytes of data and give you near-filmlike quality. The $599 **Kodak DC200** (1,152-by-864 pixels) and the $499 **Hewlett-Packard C20** (1,152-by-872 pixels) that were on the market when this book was written produced good 8-by-10 prints and stunning 5-by-7 prints. Digital cameras are getting better and cheaper so quickly, though, that you shouldn't go out and look for these models. Instead, check out ads and reviews for whatever is new.

Leading providers of digital cameras include **Kodak**, **Hewlett-Packard**, **Canon**, **Epson**, **Sony**, and **Olympus**.

In addition to the standard view finder you peer through as you hold the camera up to your eye, most digital cameras also have a color liquid crystal display (LCD) screen that shows you what the picture will look like. The LCD screen can also be used to review a picture that you have already taken. If you don't like it, you can delete it on the spot and take another.

This ability to delete pictures you don't like is useful because the number of pictures you can store in the camera is limited by how much memory it has. Some cameras have built-in memory, but most of the newer ones use little removable memory cards (sometimes called **Flash cards**) that are about an inch square and store 2, 4, 8, 16, or more megabytes worth of photos.

Resources

Canon
800-652-2666
www.ccsi.canon.com

Epson
310-257-4001
www.epson.com

Hewlett-Packard
800-637-7740
www.hp.com

Kodak
800-242-2424
www.kodak.com

Olympus
800-221-3000
www.olympusamerica.com/
   home.html

Sony
800-222-7669
www.sel.sony.com/SEL/

How many photos you can get on, say, a 4-MB memory card depends on a number of factors, including the size of the image, the complexity of the image, and the resolution you shoot at. (Most digital cameras can take photos at different resolutions, up to their maximum.) Depending on those factors, you might get anywhere from 13 to 90 images on a 4-MB memory card. Once you transfer the images to your PC, of course, you can erase the memory card and start again.

You can download pictures from your camera to your computer by connecting them via either a serial or USB port. (If your PC has a USB port, that's a better way to go, because it's much faster than a serial port.) Some digital cameras have connectors that allow you to print directly from the camera without having to go through a PC. Others let you view your images on a TV set. Other things to look for in a digital camera include whether or not it has a zoom lens or an automatic focus, how much memory it comes with, and how easy it is to transfer images from the camera to your PC.

Accessories: Making Yourself Comfortable

21 **N**ow that we've run through the parts of the computer system itself, it's time to turn to the accessories—the small but important pieces of equipment that will keep you and your computer in working order. Accessories such as mouse pads and surge protectors are just as important to your work as a good keyboard. Luckily, they're also very inexpensive.

Surge Protectors

Surge protectors are designed to insulate your computer from electrical surges that can happen during lightning storms, when your refrigerator's motor kicks in, or for no reason at all. Some electrical engineers I've spoken with claim that surge protectors are not necessary because circuits inside your PC's power supply will automatically protect your system in case of an electrical surge; others claim that they're very important. I'd certainly get one if I lived in an area where the power was unsteady. In any case, I like to err on the side of caution. You can get surge protectors for as little as $20, but the more

Plugging computer equipment into a surge protector shields it from any irregularities in your power supply.

expensive ones can offer better protection. Look for a surge protector with a UL (Underwriters Laboratory) 1449 rating, which means that it will prevent more than 500 volts from reaching your equipment.

Wrist Rests

Pound at the keyboard for a full hour and, if you type 50 words per minute, you'll enter 18,000 keystrokes. Keep that up for a full work day and that's a lot of pounding. It's no wonder that tens of thousands of computer users have complained about hand and wrist pain.

The repetitive motion of typing and clicking the mouse can lead to stiffness and minor pain in the hands and wrists. But beware: Those symptoms, if ignored, can turn into major disabling injuries. Since computers have come into widespread use, doctors have seen a burgeoning number of cases of Carpal Tunnel Syndrome, a sometimes crippling disease caused by inflammation of the wrist tendons.

The best way to avoid the trouble is to make sure your wrists are in the proper relation to your keyboard. The keyboard needs to be lower than your elbows, and your wrists should be higher than your fingers. In addition to making sure your desk is the proper height, a good way to ensure the best position is with a **wrist rest**, a simple device that elevates your hands so that your wrists remain straight while typing.

You can get a foam wrist rest at any computer store or business supply store for around $10. Fancier ones go up from there. One person I know uses a rolled up towel to serve the same purpose.

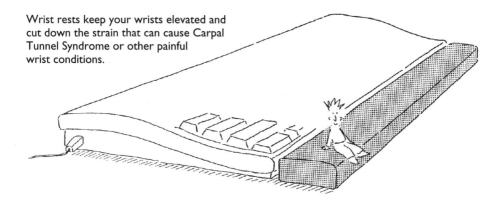

Wrist rests keep your wrists elevated and cut down the strain that can cause Carpal Tunnel Syndrome or other painful wrist conditions.

Carpal Tunnel Syndrome

Carpal Tunnel Syndrome is a serious kind of wrist injury linked to computer use. It results from inflammation of the tendons or the synovial sheaths that surround and protect the tendons.

The symptoms of Carpal Tunnel Syndrome vary, but they often include numbness, tingling, or a burning sensation in the palms, fingers, or wrists. Over time, the condition can lead to a weakening of the muscles. You could also experience loss of sensation, pain, or weakness in the arm or other parts of your body.

If you're experiencing pain or weakness in your wrist, hand, or arm, see a doctor or a chiropractor. It's probably not a full-fledged case of Carpal Tunnel Syndrome, but it's a good idea to give any pain early attention. It's also a good idea to look for a doctor who is familiar with the diagnosis and treatment of Carpal Tunnel and other repetitive-stress-related injuries.

Mouse Pads

A mouse pad is a small pad of soft material that sits under your mouse to give it better traction. Don't try to use a mouse without it. It costs just a few dollars ($2 to $10 at office supply and computer stores), and it makes a big difference.

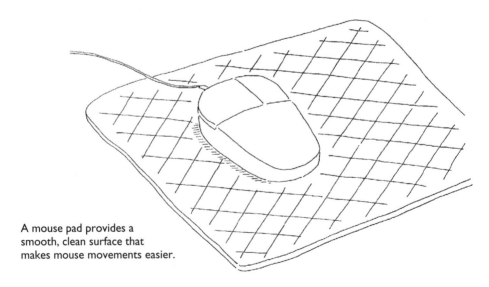

A mouse pad provides a smooth, clean surface that makes mouse movements easier.

Screen Shields

A less crucial accessory, but one that makes a big difference to some people, is a screen shield. These devices slip over your monitor screen to help eliminate glare. If you get a screen shield, try it out before you buy it to make sure that it actually helps your ability to read the screen. Some shields reduce contrast as well as glare, offsetting the benefits with other eye-straining drawbacks.

Screen shields can block the electronic component, but not the magnetic component, of monitor radiation. Some models can save your eyes as well, by sharpening the screen image.

Putting It All Together

22 OK, you've brought your PC home. Now it's time to plug it all together. That's not as difficult as it may seem. If you have a desktop PC, you just plug your various components into the plugs on the back of the PC that fit them. If you have a laptop or notebook PC, you don't even have to put it together—just install and charge up the battery.

Here's how to set up a desktop PC, step by step.

1. The first thing you should do is plug the keyboard into the system unit. The keyboard usually has a circular plug that goes into a round plug at the back of the system unit. Some machines use other arrangements, such as a phone-type jack or possibly the USB port. (I describe that in Chapter 14.)

2. Next, plug in the monitor. There are two cords coming from the monitor. One provides power; the other— the funny-looking one with nine little pins—handles the video signals.

Be careful with the video plug. They sometimes have fairly wimpy pins. It's easy to try to plug them in upside down, and if you exert too much pressure in trying to do that, you'll bend the pins. Since most

TURN YOUR SYSTEM'S POWER OFF BEFORE YOU START MESSING AROUND BACK HERE.

PLUG YOUR MONITOR'S POWER CORD INTO THE WALL OR INTO THE BACK OF YOUR COMPUTER.

PLUG THE COMPUTER INTO THE WALL LAST.

THE KEYBOARD PORT IS USUALLY ROUND. IF YOU HAVE TWO, ONE'S FOR THE MOUSE.

ON

OFF

Turn It Off Before You Connect It

With the exception of USB devices (which are designed to be plugged in while your PC is running), it's a very good idea to be sure your computer and any device you're attaching to it are turned off before you connect them. You're not likely to electrocute yourself, and you might not even damage your equipment, but why take the chance?

monitor cords are hard-wired to the monitor, you'll encounter a hefty service charge if you have to have the plug replaced. So before you start, look very closely at the plug and at the receptacle in the back of the machine. Don't exert pressure until you have aligned the plug with the receptacle. Then insert the plug slowly.

Some computers have an outlet on the back of the system unit where you can plug in your monitor's power cord. If your computer doesn't have one, you'll just plug the monitor's power cord into any electrical outlet (but not yet). Plugging the monitor into the system unit makes it easier to turn on your computer for day-to-day use. You can leave the monitor power switch on at all times and start the whole system by turning on the computer's power switch.

3. Next comes the printer, if you have one. Most printers use a cable with a large connector that goes into the parallel port of your PC. One side of the cable plugs into the printer and the other into the PC. The side of the cable that plugs into the PC is the "male" connector, which plugs into the "female" connector on the back of the PC. (The male connector is the end with the pins; the female connector has the holes.)

Some, though not very many, printers attach to your system's serial ports. These are the small, male connectors on the back of the system unit. Older-style machines use 25-pin connectors. Some newer machines use 9-pin connectors, and some have one of each. If your connector isn't right for your cables, you can always get new cables, or cable adapters, at the computer store.

Some newer printers connect through the USB port. If you have that type of connection, you can plug the printer either directly into the USB port on your PC or to a USB hub (like a power strip for USB devices) that you can purchase from a computer store.

4. If you have an external modem, it will plug into one of your computer's serial ports or into a USB port. (If it's an internal modem, it will be inside the PC.) It will usually have two phone jacks: one to connect the modem to the wall; the other lets you connect your phone through your modem.

5. If you have any other peripherals, such a scanner, you can plug them in now or you can wait and do it later. My advice is to wait. You'll have plenty to do just getting used to the basics. It might be best to leave those extra devices in the box until you're comfortable with the PC itself. That's an especially good idea if any of your peripherals require expansion boards. Before you open the system to add a board, you should be sure the system is working correctly right out of the box.

If you're plugging devices into a USB port, make sure you're plugging the right device into the right socket. This sounds obvious, but you'd be surprised at how many people destroy cables trying to force something where it doesn't go. Take it slow and look before you plug.

6. The final step, after you have everything else connected, is to plug your PC, monitor, printer, and external modem into the wall or a power strip. If you are in an area that has uncertain electrical power, you might consider a surge protector as well. (See Chapter 21 for more on surge protectors.) If you use a power strip, you can leave the switches of your computer and monitor on, and then just turn on the whole system using the on/off switch on the power strip.

And that should do it.

Use the Proper Plugs

You should plug your PC, printer, and other peripherals into a three-prong, grounded electrical outlet only. Connecting one of those three-prong cheater plugs to a two-prong outlet is not a good idea unless you also run a ground wire to a furnace, pipe, or other grounded device. Radio Shack and hardware stores sell an inexpensive device that determines whether an outlet is properly grounded.

The Software That Goes With the Hardware

In order to run any piece of hardware, Windows needs to know how to talk to that hardware. Providing those instructions is the job of the **driver**: a piece of software that comes with the hardware, usually on an accompanying floppy disk or CD-ROM. Any hardware that came bundled with your PC (probably a keyboard, mouse, and monitor) probably has the necessary drivers already installed. But if you bought the pieces separately or if you add a new peripheral to your original setup, you'll need to install the hardware driver.

Windows 95 and Windows 98 have a feature called plug and play, a technology that tries to figure out what type of new hardware you

The Dreaded Case Removal

OK, so you broke down and bought a new sound card, TV tuner, or other device that requires the installation of an expansion card. That means you're going to have to take apart your system unit to install it. Don't panic. Less technically inclined people than you have taken apart their PCs and installed hardware.

Before you break out the screwdriver, remember that, for an expert, this is an extremely easy procedure. Most computer stores will do it for under $50, so if you're really squeamish, you could always go that route. Also, check among your friends to see if any of them has ever installed hardware in a PC. If so, you can probably get one of them to come over and help.

The first thing you need to do is unplug everything. Then you remove the PC's case. Sometimes that's relatively easy but at other times it's a royal pain, depending on the way the case was designed. It's probably covered in your manual, or you can call your PC company's tech support department (or check its

website) to see if you can find instructions. Generally there are Phillips-head screws in the back of the case that you remove, and once they are all removed, you lift the case off of its chassis. This isn't always true, though. Today's cases come in all shapes and sizes and some have plastic thingies that you have to pry off. I've built several computers and know my way around inside them, but there have been times when I've had to call tech support to figure out how to remove the case.

Once the case is off the machine, you should touch the PC's power supply (the big metal box inside) before you touch any electronic components. This isn't a religious ritual; it is a way to discharge any static electricity in your body. If you've been walking around on a carpet or just sitting in a padded chair, there is a possibility that you've built up some static electricity. You know how it feels when you touch someone who has built-up static electricity—you get a mild shock. You can survive a shock like, that but some electronic have installed and what software it needs. That means that if all goes well, Windows will automatically recognize any new hardware you connect to your PC and will tell you that you need to insert the floppy disk or CD-ROM. When you do, Windows will automatically run the installation software and be on its way.

Plug and play works most of the time, but not always (in fact, it's sometimes jokingly referred to as "plug and *pray.*") If plug and play doesn't work, than you may have to call an expert or, perish the thought, read the manual that comes with the hardware to install the driver correctly.

components can't. Touching the PC's power supply discharges any static. Don't worry. You won't get electrocuted. (You *did* unplug the PC first, right?)

At the rear of the system unit there are slots. Some will have cards in them and others might be empty. Remember, too, that (as I described in Chapter 14) a PC may have several different kinds of slots: ISA, PCI, and AGP. The documentation that came with your board will tell you what kind it fits in, and the documentation that came with your PC will tell you which slot is which in the system unit. (It should also be clear just by looking at the slots; your board will only fit in the type of slot it's designed for.)

There is probably a piece of aluminum screwed down over the empty hole in the back of the unit. Your first stop is to remove the aluminum cover and put it aside. (You won't need it anymore unless you remove the device.) When you unscrew the aluminum cover, be careful not to drop the screw into the PC case, or if you do drop it,

fish it out carefully; loose screws inside your case can cause a short. Besides, you'll need the screw again, as I'll explain in a minute.

Being sure you've discharged the static electricity, take the plug in-card and insert it firmly into the appropriate slot. Press down firmly until it's completely seated. The connector from the card (assuming there is one) should be accessible from the rear of the unit.

Now screw the board into place with the Phillips-head screw.

Most manuals tell you to put the case back together now, but I don't do that until I've tested the device. With the case cover off but with the new card firmly screwed into place, connect the device you're installing and turn on the PC to make sure everything works OK. (A PC can run just fine with the case off as long as you don't spill anything into it.) If everything is working right, then you can unplug the device and put the case back together again. If it's not, it's time to check your manual or call the tech support line of the company that made the board.

Setting Up Your Workplace

23 **O**ne of the most important things to think about before you sit down at your computer is just how you're going to sit down at your computer.

You can get away with plopping a PC on a table or desk, plugging it into the wall, and sitting down any which way to type. But making things pleasant and comfortable takes some thought. And it's more important than you might think. You can actually hurt yourself if you don't have your computer set up correctly. Typing for hours in an uncomfortable hunch over the keyboard can cause neck and back pain, eyestrain, and painful injury to your wrists. In this chapter, I'll tell you how to set up a workspace that's safe and comfortable for both you and your computer.

Choosing an Area

Plan your work area from the floor up. A carpeted area will be quieter than wood or linoleum floors, but if you can, stay away from plush carpets. They generate too much static electricity, which can be dangerous for your equipment.

A Comfortable Chair

Don't skimp on your chair. A dining room chair is designed for the length of a meal, not a workday; you need something that will allow you to work comfortably at a desk for several hours at a time. The chair should let you adjust the seat height and the position of the backrest. It should be comfortable and offer you plenty of lower-back support. Check with an office supply dealer for a chair designed to be used with a computer, and test it out before you buy.

The Desk

You don't have to spend a lot of money for a custom-made computer desk. The main thing is to be sure that your keyboard is at the right height. The keyboard should be about 26 inches from the floor—or low enough that your elbows are higher than your wrists while you type. A desk that is too high can result in repetitive stress injuries to your arms and wrists (Chapter 21 has more on Carpal Tunnel Syndrome and other injuries that can result from typing all day at a badly positioned keyboard.) Most office desks and dining room tables are too high. The computer desks that you see at K-Mart and most other discount stores don't look great and may fall apart after a few years, but if they're the right height and depth, they'll do the job just as well as the fancy ones you get from office supply dealers. It's better to sit at a cheap computer desk than at an expensive office desk that's too high for your keyboard.

If you don't want to invest in a new desk, there's another option. Most office supply stores will sell special keyboard holders that attach to the underside of a desk and let you adjust the keyboard to a comfortable height. Providing a shelf for the keyboard also adds some extra desk space.

Lighting

Don't forget the lighting. Your workspace should have plenty of light, but the light should be diffused so that it doesn't create glare on your screen and strain your eyes. Adjustable lamps and lamps that let the light bounce off the ceiling work well for that purpose. If you've got a window nearby, use drapes or shades, or install antiglare film on your windows, to block the excess light.

The Monitor

OK, you've got a low desk so that your keyboard is below your elbow level, and now your monitor is so low that you've got to bend over to see what's on the screen. That can't be good.

You're right, it's not. Your monitor should be up around eye level—when you're sitting up straight. Most monitors these days come on tilt-and-swivel bases, but in many cases they don't offer a wide enough choice of adjustments. You can buy many different kinds of gadgets to take care of this problem, ranging from simple monitor platforms to elaborate adjustable arms that enable you to set your monitor in almost any position and height. If you don't want to spring for one of those solutions, however, try propping last year's Yellow Pages under the screen.

Give Yourself a Break

Even once you've set up your workspace correctly, you still need to do some thinking about how your work habits at the computer can affect your health. Computer health experts point out that even if you've got all the right equipment, in just the right position, working at the computer for extended periods can cause aches and pains. The National Institute of Occupational Safety and Health recommends that you take a 15-minute stretch break for every hour you sit at the computer in order to uncramp your muscles and give your eyes and wrists a break.

The problem seems to be that working at a computer is *too* easy. Unlike at a typewriter, you don't need to feed in new sheets of paper, raise your hands to apply white-out to a mistake, or do the other varied tasks that more traditional work requires. Constant, uninterrupted work can cause repetitive stress injuries. So take a break. It's good for you.

Your PC is all set up and ready to go. Now you're ready to do all the things you wanted to do when you decided to get a computer.

Windows is designed to make working with a PC simple by providing a set of standard ways of doing almost anything you need to do. In Part 3 I'll take you through those basic rules. Don't worry, there aren't too many.

Working With Windows

three

Starting Your Computer

24 *OK, it's finally time to turn on your PC. Ready? Just find the On switch, and you're on your way.*

If your monitor is plugged into your system unit and the monitor's power switch is in the On position, turning on your computer will usually turn on your monitor, too (and turning off your computer will turn off your monitor). If your whole system is plugged into a power strip (see Chapter 21) and the power switches are on, flipping the switch on your power strip should start up your whole system, printer, modem, and all.

While you're waiting for the Windows opening screen, the computer will be flashing all sorts of messages on the screen and flashing some lights on the system unit. This process is called **booting**. The term comes from the expression "pulling oneself up by the bootstraps." That's because the machine gives itself all the instructions it needs to go through its startup process, using intelligence that's built into its chips and stored on its hard disk.

For the most part, you can ignore all the activity that's going on. If your system beeps at you, though, it might want something from you. If you hear a beep, look on the screen to see if there is a message that tells you what to do. In some cases you are requested to "press any key." By the way, some technical support people say that users call them to ask where the "any key" is. There isn't an "any key." Just press a key—any key—on the keyboard.

At the end of the startup process, you'll see the Windows **desktop**, which I describe in the next chapter.

Congratulations! Your computer has successfully started, and you're on your way to using your PC.

How to Fix Things That Might Go Wrong During Startup

Sometimes during startup, your computer may beep at you and display a message. This list describes some of the common messages and how to respond to them.

You Turn On Your Computer and Nothing Happens

Start with the obvious. Is the machine plugged into the wall and is everything plugged into the computer? Check the monitor, the keyboard, the mouse, and the printer cables.

Disk Error

Probably the most common startup problem results in this message:

```
A:>
Non-System disk or disk error.
Replace and strike any key when ready
```

Don't panic—there's probably nothing wrong with the computer. Chances are you have a floppy disk in the floppy drive—the drive that your computer looks in first for its system files. Just remove the floppy disk and press any key on the keyboard. Your computer will continue its startup process.

You Get a Blue Screen With a Message That Says You Didn't Shut Down Properly

It also says that Windows is running ScanDisk to fix the problem. Don't worry. Everything is going to be OK if you just sit there and do nothing for a couple of minutes.

If you see this message, you probably turned off your PC without selecting Shut Down from the Start menu (the proper way to shut down, as I'll describe in Chapter 39). Or perhaps Windows crashed before you could shut it down properly. Whatever happened, don't panic. Windows has a way of fixing itself when this happens and that's exactly what it wants to do. In most cases it will load a program called ScanDisk, which checks to see if there are any problems with your hard drive and, if so, fixes them. All you have to do is wait for it to finish running. If you have an older version of Windows 95, it may require you to press a key before it runs ScanDisk. If so, then just press any key on the keyboard.

Things Seem to Be Happening, but Nothing Shows Up on Screen

If you turn your monitor on and the screen stays dark, don't panic until you've checked the brightness control. (You should find brightness and contrast controls at the side, rear, or bottom of the screen.) A lot of monitor service calls to fix "broken" monitors turn out to be false alarms—they just have the brightness turned all the way down.

(continues on next page)

How to Fix Things That Might Go Wrong During Startup (continued)

You Get the Windows Startup Menu

The Startup menu looks like the one at right.

This is the screen Windows displays if something went wrong with the startup process. It might be nothing, or it could mean a real problem. (The screen shown here is for Windows 98; Windows 95 displays something similar.)

```
Microsoft Windows 95 Startup Menu
===================================

1. Normal
2. Logged (\BOOTLOG.TXT)
3. Safe mode
4. Step-by-step conformation
5. Command prompt only
6. Safe mode command prompt only

Enter a choice: 1

```

The Windows Startup menu offers several startup options.

The best thing to do, first, is restart your computer. Just use the power button to turn it off. Wait about 15 seconds and turn it back on. Don't ask me why, but sometimes things go wrong for no apparent reason and, when you try it again, they work right.

If that doesn't work, restart the computer again, and press the F8 key for about three seconds after the machine restarts. In a moment you'll see a special Startup menu. Select Safe Mode and Windows will start, but it will look different than it usually does. This is a special way of starting Windows in which Windows loads itself but doesn't try to load some of the extra programs that generally start along with it. After Windows starts in safe mode, shut down your computer (by selecting Shut Down from the Start menu) and then turn it back on. That sometimes does the trick.

If you still get the Startup Menu, there may be a problem with one of your startup files or with a piece of software that Windows is trying to load. There are lots of possibilities so, in this case, it's time to get on the phone with your computer's tech support department. (See Chapter 5 for more on where to get help.)

You Hear a Bunch of Beeps But Don't See Anything On Screen

First check the monitor's controls to make sure it is plugged in correctly and the brightness is adjusted. If that doesn't work, you might have to call the PC maker's tech support department. That's often an indication that something is wrong, such as a loose board inside the machine.

In the rest of this section, I'm going to be telling you all about the "rules" of using Windows. But I have a secret for you. Even though I know the rules, I hardly ever think about them. I approach Windows a bit like I approach riding a bicycle. When I'm ready to make a left turn on a bicycle, I don't think about moving the handle bars and leaning my body to the left. Nope. I just do it. The same, I think, is true with athletes, pilots, and just about anyone else who has mastered their craft. While you may have to read through this section or manuals to get started, you'll soon reach the point where things just come naturally.

As you begin to use Windows you'll notice that there are some patterns. Right-clicking generally brings up choices; almost all programs have a File and Edit menu with pretty much the same commands; Alt-F4 will always exit programs and Windows itself. The list goes on. What's important here is not that you remember these or any other procedures but that, as you learn to use Windows, you'll be able to apply your learning in many situations.

It's also important to realize that you can experiment. Most of what I know about computing didn't come from reading books or manuals but from trying things. Some things work out, some things don't, but I always learn something from trying.

As you begin to learn Windows, the system might seem incredibly complicated and out of your control, but before you panic, relax. I swear it won't be long before you too are a Windows expert and moving in and out of menus and programs like you turn the wheels of a bike—without even thinking about it.

Now, on to the rules.

The Windows Desktop

25   The Windows desktop is what you see when your computer finishes starting up and is ready for work. Like a real desktop, the
Windows desktop serves as a work area that holds the various documents and tools you work with. Some of the things you see there
will remind you of items on your real desktop (like file folders),
and serve the same purpose. Others will be less familiar at first,
but you'll quickly get to know them.

Icons
*Little pictures that
represent files or tools
on your computer*

Channel Bar
*A tool for subscribing
to Internet content*

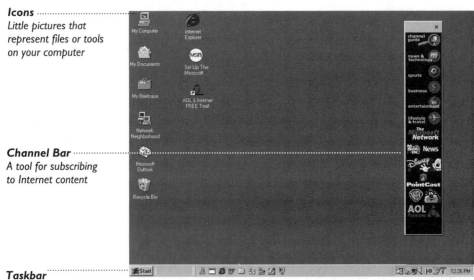

Taskbar
*A tool for managing
open files and programs*

The Windows desktop, like a real desktop, holds the documents and
tools you work with.

What exactly you see when you start Windows will vary depending
on which version you have (Windows 95 and Windows 98 are slightly
different), how your machine was set up, or maybe how the last person
who used the computer left it when he or she shut it down, but in any
case, you'll see something like the screen above.

In Windows 95, the icons look a little different, and you may be
missing a few of the items. And if someone has used your computer

The Quick Tour

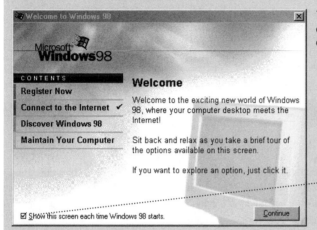

The Windows Quick Tour offers an introduction to the operating system.

Click here if you don't want this box to show up each time you start Windows.

The first time you start Windows, the first thing you'll probably see is a box that invites you to take the Windows Tour. (Depending on how your computer is set up, you might also hear some jazzy music playing to draw you in.)

Taking the tour is a good way to get a quick introduction to working with Windows, so if you're a beginner, I suggest you give it a whirl. To take the tour for Windows 95, click the Tour button on the Welcome screen. In Windows 98, click the Begin button.

In Windows 95, the Welcome screen only shows up the first time you start Windows. In Windows 98, it shows up every time you start Windows unless you tell it to go away; you can make it disappear by clicking the box at the bottom of the display.

If the Tour box isn't on your desktop but you want to take the tour anyway, you can launch it from the Start menu. In Windows 98, click the Start button, point to Programs, then to Accessories, and then to System Tools, and click on Welcome To Windows. In Windows 95, point to Start, select Help, and click on the Tour icon.

(If you're not sure how to use the Start menu yet, just keep reading. I talk about that in the next few chapters.)

before you and changed the setup, it's impossible for me to guess what icons you'll see on screen. None of that matters, though. You'll work with the desktop in the same way whether you're using Windows 95 or Windows 98 and whether or not there are extra icons on the desktop.

If you have just installed Windows 98, these are the icons you should see.

My Computer

My Computer. My Computer is your window to all the files stored on your computer. You can find out more about My Computer in Chapter 27.

My Documents

My Documents. My Documents provides a place to store files you create with your applications. There's no particular reason to store your files here, but it's as good a place as any, I guess. My Documents works just like any other folder; you can rename it and move it if you like. For more on working with folders, see Chapter 27.

My Briefcase

My Briefcase. My Briefcase is a special folder you can use to keep document versions straight when you transfer files between computers. You've got a lot of basics to get through before you start juggling files between computers, so I'm not going to go into detailed instructions for using My Briefcase here. When you're ready to use it, look in the Windows Help system (as I describe in Chapter 30) to find out more.

Network Neighborhood

Network Neighborhood. The Network Neighborhood icon may or may not show up on your desktop, but it's only used if your computer is connected to others over a local area network. If it is, you can open the Network Neighborhood icon to get access to shared files on those computers. A local area network, by the way, is how businesses connect PCs to each other so they can share data between them.

Recycle Bin

Recycle Bin. When you're done with a file, you can delete it by moving it to the Recycle Bin. For instructions on how to use the Recycle Bin, see Chapter 37.

Outlook Express

Microsoft Outlook Express. Outlook Express is the e-mail program that comes with Windows 98 and Internet Explorer versions 4.0 and later. Microsoft made the assumption that you'll probably use the program a lot and so placed a shortcut to it right on the desktop. You can double-click on it to open the program. I'll talk more about how to use Outlook Express in Chapters 42 and 43.

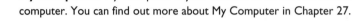

Connect to the Internet

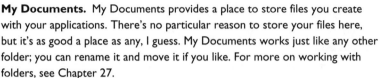

Internet Explorer

Internet Explorer. When you first install Windows, this icon is called Connect to the Internet. If you double-click on it, Windows will take you through a process that helps you connect to the Net. Once you've done that, the icon will be called Internet Explorer, and double-clicking on it will open Internet Explorer, the World Wide Web browser that comes with Windows. (I talk more about Internet Explorer and the Web in Chapter 41.) You need a modem to connect to the Internet and use Internet Explorer.

Set Up The
Microsoft ...

Microsoft Network. The Microsoft Network (MSN) is Microsoft's own online service—a gateway to content on the Internet. Before you open this icon the first time, it's named "Set Up the Microsoft Network." After you have signed on to MSN, the name of the icon changes to The Microsoft Network, and you can use it to get quick access to the online service. You don't necessarily have to use MSN to use the Internet. MSN, as I'll explain in Chapter 40, is one of several Internet service providers you can use. You need a modem to use MSN or any other Internet service provider.

The Microsoft
Network

Online
Services

Online Services Folder. The Online Services folder holds icons that let you connect to other online services, such as AOL. I talk more about online services in Chapter 40.

If you don't see all those icons on your desktop, don't worry. Someone who used the computer before you may have removed them, or whomever you bought your computer from may not have installed them. If someone has used your computer before you, you might also see lots of other icons on the desktop—you can place any file you want on the desktop for easy access.

The other item that may or may not be present on your desktop is the Channel Bar. If you don't see it there, don't worry. I'll describe what the Channel Bar is and how to make it appear when I talk about using the Internet in Part 4 of this book.

Now that you know what the desktop is and what icons are, I'll get on with telling you how to use it.

Shortcut Icons

Outlook
Express

If you see an icon with a little arrow at its bottom, that's a **shortcut** icon. Essentially, shortcuts are copies of icons that exist elsewhere on your computer. They give you easy access to that icon from the shortcut's location. One popular use for shortcuts is to place icons for often-used programs, folders, or files on the desktop, where you can get to them easily. I talk more about how and why to create shortcuts in Chapter 36.

Giving Commands in Windows

26

Windows is now yours to command. Now all you need to know is how to tell it what you want it to do.

The first thing you need to know is that there are usually several ways to do anything in Windows, and that goes for giving commands, too. But once you learn the tricks, you can apply them anywhere—to any icon, window, or menu you find, in Windows or in most application programs you use. I'll teach you the basic ways of giving commands in this chapter, and you'll apply them as you learn to do all the other basic tasks I talk about in the rest of the book.

Mouse Commands

Windows is designed to be used with a mouse. As you move the mouse around on your desktop, a pointer on screen moves along with it, allowing you to point at the object on screen that you want to use. (For more on mice, see Chapter 17.)

Clicking the mouse buttons tells Windows what you want to do with the item you're pointing at. One click means one thing, two clicks means another, and clicking with the right button means something else again. The vocabulary is pretty simple, and it's the same in Windows or in any Windows application. Here's a description of the basic mouse commands and some of the situations you'll use them in.

Clicking To "click" on something, you point to it and press, then release, the left mouse button.

Clicking is most often used to **select** something you want to act on—an icon or a button, for example. Clicking in text places an **insertion point**, which tells the program where you want to insert text you're about to type or move from another place.

"CLICK" (PUSH) THE LEFT BUTTON AND RELEASE IT TO "SELECT" SOMETHING. GOT IT?

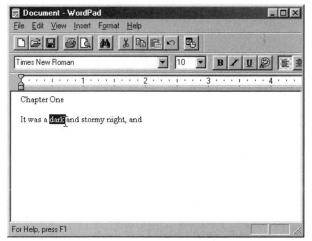

When an item is selected, it is highlighted (changed to a different color). That is the object that any command you give will act on.

TO "DOUBLE-CLICK," QUICKLY PUSH AND RELEASE THE LEFT BUTTON TWICE.

Double-clicking To "double-click," you point to an item and press, then release, the left mouse button twice in quick succession.

Double-clicking on an object—a program or folder icon for example—usually opens it. Double-clicking in text usually selects the word you clicked on.

If double-clicking doesn't work, you may be waiting too long between clicks or clicking too quickly. Try to speed up or slow down the process until you get it right.

TO "DRAG" SOMETHING, YOU "SELECT" THE ITEM, THEN HOLD THE LEFT BUTTON DOWN AS YOU MOVE THE MOUSE.

Dragging "Dragging" means pressing the left mouse button down and moving the mouse while keeping the button held down. Usually, you drag with the left mouse button down, but in special cases (you'll be told when), you drag with the right mouse button down.

Dragging a selected object usually moves it from one place to another. Dragging over text or a set of icons on the screen selects what you drag the pointer over.

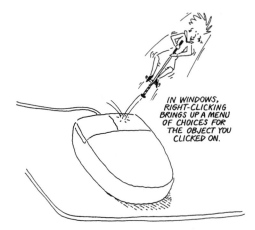

IN WINDOWS, RIGHT-CLICKING BRINGS UP A MENU OF CHOICES FOR THE OBJECT YOU CLICKED ON.

Right-clicking "Right-clicking" means clicking the right mouse button.

Right-clicking calls up a menu that lets you do something with whatever you're pointing at. For example, if you right-click on an

Some Programs Don't Follow the Rules

I'm not happy about the trend, but a growing number of programs aimed at home users break the Windows interface "rules." Some software companies, especially ones that produce consumer-oriented programs designed to edit photos, seem to think that their customers are better off using a set of icons that are unique to their program, and they don't use the standard menu bars that I talk about in this chapter.

So if you are running a program that doesn't follow any of the conventions I write about here, please don't blame me—I'm just telling you how it's supposed to be. And if a program's interface frustrates you, let the software company know how you feel. That's how *they* learn.

item on the desktop, you'll see a menu (sometimes called a **context menu**) that lets you open it, delete it, copy it, or perform other tasks on it. In some programs, right-clicking on a word calls up a menu that lets you change the font, size, or some other attribute.

Try clicking, double-clicking, right-clicking, and dragging a few objects on your desktop to get a feel for what happens.

Menu Commands

You can carry out a few common tasks using just the mouse, but most of the time, you'll use the mouse to select the item you want to act on and then tell the PC what to do with that item by choosing a command from a **menu**. When an item is selected it is usually highlighted (changed to a different color).

A **menu bar** appears across the top of any window you have open on screen. (I talk more about windows in Chapter 28.) The menu bar lists the names of all the menus available in that window. Clicking on any of the menu names shows that menu. Then, clicking on a command name executes the command.

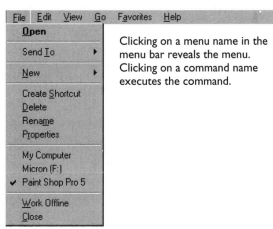

Clicking on a menu name in the menu bar reveals the menu. Clicking on a command name executes the command.

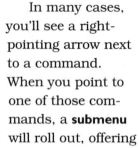

If a menu command has a right-pointing arrow next to it, pointing to that command will display a submenu.

In many cases, you'll see a right-pointing arrow next to a command. When you point to one of those commands, a **submenu** will roll out, offering a whole new set of subcommands, and some of those subcommands might lead to submenus of their own. These are called **cascading menus**. When you find the command you want, you click on it to execute it, just as you would in any other menu.

You'll see menus in several places in Windows besides the main menu bars. The Windows taskbar contains an important menu called the **Start menu**, which you use to start programs and carry out other tasks. (Clicking on the Start button in the taskbar shows that menu. I describe how to use it in later chapters.)

The Start menu appears when you click on the Start button in the taskbar.

Menus also appear when you right-click on an object. (Right-clicking, you remember, means clicking the right button on your mouse.) The menus that appear when you right-click let you carry out common tasks on desktop items.

Every window also includes a special menu called the **system menu**, which you can see by clicking on the icon at the window's top left corner. The system menu

Right-clicking on an object displays a context menu, which lets you carry out common tasks on that object.

items, which are the same in every window, let you close and resize the window. (I talk more about working with windows in Chapter 28.)

You'll also see menus in dialog boxes, which I talk about a little later in this chapter.

Reading a Menu

Menus have more information than just the name of the various commands you can choose from them. Other symbols and signs in a menu give you information about how the commands can be used. The callouts below describe that vocabulary.

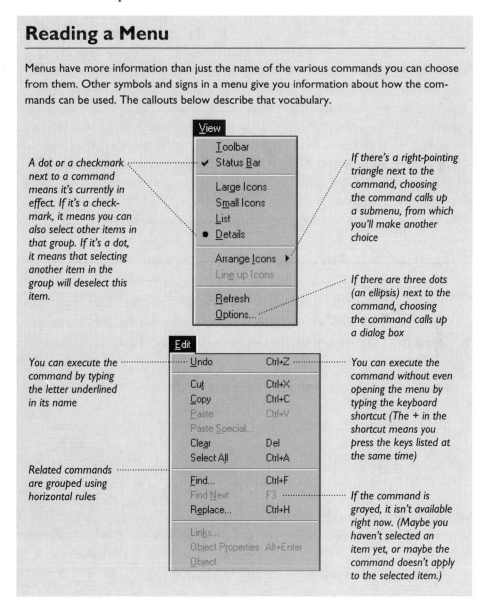

A dot or a checkmark next to a command means it's currently in effect. If it's a checkmark, it means you can also select other items in that group. If it's a dot, it means that selecting another item in the group will deselect this item.

If there's a right-pointing triangle next to the command, choosing the command calls up a submenu, from which you'll make another choice

If there are three dots (an ellipsis) next to the command, choosing the command calls up a dialog box

You can execute the command by typing the letter underlined in its name

You can execute the command without even opening the menu by typing the keyboard shortcut (The + in the shortcut means you press the keys listed at the same time)

Related commands are grouped using horizontal rules

If the command is grayed, it isn't available right now. (Maybe you haven't selected an item yet, or maybe the command doesn't apply to the selected item.)

Keyboard Shortcuts

Menus tell you what commands are available for the items you selected. Once you're used to working with Windows and know some of the common commands, however, you can issue commands without using menus by using **keyboard shortcuts**. It's largely a matter of personal taste, but after working with the PC for awhile, some people find that working with keyboard shortcuts instead of menu commands helps them work faster; if you're typing you don't need to lift your hands from the keyboard to issue a command.

Many menu commands have special keyboard shortcuts. For the ones that do, the shortcut is listed next to the command in the menu. (See the box "Reading a Menu" on the previous page for an example.)

Even commands that don't have special keyboard shortcuts can be issued through the keyboard, though. To issue a menu command from the keyboard, you just follow this procedure. At first do it slowly, one step at a time, but once you get a little pracice, you can do it very quickly.

1. Press the Alt or F10 key. That activates the menu bar.

2. On the keyboard, press the letter that's underlined in the menu name in the menu bar (usually the first letter of the menu name). That activates that menu, and the menu appears on screen.

3. Press the letter that's underlined in the command name. That executes the command.

For instance, to execute the File menu's Open command, you could just press Alt, F, O.

Many commands are common to almost every program, and in those cases, the same keyboard shortcuts should work in every program. (You'll hear more about those commands in Chapter 32, where I talk about working in applications.)

Working With Dialog Boxes

Sometimes Windows or an application program will need more information from you before it executes a command. In that case, a **dialog box** will appear after you issue the command, supplying a place where you can provide that information. When a menu command has three dots following its name, that means it has a dialog box associated with it.

For example, when you choose the Open command from the File menu, you will see a dialog box that looks something like the one at right.

The Open dialog box, shown here, appears when you select the File menu's Open command so that you can specify which file you want to open.

Dialog boxes have several different kinds of controls in them, which you will also find in application windows and other places throughout Windows and Windows programs. The illustrations below describe how to use them.

Command buttons are generally rectangular, tinted, and look sort of three-dimensional. To activate the command written on the button, you click on it.

Check boxes list options that you can either turn on or off. When the box has an *X* in it, the option is chosen. You can check a box (put an *X* in it), or uncheck it, if it is already chosen, by clicking on it.

When you can choose only one option of a set, the options are provided with **option buttons**. Clicking on one button will select it and deselect the others in the set.

Text boxes provide a space where you can type your choice.

Sometimes a text box or other field will have a **drop-down list** associated with it. The list gives possible options for the field. To see the list, you click on the text box or on the down arrow at its right. You can select an item in the list by clicking on it.

 **Tabs** mark the different "pages" of a dialog box. Clicking on a tab opens the set of options it labels.

The **question mark** in the upper-right corner of a dialog box offers help with that dialog box. Click on it for instructions. The X (the **close button**) closes the dialog box without executing the command.

When a dialog box is open, you generally have to close it before you can do anything else. (If you click elsewhere on your desktop, you'll probably just hear a beep, and nothing will happen.) If you close a dialog box with the close box, the dialog box will close without executing the command. To execute the command and close the dialog box, you need to either click on an action button or just press Enter.

Using Toolbars

Windows and many Windows programs feature a row of buttons across the top of their windows called a **toolbar**. Toolbars let you carry out commonly used commands by simply clicking on the button.

The commands the buttons represent change from window to window (they generally let you carry out the most common tasks for that window), but you'll see many of the same buttons in many different windows. Sometimes, you can find out what a button does by just

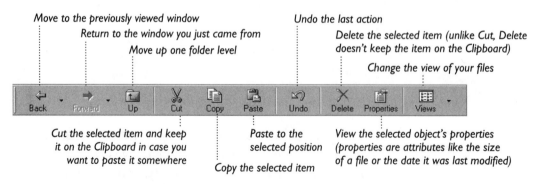

Move to the previously viewed window
Return to the window you just came from
Move up one folder level

Undo the last action
Delete the selected item (unlike Cut, Delete doesn't keep the item on the Clipboard)
Change the view of your files

Cut the selected item and keep it on the Clipboard in case you want to paste it somewhere

Paste to the selected position

Copy the selected item

View the selected object's properties (properties are attributes like the size of a file or the date it was last modified)

In Windows 98, all folder windows can display this toolbar. (You'll see a slightly different set of commands in Windows 95's folder windows.) Holding the pointer over a button for a second will display a ToolTip, naming the command the button executes.

pointing at it (without clicking) for a second. A tiny box, called a **ToolTip**, will pop up naming the command that the button executes. But sometimes this doesn't happen. Don't ask me why Windows is inconsistant. I didn't write Windows. I just write about it.

A window may have several toolbars or none at all. Just because you don't see a toolbar in a window, though, doesn't mean that one isn't available. Click on the window's View menu and look for a Toolbar command or look for the names of toolbars. Clicking on a toolbar name (and putting a checkmark next to it) displays the toolbar. Clicking again (to remove the checkmark) removes the toolbar from the screen.

Pick the Method That Works Best for You

You've now learned four ways to give a command. Look at the Copy command in the Edit menu illustrated on page 123. You now know four ways to execute that command. After selecting the item you want copied, you could

- Use the mouse to click on the menu and then the command name.
- Press the Ctrl and C keys (at the same time) on the keyboard.
- Press the Alt, E, and C keys (one after another).
- Click the Copy button in the toolbar.

All those commands have the same effect, so you can use whichever one works best for you at the time.

Seeing Your Files: My Computer and My Documents

27 **T**he *My Computer icon looks tiny and insignificant, but it's the starting point for managing all the files and settings on your computer. If you use your mouse to point at My Computer and double-click (quickly press the left mouse button twice) you'll see its contents.*

There. You've just double-clicked on an icon to open a window, one of the mouse commands I described in Chapter 26.

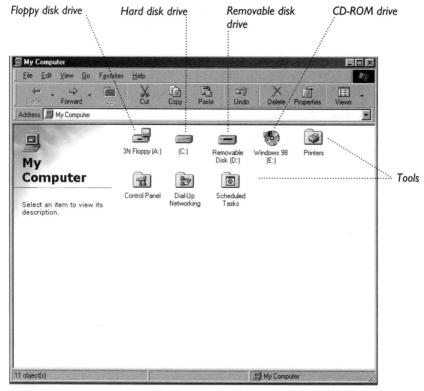

Floppy disk drive   Hard disk drive   Removable disk drive   CD-ROM drive

Tools

When you double-click on My Computer, you see the file system of your PC. Double-clicking on the disk drive icons will reveal the folders and files stored there. (This window will look a bit different if you're using Windows 95 instead of Windows 98, but it works the same way.)

If Your Windows Don't Match the Ones Shown Here

Remember how I told you that there were lots of ways to do almost anything in Windows? Well, that goes for how you view the contents of windows, too. In the illustrations in this book, I show windows as they appear using the default settings in Windows 98 (the setting Windows uses when you've just installed it). If you're using a computer that someone else has been using for awhile, or if the company that made your PC changed the settings or added extra features, your windows might look different. They might include different icons, or they might not show icons at all. To make your windows look as much like the illustrations in this book as possible, click on the My Computer window's View menu and activate the As Web Page and Large Icons commands. (Look for a checkmark next to the As Web Page command and a bullet next to Large Icons; click on them if the checkmark and bullet aren't there.) I don't, by the way, necessarily recommend that you use the View As Web Page mode. You might find your machine runs a bit faster if you don't have that checked.

The icons in the My Computer window that I'm going to focus on here are the ones that represent your computer's disk storage. The different icons represent different types of disk drives—floppy drives, hard drives, CD-ROM or DVD drives, and other drives for removable disks. Under each drive is a letter that labels it (see the box "The ABCs of Disk Drive Names," at right).

To see the items stored on each disk drive, you double-click on the drive's icon. (I'll describe how to use the other icons you see here later in the book.) For now, try double-clicking on the icon representing your hard disk (the one labeled C:). That will open a new window, showing all the files stored there. (The new

The ABCs of Disk Drive Names

The letters that label your disk drives in the My Computer window follow certain rules. A: always refers to your first floppy disk drive, and, in the unlikely event that you have two, B: refers to your second floppy disk drive. C: is always your computer's internal hard disk. After that, things get iffy. Your CD-ROM or DVD drive is probably D:, but not necessarily. If your hard drive is divided into more than one volume, then the different volumes get the next letters (D:, E:, and so on). If you have other types of disk drives, like a Zip disk or a second hard drive, they get the next letters in sequence: E:, F:, and so on. This naming system provides a simple way to refer to your disk drives from programs. You'll see it used when you learn to use paths (which I'll describe on page 131).

Each of your files appears as a separate icon in a folder window or on the Windows desktop. File icons have lots of different designs; their look depends on which application they belong to. File folders hold sets of files you want to group together.

window will probably replace the My Computer window, but once again, that depends on how your computer is set up. If a brand new window opens on top of the My Computer window, don't be surprised. I'll tell you how to change that setting later.)

All About Files and Folders

Files are what hold the information your computer works with.

A file might contain

- an application program
- your budget information
- a letter to your Aunt Hilda
- an illustration or photograph
- music, a recorded voice, or any other sound
- an animation or a short video clip
- the price, location, and inventory number of every stamp in your valuable collection

—in short, any information entered into the computer and saved there.

Just like documents in a real office, the documents, or files, on the Windows desktop are kept in order with file **folders**.

Unlike manila folders, Windows' file folders can hold any number of files; they're infinitely expandable. It's even possible to put folders

Paths: Following the Trail to a File

Before Windows 95 came along and simplified things a bit, PC users didn't have simple metaphors like folders to help them organize their files. Files could still be organized into folderlike compartments (they were called **directories** then), but no graphical user interface existed that could let you find a file by opening folders and looking through their windows. In those days PC users needed to specify the location of a file using a string of characters called a **path** (or sometimes, **pathname**).

In the path shown here, the program file called Calendar.exe is saved in the Windows folder on drive C: (the hard drive).

Why am I telling you this? Because many programs still include references to directories and paths in their dialog boxes and manuals.

A path is pretty easy to understand. It starts with the letter that labels the disk drive that holds the file (A:, B:, C:, and so on, as I described in the box on page 129), followed by the list of all the folders that contain the file, starting with the outermost folder. A backslash character (\) separates the names of the folders. The file name is at the very end of the path.

inside of folders inside of folders. You can open a folder to see its contents by double-clicking on it.

Using the My Documents Folder

My Documents

The My Documents folder offers a convenient place to store files you create.

Files can be generally divided into two categories: **programs** and **documents**. Program files are the ones you get with your computer or that get installed when you buy a new application. Documents are the ones you create using applications in the course of doing your work—chapters of your novel, birthday cards you created, whatever. (I talk more about creating documents in Chapter 32).

Many programs automatically store the documents you create in the My Documents folder on the Windows desktop. There is nothing really special about that folder. It's a folder like any other, but it's as good as any as a place to keep your documents. To view files saved in My Documents, you open the My Documents icon instead of My Computer.

Finding Files On Your System

If you're a very organized person or if you have a really good memory, you might be able to find files you need by opening My Computer and checking through the folders on your hard disk. Once you've been working on your computer for awhile, though, you might have thousands of files saved there, so Windows provides a couple of ways to help.

If you think you know which folder a file is in but you can't find the file among all the files in the window, try typing the first letter or two of its name. Windows will highlight the first file it finds that starts with those letters.

The second trick is to try the Find command, which can find a file anywhere on your system. To use the Find command, click on the Start button at the lower left of your screen (it's part of the taskbar). When the Start menu appears, select Find, and on the submenu that appears, click on Files or Folders. This command will search for files or folders on your own system.

The Find command can search through the Internet, a local area network, and your Outlook Express contacts list as well as your computer's file system.

You can also use Find to search for other computers (if your computer is connected to others on a local area network), through your Outlook Express contact list, or for subjects or people on the Internet, if you're online. (You'll learn more about Outlook Express and the Internet later in the book.)

When you select Files or Folders, you'll see the dialog box shown on the next page. Fill in any information you know about the file and click Find Now to begin your search. Windows will search your system and display a list of files that match your criteria in the list box. (You'll know Windows is done searching when the magnifying glass icon stops moving.)

Click Date to narrow your search to files
created or modified between certain dates

Click Advanced to find more options for
pinpointing your search

Select the parts of
your system you want
to search from this
drop-down list: the C:
drive (your hard disk),
Local Drives (all the
disk drives on your
system), My Docu-
ments, the desktop,
or a particular folder

Type the name (or part of the name) of the
file you want to search for

Click Find Now to
begin your search

If you don't know the
file's name but know
some text it contains,
type the text here

Check this box
to check in all
subfolders, too

Click Browse to select
a folder to search in.

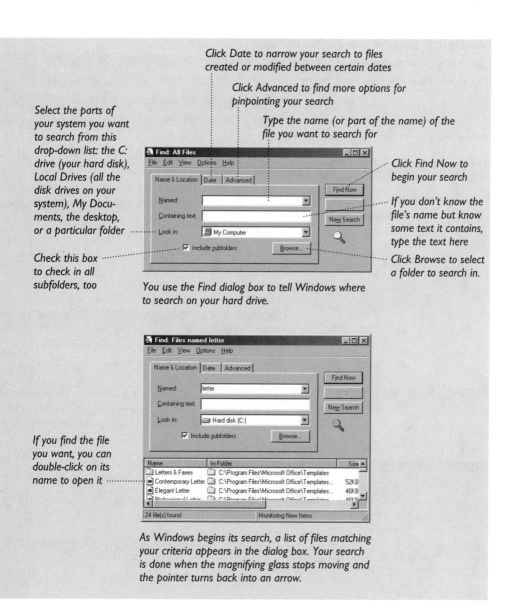

You use the Find dialog box to tell Windows where
to search on your hard drive.

If you find the file
you want, you can
double-click on its
name to open it

As Windows begins its search, a list of files matching
your criteria appears in the dialog box. Your search
is done when the magnifying glass stops moving and
the pointer turns back into an arrow.

Changing Your View of Your Files

Windows offers several ways of viewing lists of files in Folder windows. The different options and their effects are shown in the illustrations on these pages. You can select any of these views by clicking the appropriate icon in the window's toolbar, or by right-clicking in the window and choosing the view you want in the menu that appears.

Click on the arrow next to the VIew icon to show a menu of view options

Large icons

Small icons

List

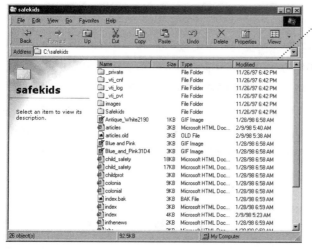

Click on a column label to sort files by that criterion, and click on it again to change the order of the list from descending to ascending order

Details

I like viewing files in the Details view because it lets me quickly sort the files by name, size, type, and date modified. That way I can easily find the files that I worked on most recently. When you're in the Details view, all you have to do to sort the listing of files is to click on the column label—the word Name, Size, Type, or Modified at the top of the window. Your view will be in either ascending (going from A to Z or from the oldest date first) or descending (from Z to A or from the most recent date first). When viewing by date modified, it helps to go in descending order because you see the most recently modified files at the top. To switch between ascending and descending order, just click on the column label again.

You can do more than just view your files in the My Computer window. Later on, you'll learn how to organize your file structure using the My Computer views. Right now, though, we'll just continue with this introduction to the tools on your desktop.

Working With
Desktop Windows

28 *Windows are views into the contents of your computer. They can display the contents of your computer's filing system (like the folder windows you opened in the last chapter) or the contents of individual files. (I talk about opening files and working with program windows in Chapters 31 and 32, when I talk about working with applications.) In this chapter I describe how to work with windows on your desktop.*

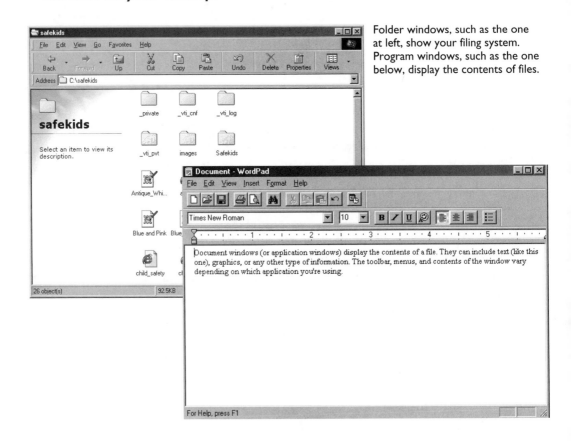

Folder windows, such as the one at left, show your filing system. Program windows, such as the one below, display the contents of files.

Window Controls

Folder windows (the ones you view by double-clicking on My Computer or My Documents) are different in some ways from **program windows**, which you open from within application programs. But no matter what kind of window you're looking at, they all have the same basic set of controls.

Each window's controls let you adjust the window to the size that works best for you, let you place the window wherever you want on screen, and provide menus of commands that let you act on the window's contents. The illustration below describes them all. Try working with each one to see its effect.

Title bar
Displays the name of the object (file or icon) you're looking at. Drag the title bar to move the window on screen

Minimize button
Click here to remove the window from the desktop without closing the file

Maximize/restore button
Click here to make the window fill the screen. If the window is already full size, click here to shrink it

System icon
Click here to view the System menu

Close button
Click here to close the window. If the window holds a file, closing the window also closes the file

Menus
Choose commands to act on the contents of the window

Scroll bars
Click in a scroll bar or drag the scroll box to view more of the window's contents (Scroll bars appear only if the window is too small to show all of its contents)

Toolbar
Click on a tool to quickly execute a command

Status bar
Lists information about the contents of the window

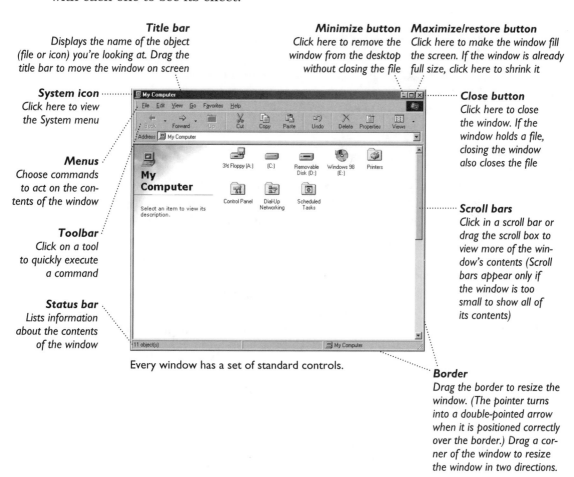

Every window has a set of standard controls.

Border
Drag the border to resize the window. (The pointer turns into a double-pointed arrow when it is positioned correctly over the border.) Drag a corner of the window to resize the window in two directions.

Quick Ways to Tidy Up Your Desktop

You can have several windows open on screen, letting you compare and work with several documents or file views at once. You can rearrange your windows on your desktop using the standard window controls (dragging the title bar to move a window to a new place or resizing a window by pulling on its border, for instance). But Windows also offers commands that let you tidy up your desktop automatically.

You can quickly **tile** or **cascade** your windows to get a view of all open windows at once. To arrange your windows this way, right-click on a blank area of the taskbar and choose Tile Windows Horizontally, Tile Windows Vertically, or Cascade from the menu that appears.

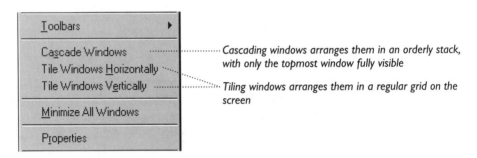

Cascading windows arranges them in an orderly stack, with only the topmost window fully visible

Tiling windows arranges them in a regular grid on the screen

Windows 98 has a handy tool that lets you get all your windows out of the way completely, letting you easily get to your desktop. Click on the icon that looks like a tiny desktop in your taskbar, and all the windows will disappear from the desktop. (No, really; it does look like a desktop if you squint hard enough; it's just so tiny you probably can't make it out at that size.) Click the icon again, and all the windows will come back, arranged just as they were before. (I'll describe more about the tools in the taskbar in the next chapter.)

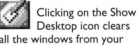 Clicking on the Show Desktop icon clears all the windows from your desktop. Click on it again and they reappear.

Switching Between Windows

To work in a window, you must first make it active. Any window you just opened will automatically become active. You can tell whether a window is active or not by looking at its title bar. The title bar of the active window will be dark (typically blue); all the others will be light (typically gray). If several windows are open on screen at once, the active window will always be on top.

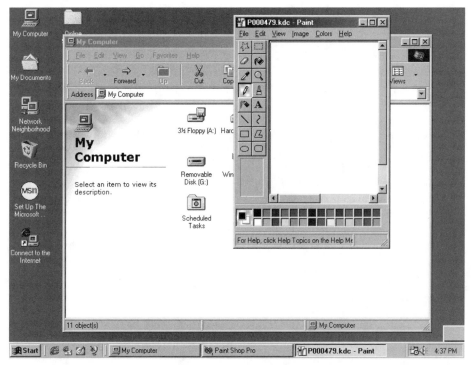

An active window will have a dark title bar. Only one window can be active at a time.

If the window you want to use is visible on screen, the easiest way to activate it is just to click in it. (If the window isn't visible, you can resize, minimize, or close the other windows on screen, using the window controls described on page 137 to bring it into view.)

If the window isn't visible, or if you just don't want to lift your hands from the keyboard to use the mouse, try presing the Alt and Tab keys at the same time. That will activate each of your windows in turn. (Keep pressing Alt and Tab to move through all the open windows.)

Another handy way to activate a window is to click on its Program button in the taskbar. I'll explain what a Program button is and other ways you can use the taskbar in the next chapter.

Using the Forward and Back Buttons in Windows 98

If you're using Windows 98, you'll see back and forward arrows in the toolbar of your folder windows. These buttons are designed to let you access other windows or folders. *Usually,* clicking the back arrow will take you to the last folder window you viewed, and clicking the forward arrow will take you through the list again. Clicking the downward-pointing arrows next to the buttons will display a drop-down menu of all the windows you've opened in that view. But notice I said usually. This should work as described if you're using Windows 98's default settings (the settings it uses when it's first installed), but Windows 98 provides a truly bewildering variety of options for how you view the contents of folder windows, and if you or someone else has changed the settings, the buttons might not work the way I describe.

Click here to view the last window you activated

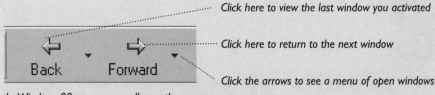

Click here to return to the next window

Click the arrows to see a menu of open windows

In Windows 98, you can usually use the Forward and Back buttons in a folder window's toolbar to activate other open windows.

Trying to describe all the different options would only confuse you here, but later, after you've become comfortable with using Windows, you might look under a folder window's View menu, click on Folder Options, and try some different settings. If you get confused, you can always set things back to the default by making your settings match the dialog box shown at right.

To make your windows act as they did when you first installed Windows 98, use these custom settings. To get this dialog box, choose Folder Options from the View menu of any folder window. When the Folder Options dialog box appears, choose Custom and click the Settings button.

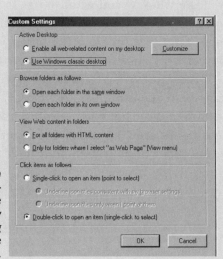

The Taskbar

The taskbar is your computer's main control center, letting you
start new programs, move to favorite places on the Internet, get
help, find files, manage windows and programs on screen, and shut
down your PC.

29

Quick Launch Toolbar

Start button

Program buttons

System Tray

| Start | Main Gallery | Img0017 - Paint | 4:40 PM |

The taskbar is the control center of your computer.

The Start Button

The **Start button** (the leftmost icon on the taskbar) is
your main tool for starting programs, getting help,
finding files, and performing many other common
tasks on your PC. How does it do all that? Try clicking on it, and you'll see the **Start menu**.

You'll be using the Start button more as you learn
how to open files, shut down your computer, and
carry out other tasks in the other chapters in this
section. Right now, though, we're just concentrating
on getting an overview of the taskbar's various components.

The Start menu lets you
start programs, open
documents, change the
look of your desktop,
find files, and shut down
your computer.

The Quick Launch Toolbar

If you're using Windows 98 or Windows 95 with
Internet Explorer (version 4.0 or higher), you should
see the Quick Launch Toolbar, just to the right of the
Start button. This is a mini ver-
sion of the toolbars you learned
about in the last chapter. Like
any other toolbar, this one
includes icons you can click on
to execute common commands.
When you first use Windows 98,

Start Outlook Express   Show Desktop

Start Internet Explorer   Show Channels

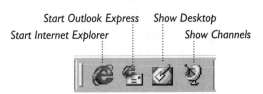

The Quick Launch Toolbar lets you quickly
launch Internet programs and clear your desktop.

the Quick Launch Toolbar includes icons for opening Internet Explorer, Outlook Express, and the Channel Bar (Internet tools that come with Windows, which I describe in Part 4), plus the button you learned about in the last chapter that clears your desktop of windows. Try clicking on the buttons to see what happens.

You can add or remove icons from the Quick Launch Toolbar. To add an icon, you simply drag it from the desktop or a folder to the bar. To remove an icon, simply right-click on it and select Delete from the menu that appears. (Don't worry: You're not deleting or moving the real file; you're just adding or deleting the icon.)

Program Buttons

The central part of the toolbar is reserved for **Program buttons**. These buttons represent every program that is running and every folder window you have open. Clicking on a Program button lets you select the program or folder window it represents. When a program or folder window is minimized, it appears only as a program button on the taskbar.

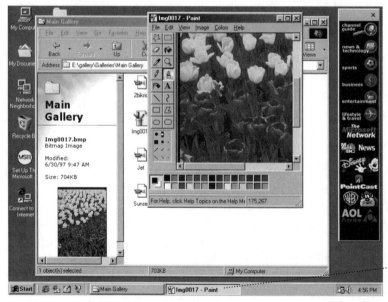

The Program button for the active window looks like it's "pressed in"

When you have windows open on screen, the taskbar holds a button for each one, letting you quickly select the one you want to work with.

(You minimize a window by clicking its minimize button, as you learned in the last chapter.) Clicking on the Program button of a minimized program window opens that window on screen and activates it so it's ready for use.

The System Tray

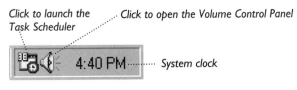

Click to launch the Task Scheduler

Click to open the Volume Control Panel

4:40 PM ······· System clock

The System Tray holds icons for Windows utilties— programs that help you manage the computer itself.

The System Tray, at the far right of the taskbar, holds icons for Windows **utilities** (programs that help you manage the computer itself). When you first start Windows, you'll see an icon for the Task Scheduler, a system volume control, a digital clock, and perhaps one for changing your PC's display settings. You may see other items depending on how your computer was set up by the manufacturer.

Now that you see how handy this taskbar is going to be, you'll be glad to hear that it's available to you at all times for carrying out important tasks. Think of it as the dashboard of your computer.

In Chapter 36, "Customizing Your Desktop," you'll learn ways you can make your taskbar even more useful.

Getting Help From Windows

30 *Almost any time you're stuck, you can get help from Windows itself. The Windows system has lots of built-in features that describe its capabilities and lead you through the most complicated procedures, all just a command or keystroke away.*

The Windows Help System

Windows' most comprehensive help system is available from the Start menu. Clicking on the Start button and then on the Help command brings up a dialog box in which you can find out about any Windows feature.

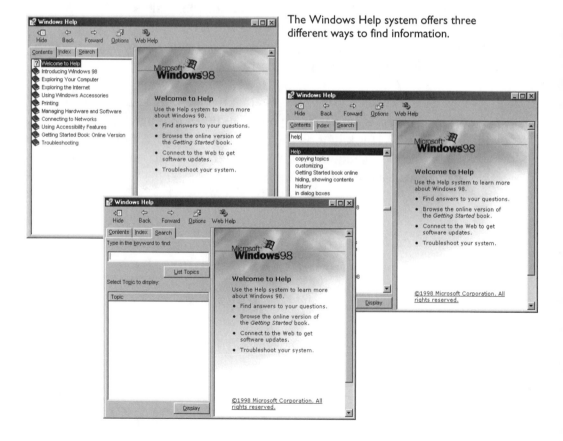

The Windows Help system offers three different ways to find information.

Help in Applications

Most Windows applications offer their own help systems, using the same conventions used in Windows itself. You'll find a searchable help system, ToolTips, help boxes that pop up when you press F1, and Wizards in Windows applications as well as Windows itself. The only difference is that you'll get to an application's help system from the application's Help menu, not from the Start menu.

The three tabs in the dialog box offer three ways to find information.

The Contents tab brings up the help system's table of contents, which lists the major topics. Double-clicking the book icon next to any topic shows subtopics. Clicking on a topic opens the help text in the display area on the right.

The Index tab brings up a more detailed index; you can move directly to a topic you're interested in by typing the first few letters of it in the text box at the top. Click List Topics or double-click on an entry to display information about a topic you want information on.

The Search tab lets you search for a word anywhere in the help system. A list of entries containing that word appears in the list area below the search box. Double-click on the one you want to display the information.

ToolTips and Help Boxes

You've already seen the ToolTips that appear when you point to buttons in toolbars and other Windows icons. ToolTips usually just name the item you're pointing to. You can call up more detailed information about an item by selecting it (clicking on it) and pressing the F1 key. Try it whenever you can't figure out what to do in a dialog box or what an icon is for.

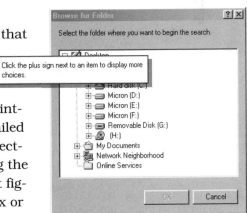

In many cases, clicking on an object and pressing F1 will call up a help box describing that item's use.

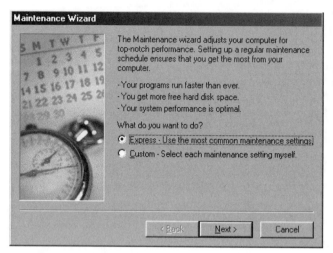

Wizards lead you through multi-step procedures. To use a Wizard, just read the instructions it presents and click Next to move through the steps.

Helpful Wizards

In Windows, **Wizards** aren't magical people in strange hats but help systems that take you step by step through multiple-step procedures like installing software or backing up your hard disk.

A Wizard looks something like a dialog box, displaying instructions and offering choices. You just do what it tells you and answer the questions it asks; the Wizard will make sure it's done correctly. In some cases, a Wizard will totally automate a process; you just sit back while it carries out the task. In other situations, a Wizard is more of an advisor that helps you along the way. Clicking Next in a Wizard window moves you through the process.

Opening Programs

**So *far we've mainly talked about using Windows itself. But
the real fun (and productivity) starts when you actually use
programs—or "applications" as we say in computerspeak.
Applications are what you use to work and play on the computer—to write a letter, plan a budget, explore the Internet,
design a birthday card for your mom, whatever.***

To use a program, you have to open it first. (People also call it "running" a program or "launching" it.) And like just about everything else
in Windows, there's lots of ways to do it. I'll give an overview here. All
the ways I describe below will have the same effect: the program will be
loaded into memory, a document window containing that program's
menus and toolbar will open on screen, a Program button for that window will appear in the taskbar, and you can start your work.

When you open a progam, a window for that program opens on the desktop, and a Program
button appears in the taskbar. You can have several programs open at once—as many as you
have available memory for.

Using the Start Menu

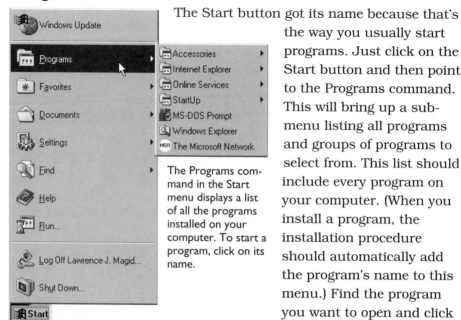

The Programs command in the Start menu displays a list of all the programs installed on your computer. To start a program, click on its name.

The Start button got its name because that's the way you usually start programs. Just click on the Start button and then point to the Programs command. This will bring up a sub-menu listing all programs and groups of programs to select from. This list should include every program on your computer. (When you install a program, the installation procedure should automatically add the program's name to this menu.) Find the program you want to open and click on its name to open it.

Using the Run Command

The Start command includes another way to launch programs—the Run command—that is sometimes even handier to use than the Programs submenu. To use the Run command, you just click the Start button, and then click Run in the Start menu. In the Run dialog box, you can either type in the name of a program you wish to run or use the Browse option to find the program on your hard drive and then run it.

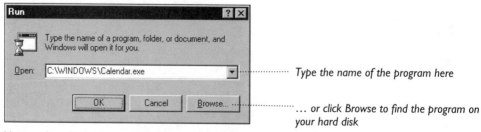

Type the name of the program here

... or click Browse to find the program on your hard disk

You can launch a program by typing its name in the Run dialog box. You can also use Run to open files and folders.

Double-Clicking on an Icon

You can also run a program by double-clicking on its icon—or on the icon of a file created by that program. That's often the quickest way to do it, because you're taking care of two things at once—opening the program and opening the file you want to work on. I talk about how to open files in the next chapter, "Working With Applications."

Closing Programs

When you're done working with a program, you can close it (also called "exiting" or "quitting" it). You don't have to exit a program when you're done with it, but I usually do just to save memory space on my computer.

The way you exit a program is the same in most Windows applications: You either choose Exit from the File menu or you use the keyboard shortcut (press Alt and F4 at the same time). When you exit a program, your PC will close every file that belongs to that program.

If you don't close a program yourself, Windows will close all your open programs when you shut down your computer (a procedure I talk about in Chapter 39).

Working With Applications

32 *The steps you take to draw a picture in a graphics program are different from those you go through to write in a word processor or those you take to map your family tree in a genealogy application. But no matter what program you're using, there are a few basic tasks—things like creating, opening, saving, printing, and closing files; moving, copying, and deleting parts of files; and exiting the program—that you'll always need to do. And to make your work easier, you carry out these tasks in the same way in most Windows applications. In this chapter, you'll learn how.*

Creating a New File

Creating new files is easy. In most cases, you'll find a New command in your program's File menu that does the job. Choosing it will open a blank file in a new window. Often, a program will create an empty file automatically when you start the application.

The New command in the File menu of a Windows program opens a new file.

Opening an Existing File

You can open an existing file—one that has already been created and saved on your hard disk—by double-clicking on its icon in a folder window. If the program that created the file isn't already open, opening the file in this way will also open the right program.

If the program that created the file is already open, you can open an existing file by selecting Open from the program's File menu. An Open dialog box will

The Open command in the File menu of a Windows program lets you open an existing file. You can type the path and filename (if you know it) or you can click the Browse button to find it on the disk.

appear, from which you can select the file you want to open using the Browse button.

Working With Program Windows

Program windows look a lot like folder windows, and as you learned in Chapter 28, they work in many of the same ways. There are a few differences, though, that I'll explain quickly here.

When you open a new or existing file from within an application, a window holding the file opens inside the main program window. This **child window** has many—but not all—of the same controls as the main program window. You can switch between windows using the program's Windows menu. When you minimize child windows, they appear as buttons at the bottom of the program window.

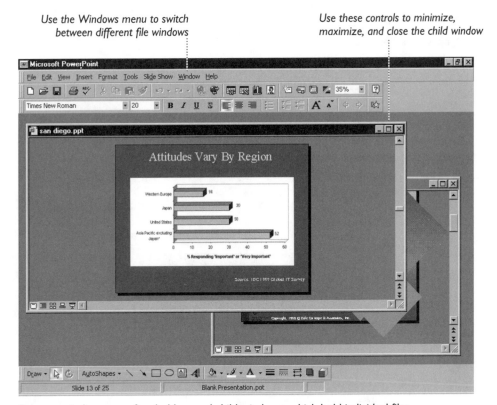

Use the Windows menu to switch between different file windows

Use these controls to minimize, maximize, and close the child window

Program windows can often hold several child windows, which hold individual files.

File Formats and File Extensions

Once you start working with application programs, you'll notice that you can't open just any file with any program. Programs can only work with files that are in a **file format** they recognize. Almost every program has its own proprietary format in which it saves the files it creates. Application programs can usually open files in a few different formats—their own proprietary format and some others as well.

Windows uses a **file extension**—a three-character code following a period in the file's name—to identify which program each file belongs to. For the most part, the extension is put there automatically by the program whenever you save a file. The list of common file extensions below shows some of the extensions you'll see on document files for different kinds of programs. (Although it is sometimes possible to override the default extension by typing one of your own when you save a file, that's not usually a good idea. If you change the extension, a program may not know that a file belongs to it and may have trouble opening it.)

Common File Extensions

Proprietary Formats

.DBF	dBase (database)
.DOC	Microsoft Word or Windows WordPad (word processor)
.WKS	Microsoft Works or Lotus 1-2-3 spreadsheet
.XLS	Microsoft Excel (spreadsheet)
.WPS	Microsoft Works word processing file

Interchange Formats

.BMP	bitmap graphic
.GIF	bitmap graphic
.HTM	a Web page
.JPG	bitmap graphic
.TIF	bitmap graphic
.TXT	plain text
.CSV	a kind of text file used by spreadsheet programs

Program Files

.EXE	the main program file for an application
.DLL	stands for Dynamic Link Library. All you need to know is that it's put there by a program and that you mustn't delete it. The same is true with .DAT, .IFN, and .SYS files. Don't mess with them unless you really know what you're doing.
.DAT	special data that the program itself uses
.INF	"Information" that the program uses to store certain default settings
.SYS	system files created by Windows
.WAV	sound files used by Windows programs (you can also create your own)

Although you don't necessarily see the file extensions when you look at files on the Windows desktop, they're there, behind the scenes. If your folder windows don't show file extensions on the file names, you can tell Windows to show them. In Windows 98, choose the Folder Options command from the View menu in any Folder window. In the dialog box that appears, click on the View tab, and then click the box next to the line "Hide file extensions for known file types." In Windows 95, select Options from the View menu, click on the View tab, and click to remove the check mark next to "Hide MS-DOS file extensions for the types that are registered."

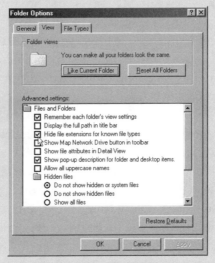

If you don't see extensions on your file names, you can tell Windows to show them using the View menu.

The fact that every program has its own format can make sharing information between programs complicated. Often it isn't a problem, especially when you're working with files from popular word processing programs, spreadsheets, or graphic programs because most of these programs are able to open each other's files. Sometimes, though, you won't be able to open the other program's files at all, and sometimes the file will open, but it will look different in the new program. The layout might be messed up, or it might not even be readable, with a lot of strange characters scattered throughout.

If you want to share a file with a friend who uses a different application, ask them what formats their program can open. Usually, the two programs will have at least one format in common, so you can save your file in a format your friend's program can use. If you want to share text files between incompatible programs, you can always save the file in **plain text**, also called **ASCII**, format. (Such files have the extension .TXT.) Almost every text-based program can also save and read files in plain text format, in addition to its own application format. Plain text files include just the content information, not the formatting, so you will lose all the bold-face text, paragraph indents, and other design information, but the content should come across fine.

Other kinds of files have similar types of interchange formats. For bitmapped graphics, you can use the .BMP, .GIF, .JPG, or .TIF formats. For spreadsheet and database files you can use the "comma-delimited ASCII" format or, better yet, the .WKS (Lotus 1-2-3) or .XLS (Microsoft Excel) format, which are recognized by most spreadsheet and database programs.

Saving Your Work

When you open a file, whether you're creating a new one or opening one that already exists, the program creates a space in your computer's memory where it keeps the information while you work with it. Remember what I told you about memory back in Chapter 12, though: Anything in memory exists only as long as the computer is on. To keep the file safe when you turn off the computer, you must give it a name and **save** it to disk.

You can save a file by selecting Save from the File menu. The keyboard shortcut—the gesture that should become automatic—is usually Ctrl+S (pressing the Ctrl and S keys at the same time). The first time you save a document, Windows will display the Save As dialog box, where you can name the document and select the folder you want to save it in. Every time you save after that, the program will save your changes in the same document and in the same directory.

Many programs help you out with an automatic save feature, which saves the file every few minutes. (You can usually set the interval or turn the feature off in the program's Preferences dialog box.) This can be a lifesaver if you're absent-minded.

Just under the Save command in the File menu you'll notice another command, Save As. You can use this command to save a file

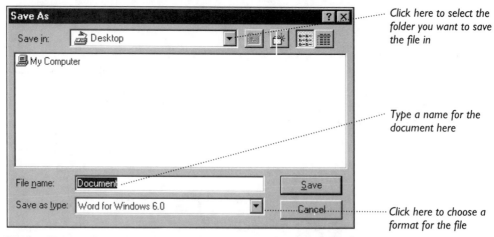

Click here to select the folder you want to save the file in

Type a name for the document here

Click here to choose a format for the file

The first time you save a document, you must give it a name and choose the folder you want to keep it in. (Here I show the Save dialog box from Windows WordPad, but the Save dialog box will look similar in most Windows programs.)

Why You Should Save All the Time

I'm not naive or egotistical enough to believe that you're going to pay attention to everything I say, but in this case, please do—it's very important.

Common sense might suggest that you save your file to disk once you've finished working on it. Wrong. *You need to save your file every chance you get:* when you get up to stretch, when you stop work for a minute to think about what you're going to do next, when you switch between programs, and especially when you answer the phone. It should become an automatic gesture. When you create a new file, it's a good idea to give it a name and save it right away, before you even start to work on it. Once it's saved the first time, you can save it easily at short intervals.

Why? Because more often than you might expect, something goes wrong. If your cat trips over the power cord, if a three-car pileup a mile away takes out a power line, or if your computer just freezes up (which it sometimes will, believe me) and you need to restart it, you will lose everything that isn't saved to disk. Perhaps the most important time to save is just before you print a document, since printer problems are probably the most frequent reasons computers freeze up. Another time to save is if you want to start using another application program. If that program "crashes," it could bring your whole system down with it. That's not supposed to happen, but life doesn't always work out the way we plan.

Invariably, thanks to Murphy's law, foulups become almost inevitable just before a deadline, or when you've just created something that will win you international fame—and you haven't saved. Don't worry about saving too often. That's impossible.

under a new name, in a different format, or in a new location. This lets you use one file as a template for several others. If you want a new document to be patterned on an older one, you just open the old file, select Save As, give the file a new name in the Save dialog box that appears, and click OK. This results in two files: the old one, still saved under the old name, and a new one, under the new name, that you can edit to create a new version.

Naming Files

When you save a file the first time, the program will ask you to give the file a name. You can use any name (up to 256 characters long in Windows 98, up to 32 characters long in Windows 95, including spaces). Only a few alphanumeric characters (listed below) are forbidden:

Forbidden Characters in Windows 95 and Windows 98

\	backslash
/	forward slash
:	colon
*	asterisk
?	question mark
<>	angle brackets
|	bar

Before Windows 95 came along, the rules were a lot more strict. There were more forbidden characters, and file names could be no longer than eight characters, plus the three-character file extension, which follows a period in the file name. (I talked about file extensions on pages 152 and 153.) Thus, you'd have file names like LTR2JANE.DOC for the letter you wrote to Jane in Microsoft Word, JUNBUGET.WKS for the June budget spreadsheet you created in Lotus 1-2-3— you get the idea.

Windows 95 and 98 lets you use long file names, but not all Windows programs do. The longer file names shown in the first dialog box (Letter to Bob, Letter to Darcy, Letter to the Editor, and Letter2 to Darcy)...

...are truncated when viewed in the dailog box of an older program. A tilde (~) in the file name shows that it has been truncated.

To rename a file, right-click on the file name, select Rename, and type a new name.

Why am I boring you with the history lesson? Because some programs still adhere to the old MS-DOS rules and (for reasons that I don't quite understand) have never gotten around to updating their file-naming abilities.

If you try to name a file with invalid characters or try to use a long file name in a program that doesn't allow it, you'll get an **error message** warning you of your mistake.

Once you've named a file, you're not stuck with the name you've selected. You can change the name at any time by selecting the file, right-clicking, selecting Rename, and typing a new one.

Cutting, Copying, and Pasting

Cut, Copy, and Paste are the three commands you'll use most often when you're editing a document. Cut removes the selected material from your document, while Copy stores a copy of the selected material in memory but leaves it in its original position. Paste places the cut or copied material into a new position—within the same document, in another document, or even in a document from another program. For example, you could copy part of an e-mail message and place it in your word processing program, or vice versa.

The commands for these three actions are the same in most Windows programs. You'll find them in the Edit menu, or you can just learn the keyboard shortcuts: Ctrl+X for Cut, Ctrl+C for Copy, and Ctrl+V for Paste. To move or copy any part of your file, you follow this procedure:

Edit	
Undo	Ctrl+Z
Cut	Ctrl+X
Copy	Ctrl+C
Paste	Ctrl+V
Paste Special...	
Clear	Del
Select All	Ctrl+A
Find...	Ctrl+F
Find Next	F3
Replace...	Ctrl+H
Links...	
Object Properties	Alt+Enter
Object	

You'll find the Cut, Copy, and Paste commands in the Edit menu. If the Cut or Copy command is dimmed, you probably don't have anything selected. If the Paste command is dimmed, there's nothing on the Clipboard to paste.

1. Select the text you want to cut or copy.
2. Give the Cut or Copy Command (depending whether you want to move or copy the selection).
3. Click on the position where you want to insert the material, or select any part of the document you want to replace with the new material.
4. Give the Paste Command.

The Windows Clipboard

Where does the material you cut or copy go while it's waiting to be pasted into a new position? To a place called the Windows **Clipboard**, a special part of your PC's memory invented for that purpose. Material that you cut or copy remains on the Clipboard until you cut or copy something else. That means that once you cut or copy something, you can paste it over and over again without copying it again each time. The Clipboard can hold all kinds of information: text, pictures, spreadsheet data, or anything else. But if you want to paste something that you've cut or copied, make sure you do it before you cut or copy anything else or you'll lose it.

Some programs have a Show Clipboard Contents command, but you usually can't see what's on the Clipboard. If you ever want to find out what's on the Clipboard, you can just do a paste operation in your document.

Keyboard Shortcuts

Most Windows applications use the same keyboard shortcuts for common commands. Some of the most useful ones are listed here.

Activate menu bar	Alt or F10	Display system menu in current window	Alt+Spacebar
Close the current window or exit a program	Alt+F4		
Copy	Ctrl+C	Display the shortcut menu for item	Shift+F10
Cut	Ctrl+X	Bring up Start menu	Ctrl+Esc
Paste	Ctrl+V	Switch to the last window you used	Alt+Tab
Delete	Delete Key		
Display Help	F1	Undo	Ctrl+Z

Undoing What You Just Did

Another common editing command you'll learn to love is the Edit menu's Undo command (Ctrl+Z). It does just what it says: It undoes your last action, whether that's typing, deleting part of your document, adding a new color to a picture, or any other operation.

In some programs, you can even undo an Undo command (in effect, redoing whatever you just did undid) by giving the Undo command again. (In such programs, the command usually changes to Redo in the Edit menu.) In other programs, which have "multiple undo" capabilities, you can undo more than just your last action. Giving the Undo command again and again lets you undo several editing steps, which enables you to return to an earlier state of the file if you decide you've taken a wrong turn in the editing process.

Printing a File

The Print command is almost always in the File menu, and the keyboard shortcut is usually Ctrl+P. Of course, in order to print a file, you need to have a printer attached to your PC. (See Chapter 19 for more on printers.)

Giving the Print command will bring up a Print dialog box, from which you can select options such as print quality and the range of

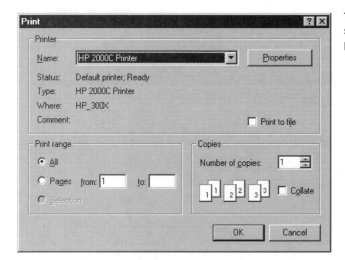

The Print dialog box lets you specify information about the print job.

pages you want to print. The options in the Print dialog box will vary depending on which application you're using and the capabilities of your printer. A very basic one (from Windows WordPad), is shown above.

Closing a File

When you're done working on a file, you close its window. You can do this by clicking the window's close button, as you learned in Chapter 28. Or you can use the application's Close command (Ctrl+W), which you'll find in the File menu.

When you close a file, the computer removes the file from its memory. This is a different from saving it, and if you don't save your work before you close the file, any work you've done since the last save will

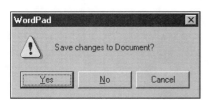

If you try to close a program without saving your work, most programs will ask you if you want to save your changes before you leave the program.

be lost. If you haven't saved all your changes when you give the Close command, the program will usually notify you of that and ask you if you would like to save your changes before closing. If you don't get the "Save changes?" dialog box when you close a file without saving first, that's probably because your program has an automatic save feature that has already done the job for you.

Minimize, Close, or Exit? They're All Different

A lot of computer novices get confused between the actions of minimizing a window, closing a file, and exiting a program. After all, all three remove the file's window from your desktop. But each of these commands has a very different effect.

Minimizing a window doesn't actually close the file, or even the window. When you minimize a window (by clicking the minimize icon in the window's title bar, as you learned in Chapter 28), the window remains on screen as a Program button in the taskbar. (I described that in Chapter 29.) The file and the program stay open in memory, just as if the window were still on the desktop.

Closing a window is a bit more extreme. When you close a window (by choosing Close from the window's File menu or clicking on its close icon), the window and the file inside it are closed (removed from memory), and the file's Program button is removed from the taskbar. To keep your work, you need to save your changes before you close the file, and to work on the file again, you need to open it all over again. But closing a window—even if it's the only window open for a particular program—doesn't exit the program.

Exiting a program closes any windows associated with that program and removes those files, and the program itself, from the computer's memory. As you learned in Chapter 31, you can exit a program by choosing the Exit or Quit command from the File menu (Ctrl+Q) or by shutting down your computer.

Working With Multimedia

Your PC isn't just a data machine—it's a multimedia theater and studio that lets you listen to music, watch videos, and even create your own multimedia productions. We're getting to the point where the PC can actually replace your TV, stereo system, and VCR. The PC on my desk has a built-in TV tuner and a DVD drive that plays movies and audio CDs. Windows also includes players for almost any kind of multimedia file you can find on CDs or the Internet. In this chapter, I'll introduce you to some of its multimedia features.

33

Playing CDs and DVDs

CD-ROMs are exactly the same shape and size of the audio CDs that you play on your stereo. In fact, they store their digital data in basically the same format as audio CDs do. To take advantage of that, Windows includes software that makes it even easier to play an audio CD on your PC than on your stereo system. Just pop in the audio CD in the computer's CD-ROM drive and it should start to play automatically. (It should work the same way with software CD-ROMs, too.) If the CD doesn't start playing on its own, you can go to the Start menu, select Programs, Accessories, and Entertainment, and click on CD Player. You can then run the CD manually.

If you have a DVD drive, you can play movies on DVD the same way. Just insert the disk and it should start to play. (Again, if it doesn't work like that, you'll have to launch the player yourself. Look again in the Programs, Accessories, and Entertainment submenus of the Start menu, but I can't tell

Windows' CD Player software lets you control playback of CD-ROMs or audio CDs.

WebTV: A TV Tuner on Your PC?

The latest multimedia addition to Windows is WebTV for Windows, which you'll find in Windows 98. Because of the name, it's easy to confuse it with Microsoft's other (and very different) WebTV product, which is a hardware unit that lets you access the Internet over your TV set.

WebTV for Windows consists of three components. One part of it, which only requires an Internet connection, allows you to go to the Web to get information about what's on TV. The other two parts of WebTV for Windows require that your PC have a TV tuner card. (Some machines come with tuners, and you can also purchase one that plugs into one of your PC's expansion slots.) With a tuner, you can use WebTV for Windows to watch TV on your PC screen (either in a tiny window or full-screen) and to download special Web pages that come along with your TV signal.

Neither of these functions is all that exciting to me. Although it's nice to be able to get Web pages along with the TV signal, it really doesn't add anything to what you can already do on the Internet if you have a modem. And being able to watch TV on your PC, for most people, seems pretty silly. Unless you're really short of space (such as in a dorm room), you're probably better off putting a TV in the same room as your computer.

you what the program will be named because it's different for each type of computer.)

Personally, I'd rather not watch a movie on my PC—my living room has a TV with a much bigger screen and much more comfortable seating arrangements. I am tempted, though, to get a DVD player the next time I get a notebook PC. That way I'll be able to watch full-length movies while winging my way over the Atlantic. Considering how bad some airplane movies are these days, it's not such a bad idea. Too bad you can't also use a notebook PC to cook an inflight meal.

Playing Sound and Video Clips

You'll find sound and video files in other places besides CD-ROMs and DVDs. You can download sound and video clips from the Internet. There are even sound and video clips already stored on your PC.

Sound and video clips come in a variety of formats (see the box on the next page). The most common kind of sound file is probably .WAV ("wave), a format for storing digital audio signals. Another popular format is .MID, which stores MIDI (musical instrument digital

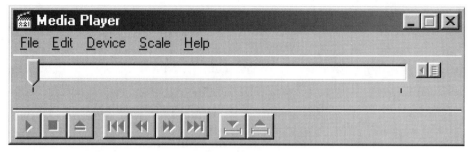

The Windows Media Player plays several sound and video formats.

interface) code, a set of instructions that tells a MIDI-capable instrument what to play.

Windows comes with several wave files and at least one or two MIDI files. Want to hear them? Use the Find command (covered in Chapter 27) to locate files ending in .MID and .WAV and, when they come up, just double-click. If all goes well, you'll hear music, because Windows comes with a program, called Media Player, that plays these and other sound formats.

Media Player also plays video formats, including the popular .AVI (audio-video interleave) and MPEG (an abbreviation for Motion Picture Experts Group, the group that came up with the format). Double-clicking on almost any video format will open a built-in player (either Media Player or a special player that comes with your PC) and play the clip.

Sound and Video Formats

Sound and video files come in lots of different formats. Some of the most popular are listed here. You will be able to play many of these using Media Player or another player that comes with your system. If you double-click on the file and nothing happens, you may need another piece of software. If you downloaded the clip from a website, the site will usually provide a link to any player you need. If you got the file from another source, you can usually download a shareware or freeware player from the Net. (Check the sites listed in the box on page 251.)

Format	*Extension*
Sound	
MIDI	.MID
Real Audio	.RAM
wave	.WAV
Video	
Windows video	.AVI
MPEG	.MPG
Quicktime	.MOV
RealVideo	.RAM

Recording Your Own

It's possible to digitize and edit your own videos on your PC, but that requires some special hardware and software I don't have the space to go into here. Your PC does, however, come with a mini recording studio for sound clips. It's called Sound Recorder, and you'll find it (you guessed it) in the Programs submenu of the Start menu. (In Windows 98, click on Start and then choose Programs, Accessories, Entertainment, and Sound Recorder from the cascading menus. In Windows 95, choose Programs, Accessories, Multimedia, and Sound Recorder.)

Sound Recorder is very easy to operate, with an interface like an analog tape recorder. Make sure you have a microphone plugged in, then simply run the program and, when you're ready to record, click on the red Record button. You can stop the recording by pushing on the rectangular black Stop button, and you can use the arrow keys to rewind and fast forward. You can listen by pressing the Play button; when you're done, just save your file and give it a name. Watch out, though. Sound files can take up a lot of space on your hard disk. This is a good way to record short audio clips, but it's not a substitute for a tape recorder if you need to store a lot of audio.

Windows' Sound Recorder software provides a digital version of a cassette tape recorder.

Don't Hear Anything? Check the Volume

If you don't hear a sound coming from your PC when you think you should, it could be as simple as your speakers being off or unplugged or as complicated as a sound driver not working properly. After you've determined that the speakers are connected, check to see if the volume is set too low on the PC. On most systems there is a volume control icon in the System Tray (in the lower-right corner of the taskbar). It usually looks like a speaker. If you click on it, a slider will appear that you can adjust to change the volume. The exact look of the volume control might depend on what kind of sound card you have in your computer. (A standard setup is shown in the illustration below.) The Volume slider controls all sounds, but you may also need to adjust the Wave slider or other sliders depending on how your system is set up and what you hear. You may need to experiment a bit.

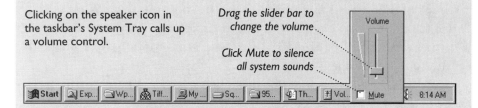

Clicking on the speaker icon in the taskbar's System Tray calls up a volume control.

Drag the slider bar to change the volume.

Click Mute to silence all system sounds

Some PCs also have volume controls in the monitor, on the system unit, or on the speakers themselves. Make sure none of the controls are turned all the way down. Read your instruction manual to see if your PC has a different way to adjust the volume.

Double-clicking on the speaker icon calls up a sophisticated sound mixer, like the audio control panels used in radio stations. You can learn how to use the sound mixer by pulling down the Help menu from the window's menu bar. If you're not hearing any sound, though, look for a checkmark in the box marked Mute below each control. If the boxes are checked, Windows turns off the volume completely. Click the boxes to remove the checkmark.

If this doesn't work, you probably have a problem with your sound driver. That means it's time to call your PC company, the company that made your sound board, or some other expert.

Organizing Your Files

34 *Your hard disk works like a giant warehouse for all your work and tools. When you first buy your computer, that space is almost empty, except for the few things the manufacturer or dealer has preinstalled on the hard disk—Windows and perhaps a few applications. As you use your PC, though, you'll fill your hard disk with hundreds of program files, text files, picture files, and font files. Things can get out of hand pretty quickly unless you develop a few good housekeeping habits.*

Luckily, Windows has provided just the tool you need. What is it? Those folders that you learned about in Chapter 27. Anytime you sense your files getting out of control, it's time to start rustling up a few folders and putting things away.

How you use folders depends on how organized a person you are. Some people will be organizing and reorganizing their folders all the time, whenever they start thinking about their work in a different way. Others will build a very basic structure and work with it as long as they own their computer. Either way is fine; the beauty of folders is that you can set them up in any way that suits your working style.

Creating New Folders

You can create a new folder whenever you need one. If you're in a folder window, you can do it by selecting New from the window's File menu or by right-clicking (clicking the right mouse button) anywhere within the window. Either way, that brings up another menu. Choose Folder from that submenu, and a new folder appears on your desktop.

Any folder you create is automatically called New

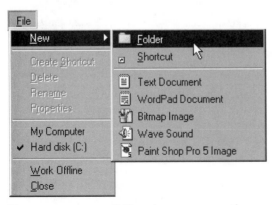

You can create a new folder whenever you need one.

Folder. You can rename it anything you want, though. If you've just created a new folder and want to rename it right away, just type the new name and press the Enter key. You can also rename folders at any other time by selecting the folder (by clicking on it) and selecting Rename from the File menu (or right-clicking on it and selecting Rename from the context menu that appears). You can rename any of your files the same way.

Moving Files Between Folders

In addition to creating new folders for new projects, you'll probably also want to reorganize your files by moving them from one folder to another. If your Letters folder has so many files that it's hard to manage, for example, you may want to split it into two folders: Letters to Family and Business Letters. Or when a project you're working on really gets going, you might want to start creating subfolders in the main project folder to sort the files into manageable chunks—a process that you might repeat several times during the course of the project.

Moving and copying files into new folders and locations on your disks is one of those tasks you can do in a number of ways. If you don't want to dig through My Computer or My Documents for the folders you want to move a file to, you can right-click on the file and choose Cut or Copy from the menu that appears, and then move to the window in which you want to place the file, right-click again, and choose Paste. (It's the same way you cut or copy material from one file to another.) You can also use the keyboard shortcuts for Cut, Copy, and Paste (Ctrl+X, Ctrl+C, and Ctrl+V, respectively) to use the same method.

To move or copy a file, you can right-click on the icon and choose the command from the menu that appears.

If the icon you want to move and the destination location are both visible on the desktop, you can just drag the icon to the new location. (If you're placing the icon in a folder, you can drag the icon to the folder icon or to the folder's open window.) If the new destination is on a different disk than the original location, Windows will assume you want to copy, rather than move, the file. (It's a reasonable assumption because when you move a file to a different disk, you're usually

letter to Patty

To move an icon into a folder, you can just drag the icon onto the folder icon. When the folder icon is highlighted, release the mouse button to drop the icon in.

either making a backup copy, copying a file for a friend or colleague, or putting the file on a removable disk to bring to a different computer.) A plus sign will appear next to the icon as you move it to show that Windows is making a copy of the file.

To control whether you copy or move the file, you can right-click on the icon and drag it to the new location. (Notice that, in this case, you *right*-click on the item rather than clicking with the left mouse button to drag it.) When you let go of the mouse, Windows will ask if you want to Move Here (meaning move to the new location), Copy Here, Create a Shortcut Here, or Cancel. Click on the option you want.

Selecting Multiple Files

If you want to copy or move a number of files or folders, you can save yourself some work by selecting all the files you want to work with at once.

Usually, clicking on a new file after you've already selected another one will deselect the first one and select the last one you clicked on. (Windows assumes you just changed your mind.) However, if you press the Shift key as you click on the additional files, Windows won't deselect your earlier choice. This way you can select as many files as you like. (And you can deselect a selected file, without deselecting all of them, by Shift-clicking on a highlighted icon.)

If the files are contiguous in the folder window, you can draw a selection rectangle around them—just click outside the group of icons you want to select and drag the mouse across them. When all the icons you want to select are highlighted, release the mouse button.

You can use this technique with any file operation—deleting, opening, or performing any other task for which you select files before you act on them. Shift-clicking and dragging a selection rectangle also work to select multiple objects in many applications.

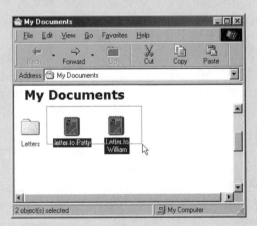

To select contiguous icons in a folder window, you can drag a selection rectangle around them.

Organizing Tips

I know. I said that how you organized your folders was completely up to you. The following suggestions aren't hard and fast, but they have been gleaned from years of experience, so keep them in mind as you organize your filing system.

Keep document files in a different folder from application files. The natural instinct of novice computer users is generally to save Microsoft Word files in the Microsoft Word folder, for instance, but that's not a good idea. You should create new, special folders for the documents you create yourself.

The reason is this: Your hard disk will basically include two kinds of files—ones you can edit and ones you should never touch. The first group includes your document files. The second group—the ones you shouldn't touch—these all the files that come with an application, including the program file itself and any associated files, such as dictionaries and help files. Keeping the files you shouldn't touch in their own folders keeps them out of harm's way. It also makes it easier to find the document files you need.

Windows encourages you to keep your document files separate by providing the My Documents folder to store them in. Many Windows programs use that folder as a default location for files in the Save dialog box. You don't have to use the Documents folder that way, but it's as good a place to use as any. You can create your own subfolders within My Documents to organize your work.

Don't mess with the folders that program installation files create. When you install a program, the installation program will generally create a folder specifically for the application's files. You should leave those folders just as the program created them: Don't delete any files, rename the folder, or move that folder inside another folder. The application will need to use files that are in that folder, and it makes certain assumptions about the folder's name and whereabouts. For example, your word processor will look for its dictionary file to perform a spelling check. If you've moved the application folder to a new location, you're out of luck. It's possible to fix, but make it easy on yourself and stick with the default organization.

Keep only one copy of each file on your hard disk. If you save a file in a folder that already includes a file of the same name, the program will generally ask you if you want to replace the old file with the new one. If you save the new file, or a new version of the file, in a different folder, Windows will just save it, no questions asked. This means that it's possible to have several versions of a file on your hard disk. This is a bad idea unless you are doing it for backup purposes. If you do want to keep a backup copy of a file on your hard disk, make sure you put it in a folder called Backup or something similar. That way, you'll know that the only files in that folder are backup copies. Another option is to give the file a special name like "Backup of Proposal." Yet another option is to keep just the latest version on the hard disk, with a backup copy on another disk entirely. You'll soon find out that nothing is worse than working on—or actually distributing—a document that you think is the latest version, but in fact isn't. In Chapter 36, I tell you about creating shortcuts, a nifty way to keep files in every folder you want to put them in without risking those kinds of problems.

Keep your folder structure simple. If you're a hyperorganized type, you can get really carried away creating folders inside of folders. My advice is, don't. If you create a folder structure more than three levels deep, you'll find yourself spending an awful lot of time clicking away to find what you want. If you plan it right, you can probably create all the divisions you need with no more than three levels.

Backing Up

GRANDMA, TELL US A
REALLY SCARY STORY.

OKAY, HERE'S ONE ABOUT
A YOUNG ASTRONAUT WHO
TRIES TO SAVE TIME BY
NOT BACKING UP MISSION-
CRITICAL FILES.

WHOA!

35

In PC-speak, "backing up" doesn't mean going back to where you started. It means taking steps so that you never have to.

Keeping your work in electronic form has the advantage of keeping it compactly stored, in a form that's easy to work with. The disadvantage is that electronic components are subject to all sorts of dangers. The magnetic data on a floppy disk can be scrambled if you leave the disk near a television set, lying on top of your computer, or in other places near magnetic fields. Hard disks are subject to their own perils. It may never happen to you, but I know lots of people (including yours truly) who have, at least once, turned on their PC only to discover that their hard disk wasn't working. If that happens to you, you had better have a backup copy of your files or, well, you're in trouble. Remember, when you're talking about electronic files, one copy is never enough.

Backing Up Your Hard Disk

If, like most people, you keep all your working files on your hard disk, you'll need to make extra copies of all those files. And you can't rest after you've backed up everything just once. Since those files are added to and changed all the time, you'll also need to back up your new work periodically.

How often you need to back up depends on how much work you do each day. Businesses that store many workers' files on a central hard

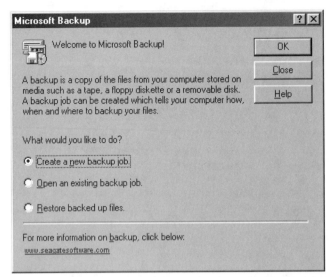

The Backup Wizard leads you through the Backup process. (The one shown here is from Windows 98. The Backup Wizard for Windows 95 looks a bit different.)

disk back the disk up at least once a day. If you're working intensely on a single document, you'll probably want to back up that document every evening or even every few hours. If your work is less intensive, you can get away with backing up every week or so. The best rule to follow is: Back up whenever you'd be distraught if you lost the work you've done since the last backup.

The simplest way to back up your daily work is to keep a backup disk in your computer's floppy drive or Zip drive and save a copy to that backup disk whenever you close a file.

It's also a good idea to make regular backups of everything on your hard disk, or at least everything you've changed since the last big backup. Windows comes with a good backup program that automates the process. You run it by choosing Programs from the Start menu, and then, from the submenus, choosing Accessories, System Tools, and Backup. When you click on Backup, the Backup Wizard will guide you through the process. The Backup Wizard also leads you through the process of copying files from your backup disks to your hard disk, should the need arise.

Usually, you'll back up to some kind of removable disk (which I talked about in Chapter 13).

Creating a Backup Startup Disk

One special kind of backup you should always have on hand is a floppy **startup disk**—a floppy disk that has the files (called **boot files**) that your computer uses to start up. That way, if your hard disk crashes or if something goes wrong with Windows (it *could* happen), you will be able to start up your computer. If you don't have your system files on a floppy, you won't even be able to do that.

You can't just copy the boot files to a floppy. You need to run a special program provided with Windows to create the startup disk. The easiest way to do this is to double-click on My Computer and again on Control Panel. In the Control Panel window, double-click on the Add/ Remove Programs icon. Then, in the dialog box that appears, select the Startup Disk tab and click the Create Disk button. Windows will tell you to put a floppy disk in drive A:, and it may also tell you to insert the Windows 98 (or Windows 95) CD-ROM. Go ahead and insert a blank disk (or one that doesn't hold any information you'll need again) and, if necessary, the Windows CD. Click Next, and Windows will create the backup system floppy for you.

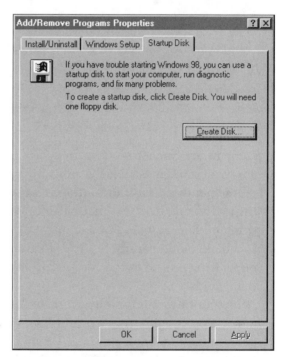

You can create a backup startup disk using the Add/ Remove Programs Control Panel program.

Storing Backups

Software manuals always tell you to store your backup disks "in a safe place," but they never say just what that is.

A safe place for disks is somewhere where they won't be subjected to excessive heat or cold, are away from magnets and sources of electrical bursts, and won't get dusty. The boxes that the disks originally

Locking Backup Floppies

It's easy to save information on a floppy—sometimes too easy. In some cases, you won't want the information on a floppy disk to be altered—you'll want it to stay in just the condition you saved it in. That's true, for example, for copies of a project you've finished, the original program disks for software, your tax records, or business transactions that you've archived to floppy disk. How do you keep the original files from being changed once they're opened on the computer?

Floppy disks have a built-in mechanism for keeping files safe from accidental changes. It's called locking a disk or **write-protecting** it. When a disk is locked, your computer can read files from the disk, but it can't write (that is, save files) to it.

Locking a disk is totally reversible. You can lock and unlock a disk over and over again.

YOU "LOCK" A 3½" DISK BY SLIDING THE BUILT-IN WRITE-PROTECT TAB UP TO UNCOVER THE HOLE.

came in are fine for storing them. You can also buy disk storage boxes at any computer or office supply store.

Remember that information is saved magnetically on disks, so anything that creates a magnetic field is dangerous. Things you wouldn't think of, like a ringing phone or an electric pencil sharpener too close to a disk, could scramble the data stored on it. Don't leave your backup disks lying on top of the computer, either, because it, too, creates magnetic fields.

A lot of people that airport metal detectors might damage their disks. I don't think that's a problem. I've taken floppy disks, the hard disk on my notebook computer, and even audio and videotapes through metal detectors thousands of times, and I have never lost any data.

If you want to be really safe, you need to keep a set of backup disks or tapes off your premises. I hope it will never happen, but if there is a fire or other catastrophe, having a backup in the same room as your computer won't do you any good.

Customizing Your Desktop

Windows has more in common with your office than just a handy desktop. Like your office, your Windows workspace can be decorated to suit your personality and mood. The Windows desktop can be customized with inventive color schemes, fresh wallpaper, and playful sound effects, and you can adjust its behavior to fit your particular way of working. In this chapter, I'll show some of the ways you can adjust Windows to your own tastes.

36

Changing Your Monitor Setting

On most monitors, you can change the number of pixels (picture elements, or the individual dots of color that make up the picture) shown on screen. A higher resolution (more pixels) results in more information on the screen. The other result, though, is that every element is shown at a relatively smaller size, which could make type harder to read. A lower resolution increases the size of the individual elements but limits

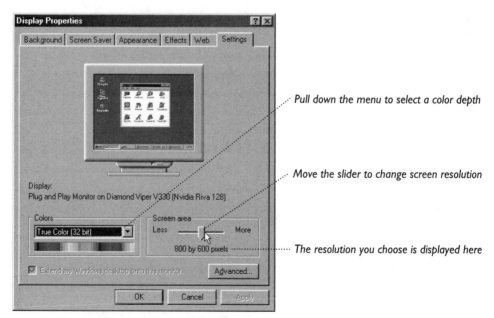

Pull down the menu to select a color depth

Move the slider to change screen resolution

The resolution you choose is displayed here

The Settings tab in the Display Properties dialog box lets you set the bit depth and resolution of your monitor.

the amount that can be shown on screen. If your display adapter and monitor allow it, you can adjust the resolution to find the setting that fits your own preference (and eyesight).

To change the resolution, click on the Start menu, select Settings and then Control Panel, and click on the Display icon (it looks like a monitor) to call up the Display Properties dialog box. You can also get this dialog box by right-clicking on the desktop and selecting Properties from the menu that appears. In the dialog box, click on the Settings tab.

On the left side of the dialog box is a drop-down menu from which you can select the number of colors you want your screen to display. (How many colors are available depends on the capabilities of your display adapter, as I explained in Chapter 15.) The more colors, the richer the image, but going with more colors may slow down your system a bit. Again, your best bet is to experiment.

On the right side of the dialog box, you'll see a slider labeled "screen area." A number below it tells the current screen resolution. Moving the slider chooses a new resolution. Usually, you can choose from three or four different settings. Most people choose 800 by 600, but if you have really good eyes or a big monitor, you can get more on your screen by selecting 1,024 by 768. Try a few settings and see which works best for you.

Redecorating the Desktop

Windows' default decorating scheme is low-key and businesslike. If that's not your style, you've got some pretty wild alternatives to choose from.

If you have Windows 98 (or the Windows 95 Plus Pack), you can choose from a variety of prepackaged decorating "themes," which do a wholesale revamping of your background, sound effects, mouse pointer design, and other elements to create a coordinated look. If your PC has this capability, you'll find it in the Control Panel folder in My Computer. To use it, double-click on My Computer, then on Control Panel, and then on the Desktop Themes icon. The dialog box that appears lets you choose from a drop-down menu of themes and pick and choose which elements of that theme you want to use on your own desktop.

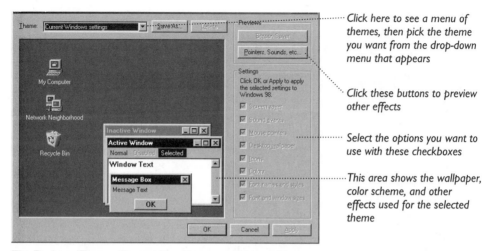

Click here to see a menu of themes, then pick the theme you want from the drop-down menu that appears

Click these buttons to preview other effects

Select the options you want to use with these checkboxes

This area shows the wallpaper, color scheme, and other effects used for the selected theme

The Desktop Themes Control Panel lets you easily combine a coordinated set of preset desktop effects.

If you don't have the Desktop Themes software, or if you just want to do your decorating yourself, you can create a unique look by defining the wallpaper, screensaver, and other settings one at a time in the Desktop Properties dialog box. Again, right-click on an empty part of the desktop and choose Properties from the menu that appears, or choose

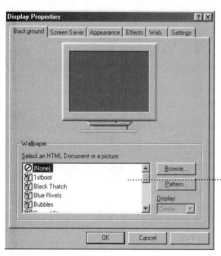

Settings, Control Panel from the Start menu and double-click on the Display icon. You used the Settings tab in this dialog box to set your screen resolution. The other tabs are used for more colorful effects, as shown in the illustrations at left and on the next page.

Choose a pattern or a wallpaper from these lists. (Use the scroll bar to see the full list of choices.) To remove a pattern or wallpaper, select None from the top of the list.

The Background tab of the Desktop Properties dialog box lets you choose a pattern or "wallpaper" (a more elaborate graphic) for your desktop.

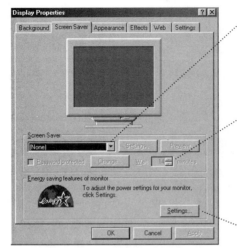

Click here to see a list of screen savers

Click here to increase or decrease the amount of time the computer must be idle before the screen saver kicks in

Click Settings for more screen saver controls

The Screen Saver tab of the Desktop Properties dialog box lets you choose an animated image that will take over your screen when your computer is left idle for awhile.

Click here to see a list of preset color schemes

Click here to choose colors for individual items

Click here to see a menu of colors

Click here to choose a new font

The Appearance tab of the Desktop Properties dialog box lets you choose a color scheme and new fonts for your desktop.

You can use the Apply button to see the effect of your selections on the desktop without closing the dialog box. When you're happy with your choices, click OK.

Personalizing Your Settings

If you share your computer with other people, and those people have different decorating tastes than you do, it could be annoying to have to reset all your desktop preferences each time you work at the computer. For that reason, Windows has a feature that lets you save your settings under your own name and then reset them automatically each time you turn on the computer. You'll find the tool for doing that in the Control Panel folder. To activate it, double-click on My Computer, then on the Control Panel folder, and then on Users. The Multiuser Settings Wizard appears to help you through the process.

The Multiuser Settings Wizard takes you through the process of setting up a password that you can use to invoke all your customized preferences each time you start the computer.

When you finish the process, you will need to restart the computer. When the PC starts up again, it will ask you to sign on with a password (which you created during the setup process). You can assign a password (don't forget it or you'll be locked out) or just leave the password area blank. Signing on this way executes all the settings you've chosen.

You can create personalized settings for as many different people as you like by clicking the New User button in the Wizard's opening screen and repeating the setup process for each user.

If you come to the computer and find someone else has used it and set it up with their own settings, you can either restart the computer (using the Shut Down command in the Start menu, as described in Chapter 39) or just use the Log Off command n the Start menu to log the last user off and then log on as yourself without going through the startup process.

Customizing the Taskbar

Having the taskbar always on screen is one of the things that makes Windows so easy to use. The Start menu, program buttons, and other controls there make it easy to carry out important tasks. Here are a few tricks for making the taskbar even more useful.

In Chapter 29, you learned how to add and remove icons from the taskbar's Quick Launch Toolbar. Now you'll learn how to add new

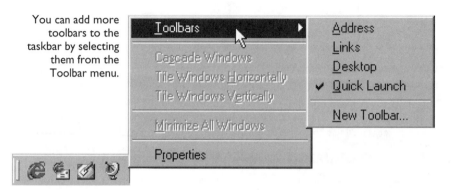

You can add more toolbars to the taskbar by selecting them from the Toolbar menu.

toolbars. The secret? Right-click on an empty part of the taskbar (make sure you click on an empty space on the taskbar, and not on the Start button, a program button, or an icon) and point to Toolbars on the menu that appears. You'll see a submenu that lists four toolbars. A checkmark indicates which toolbars (if any) are already showing. To select others, just click on their names.

You can even change the size of toolbars in the same way you resize a window or the taskbar itself, by dragging the border.

Another taskbar trick is to make the taskbar disappear—but just until you need it. Turning on the taskbar's Auto Hide feature hides the taskbar until you move your mouse to the taskbar's usual position. When you point to that area, the taskbar rolls back into view. To activate Auto Hide, right-click on an empty spot on the taskbar (just as you did to add extra toolbars), and choose Properties from the menu that appears. In the Taskbar Properties dialog box, check the box next to Auto Hide and click OK to activate the feature. If you find the Auto Hide feature too confusing, or if you just don't like it, you can always turn it off again, by clicking to remove the checkmark next to it in the Taskbar Properties dialog box.

Activating Auto Hide in the Taskbar Properties dialog box hides the taskbar until you point to the bottom of the screen.

You can position the taskbar at the side of the screen by just dragging it there.

Another method for getting the taskbar out of your way is to simply drag it to another side of the screen. Just point to it with your mouse (again, making sure you're pointing to an empty spot on it), press the left mouse buttton down, and drag the taskbar to its new position. If you don't like it there, just drag it back.

You can make your taskbar bigger—or smaller again—in the same way you resize a window, by positioning your pointer over the taskbar's border, waiting for the double-headed arrow to appear, and then dragging until the taskbar is the size you want. If you have lots of windows open on screen or lots of toolbars displayed, this gives the taskbar more room to display Program buttons and makes each button easier to read.

You can resize the taskbar by dragging its border.

Adding Shortcuts

A shortcut is a sort of "ghost" icon that acts just like the real one. You can double-click on a shortcut, for example, to open the object that the shortcut represents. By putting shortcuts to items in places that are easy to access (such as on the

A shortcut acts just like the original icon it is created from. Shortcut icons have an upward-pointing arrow at their bottom left corner.

desktop), you save time you would otherwise spend opening and closing folders in which the original object is buried.

You can make shortcuts of any icon: a disk, folder, file, program, or anything else you want quick access to. By putting a shortcut of the object (instead of the object itself) on the desktop, you keep the original object safe in its folder and with the other files it needs to work correctly. You also avoid the confusions that can be caused by having multiple versions of a file scattered throughout your hard disk. And unlike a copy of the object (which would act the same way), a shortcut takes up very little storage space.

One way to make a shortcut is to right-click on the original object's icon and choose Create Shortcut from the menu that appears. That will create a shortcut in the same directory as the original file. You can move (drag or cut and then paste) that shortcut to wherever you want it.

If you're making a shortcut of a program icon to place on the desktop, there's an even easier way. You can just drag the program icon to the desktop, and Windows automatically creates a shortcut there.

Another option is to right-click on any icon and drag it to a new location. (This is one of those occassions when you hold the *right* mouse button down to drag, instead of the left.) When you let go of the right mouse button Windows will ask you if you wish to Move Here, Copy Here, Create Shortcut Here, or Cancel. Select Create Shortcut Here and you'll have a shortcut to the item. Be careful not to select Move Here, since moving an icon to the wrong location could cause a program not to work.

You can have several shortcuts to the same thing; you can, for example, put shortcuts to the Calculator in any folder where you might need it. By default, shortuts are named "Shortcut to" plus the name of the original icon. You can rename a shortcut whatever you like. (Right-click on the icon, choose Rename from the menu that appears, and type a new name.) And when the shortcut is no longer useful, you can delete it; the original stays safe in its original folder. Just be sure that the icon you're deleting has a little arrow pointing to it, showing that it's really a shortcut and not the program itself.

Customizing the Start Menu

As you learned in Chapter 29, the Start menu provides a handy way to quickly do common tasks like starting programs. Once you've worked with your PC for awhile, you may wish you had even more commands listed there. What if you could choose a command from the Start menu to quickly open a certain folder that you use all the time, for instance? Or maybe you think it would be nice to have a program that you use every day listed at the top level of the menu rather than having to choose Programs and then go through the submenus to start it. The good news is, you can. You can add, substract, and rearrange commands on the Start menu however you want.

The easiest way to customize the Start menu is to add items to it. Just drag the icon of any file, folder, or program onto the Start button, and Windows will add a menu command that opens that icon to the top level of the Start menu.

The basic set of commands in the Start menu needs to stay where it is, but in Windows 98 you can rearrange items that you add to the Start menu yourself. To move an item into a new position on the Start menu, just drag it into its new place. Click the Start button, then point to the command you want to move, and hold the mouse button down while you drag it to a new position.

To delete an item you've added, right-click on the Start button and choose Open from the menu that appears. You'll see icons for the items you've added. You can put a group of

You can view the commands you've added to the Start menu in a folder window. Right-click on the Start menu and choose the Open command to open the window.

commands into a folder to create a submenu and delete commands you've added by moving them into the Recycle Bin.

Changing the Name of Your Hard Disk

You can change the name of your hard disk (or any other disk attached to your computer). Double-click on My Computer, right-click on the icon of your hard drive, and choose Properties from the menu that appears. This calls up the hard disk's Properties dialog box.

You can change the name of the hard disk by typing a new name in the Label box and clicking OK. You can use as many as 11 characters, including spaces. Next time you open My Computer, the hard drive will be labeled with that text.

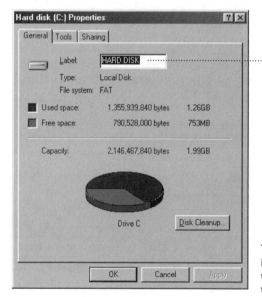

Type the new name for your hard disk here

The hard disk's Properties dialog box offers information about the hard disk and the tools for working with it. You can change the hard disk's name here.

Housekeeping Tasks

Okay, it's not all fun and games. Another way that your computer **37** *is like your office is that it can get awfully cluttered and hard to get around in if you don't do some housekeeping once in awhile.*

I've already talked about some basic housekeeping tasks in earlier chapters, such as rearranging folders and files and backing up your hard disk. In this chapter, I'll run through a few more routines you'll probably want to perform fairly regularly to keep your workspace in shape.

Deleting Files

Sooner or later you're going to want to delete files from your hard drive. You might do it to save disk space (hard disks are big, but they do fill up eventually), or just to keep things uncluttered. When you're done with a project, for instance, you might want to archive the files associated with it to a backup disk and remove them from your hard disk to make room for more current files.

To delete a file, you drag it to the Recycling Bin on the Windows desktop. When the Recycle Bin is highlighted, release the mouse button to drop the item in.

As with almost every other common Windows task, there are lots of ways to delete a file, and you'll probably use them all, depending on which is most convenient at the time.

If you're looking at a set of files in a folder window, the easiest way to delete a file is to just drag it to the Recycle Bin icon on the desktop. Dropping a file in the Recycle Bin removes it from its location in your filing system and stores it in the Recycle Bin until the bin is emptied (an action that I'll cover next).

If the Recycle Bin isn't handy (if it's buried under windows or otherwise not convenient to use), you can simply select the file and press the Del key. You can also use the Delete command in the window's File menu, or you can right-click on the file and select Delete from the menu that appears.

No matter what method you use, the result is the same. Windows will ask you if you're sure you want to send the item to the Recycle Bin, and if you click Yes, that's where the file is sent. Anything you send to

Files are deleted permanently (and disk space they use is freed up) when you empty the Recycle Bin.

the Recycle Bin stays there until you empty the bin, so you can change your mind about deleting it if you need to. You can "undelete" a file by dragging it back out of the Recyle Bin. (Double-click on the Recycle Bin to open it.) You can also remove individual files and folders from the Recycle Bin by right-clicking on the file's or folder's icon and choosing Restore from the menu that appears, or by cutting and pasting the icon to a new location on the disk.

You can delete single files, whole folders, or groups of files and folders this way. Deleting a folder deletes all the files in the folder as well as the folder itself. To select more than one icon at a time, remember that you can press Shift while you click on each icon, before dragging the files or selecting a command from a menu.

When you're absolutely sure you're ready to delete the files you've moved to the Recycle Bin, you empty the bin, deleting for good all the files and folders it holds. To do that, you just right-click on the Recycle Bin and choose Empty Recycle Bin from the menu that appears. Before it deletes the files, Windows will present a dialog box asking whether you're sure you want to empty the bin. If you're sure, click Yes, and the files will be deleted permanently.

Is the File Really, Really Deleted?

Although I just said that emptying the Recycle Bin permanently deletes the file, there are sometimes ways to bring back files even if they have been deleted. There are programs, such as Norton Utilities from Symantec (which I talk about more in Chapter 58), that come with an "unerase" feature. It doesn't always work, but sometimes you can bring back files like this even after you've emptied the Recycle Bin. This is good to know for two reasons. First, if you're ever in trouble because you deleted an important file and then emptied the Recycle Bin, call an expert before you do anything else. It might be possible to bring it back. I also point this out to remind you that other people, under some circumstances, can unerase files on your disk. Think about this if you have something that's really secret and you think that someone might be willing to go through a lot of hassle to uncover it. Police have used unerase programs to get the goods on criminals who thought they had completely deleted the evidence.

Emptying the Recycle Bin "recycles" the space on your hard disk, freeing it up for use by newer files. If you're running out of disk space, emptying your Recycle Bin is one of the easiest ways to free some up.

Removing a Program from Your Computer

If you decide you don't need a program any more—because you've replaced it with a different one or you just don't use it much and need the extra space on your hard disk—you can uninstall installed programs. You can't, however, just delete the program icon. Chances are, the installation procedure placed a lot of helper files in different locations throughout your hard disk. Using the Uninstall feature in Windows makes sure that all the program's files are removed.

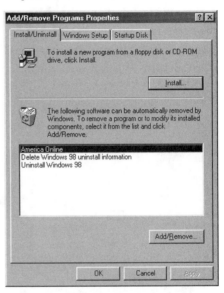

Deleting a program using Windows' Uninstall feature deletes all the files associated with that program, no matter where they're stored on your hard disk.

To uninstall a program, click on the Start button, choose Settings from the Start menu, and choose Control Panel from the submenu. Then, in the Control Panel window, double-click on the Add/Remove Programs icon. In the dialog box that appears, click on the Install/Uninstall tab. In the bottom part of the dialog box, you'll see a list of programs that are installed on your computer that can be uninstalled. Select that program's name and click on the Add/Remove button, and Windows will delete the program, and all its associated files, from your disk.

If the program you want to remove isn't listed in the dialog box, you'll have to uninstall the program manually, by deleting its folder from your hard disk. If you delete a program manually, you may run across some leftover files associated with it. If you do, delete the files you find.

Before you delete a program, make sure that you have a backup of the original CD-ROM or floppies somewhere, at least for a while. That way, if you change your mind or find some old files that you need the program to open, you can reinstall the program.

Changing the System Date and Time

Your PC has a battery-powered clock that keeps track of the date and time even when the machine is off. That system date and time is what shows up on the taskbar clock. It's also used to keep track of creation and modification dates for files, so having the correct date and time is important. Windows automatically updates the clock when the time changes from Standard Time to Daylight Savings Time and back again, but PC clocks have a habit of running slow or fast, so you'll probably need to set the time every couple of months.

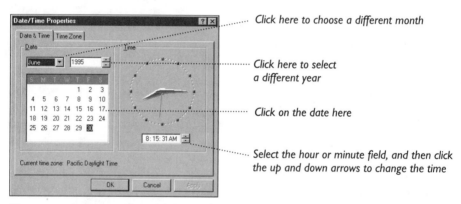

Click here to choose a different month

Click here to select a different year

Click on the date here

Select the hour or minute field, and then click the up and down arrows to change the time

You can set the correct date and time in the Date/Time Properties dialog box.

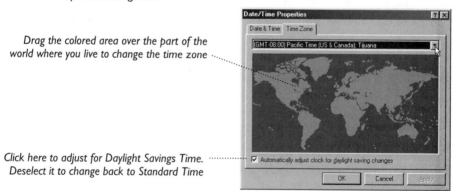

Drag the colored area over the part of the world where you live to change the time zone

Click here to adjust for Daylight Savings Time. Deselect it to change back to Standard Time

You can automatically adjust for changes of time zone (if you're on the road) or for Daylight Savings Time in the Time Zone panel.

To set the system clock, just double-click on the clock in the taskbar. The Date/Time Properties dailog box will appear. That's where you can adjust the date and time.

Checking for Disk Problems

If your machine crashes, or if you turn off the power without shutting down properly, some damage could be done to your files, though it isn't very likely. A quick way to find out if everything's all right is to run ScanDisk, a disk-checking program that comes with Windows.

To run ScanDisk, click on the Start button, and choose Programs, then Accessories, then System Tools, and finally, ScanDisk from the cascading menus. You'll see the ScanDisk dialog box, from which you can choose the options you want to use. Choose the Automatically Fix Errors option, make sure the correct drive is chosen, and click Start. ScanDisk will check your files for errors. When it's done, it will provide a summary of any problems it found and fixed, along with information about how your disk space is being used.

When you're done reading the report, just click on the Close button in the summary box and in the ScanDisk dialog box.

ScanDisk is a good tool to use if you find you're having trouble opening any of your files or programs. In those cases, make sure you choose the Thorough option, which takes a bit longer but checks the disk surface as well as the files.

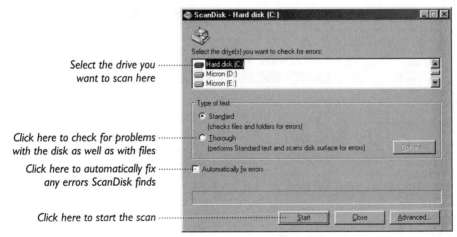

Select the drive you want to scan here

Click here to check for problems with the disk as well as with files

Click here to automatically fix any errors ScanDisk finds

Click here to start the scan

The ScanDisk program checks the file system of your PC for problems.

If You're Missing ScanDisk

If ScanDisk or any of the other Windows tools I mention in this section aren't listed in the Programs section of your Start menu, it could be they just haven't been formally installed yet. To install a program that comes with Windows, you can use the Add/Remove Programs utility in your Control Panel. (You can open the Control Panel and find the icon by clicking Start and then choosing Settings, and then Control Panel from the Start menu, or by double-clicking on My Computer and then the Control Panel icon.) Select the Windows Setup Tab, and then select the program you want to install from the list and click Install. When the process is done, the program should be available in your Start menu. Be sure you have your Windows installation CD ready just in case it's needed.

Updating Windows Over the Net

If you have Windows 98, then you don't really have to worry about the operating system and many of the drivers for your printer and other devices becoming out of date. That's because Windows 98 is able to update itself with a little help from the Internet.

A feature in Windows 98 called Windows Update automatically analyzes your computer and checks against a database over the Internet to see if anything on your system should be updated. It shows you a list of items that may be out of date and new features for Windows that are

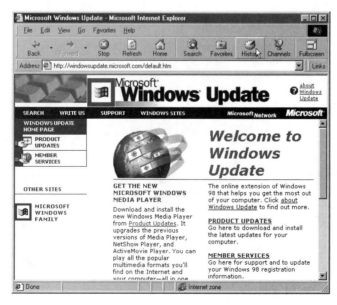

The Windows Update website includes updates and fixes for your Windows software. A special program will check your system to find out whether it needs updating.

newly available. It also has a "revert" feature in case you decide you want to undo something you've updated.

To access Windows Update, click on the Start menu, select Settings, and then select Windows Update. If you're online, Windows 98 will take you to a website that will guide you through the update process.

Click on Product Updates and wait until you get to yet another Web page, which asks you if you wish to let Windows Update analyze your computer. It will then tell you what updates are available. Pay special attention to anything it lists in the Critical Updates category. These are bug fixes that you should take care of right away. Also check out the optional upgrades, which add new features to your system.

Place a checkmark next to anything you want to upgrade, go to the bottom of the screen, and click Download. You'll go to another screen which shows estimates of how long it will take to download each item. Click Start Download and wait while Windows heals itself.

If you're not sure how to get on the Internet or how to use a website, read on. I cover that in Part 4 of this book.

If You Get Stuck

38 *Sometimes, especially when you're just getting the hang of using a computer, you'll run into a situation that completely baffles you but is actually quite easy to fix. This chapter will run through a few of the most common such problems.*

You're Working With an Application Program and the Computer Just Beeps at You Whenever You Press a Key

This is a pretty common occurrence. The program is working OK, but you just can't figure out how to get back to the main menu or even how to exit the program. First try pressing the Esc (short for Escape) key one or more times. As good as its name, the Esc key usually backs you out of whatever situation you're in, one step at a time.

If that doesn't work, your computer is probably frozen, and you'll need to apply more desperate measures. (See the next item.)

Your Computer Freezes Up

Sometimes you'll press the keys on your keyboard, or move your mouse, and nothing happens. There's often no apparent reason. Programs sometimes just "lock up." It could be a **bug** or some combination of actions that you just can't figure out.

If that happens, first give the computer about a minute to try to work things out by itself. Sometimes the software just needs time to catch up.

If you test it again after waiting and, still, nothing happens, try holding down the Ctrl, Alt, and Del keys all at the same time. This might cause you to lose any work you did since you last saved the file (good thing you saved recently!), but it can't be helped. Sometimes you can shut down just the troublesome program without shutting down Windows itself or other

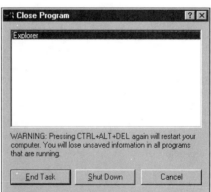

If you press Ctrl, Alt, and Del all at once you get this dialog box, which allows you to exit any program that's giving you trouble.

programs that are running. (Press the End Task button, or press Return, when you see the Close Program dialog box.)

That's the way it's supposed to happen, but if things don't work out quite that way, the computer might go through its startup procedure again. If you saved your work, you should be OK. It's very unlikely that a problem would cause you to lose any work that's already been saved.

Once in awhile, even Ctrl+Alt+Del won't work. The next maneuver is to push your PC's "reset" switch, if it has one. If that doesn't work (or if you can't find the switch), turn off the power for a few seconds (until it sounds like it has really stopped), and then turn the computer back on. Unless there is a serious problem, the machine should restart as it normally does, although it will probably run ScanDisk automatically. That's OK. If it doesn't start properly, something might be wrong with your Windows startup files. See the box "Things That Might Go Wrong During Startup" on page 11 for what to do then.

If all that doesn't work, you're going to need help from an expert. See Chapter 5 for more on how to get it.

You've Messed Up a File You're Working On

Most Windows programs have an Undo command (in the Edit menu) that undoes the last thing you did. With Undo, you can reverse any simple command you just completed. For example, you can remove the last sentence you typed or reinstate the text you just deleted.

Unfortunately, in some cases, the Undo command won't work. If what you did was complicated or if it involved a lot of steps, Undo might not be available. And if you've done anything else since the command you want to retract, you're out of luck. Generally, Undo only works on the action you've just finished, although some programs have a multiple undo feature that can step backward through several actions.

If the problem is past fixing with Undo, you can always go back to the last version you saved to disk (the state the file was in when you last gave a Save command). To do that,

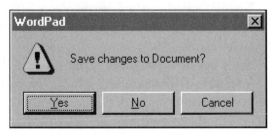

If you click No, the program will discard all the changes you made since you last saved the file.

just close the file without saving your changes. When you open it again, it will be the earlier version. (Some software has an automatic save feature that saves your file at regular intervals. If you're using software that does that, it will be hard to tell just what state the file was in when it was last saved, but this method is still worth a try.)

You Have Much Less Disk Space Than You Think You Should Have

First, check to see if you've emptied the Recycle Bin. When you delete a file, you don't really erase it. Instead, you just copy it into the Recycle Bin on the Windows desktop. Right-click on the Recycle Bin and you'll be able to empty it.

If that doesn't do it, try restarting your computer (by selecting Shut Down from the Start menu). Sometimes unnecessary files are automatically erased when Windows shuts down.

If you have Windows 98, run Disk Cleanup (you'll find it in the Programs section of your Start menu, under Accessories and System Tools). It will delete files that you definitely don't need. The disk cleanup program is run automatically whenever the Maintenance Wizard does its work.

If that doesn't work, use the Find command in the Start menu (see Chapter 27) to locate any files that end in .TMP. These are temporary files that programs create (and are supposed to delete). They often don't get deleted properly and they clutter up your disk. Select all of these temp files and drag them to the Recycle Bin.

Finally, if you're still low on disk space, consider deleting some programs or data files that you never use.

The PC Suddenly Seems Very Sluggish

There are a couple of possibilities. Some older machines have a "Turbo" switch that—when in the off position—will slow them down. It was put there because some really old programs actually run better on a slower machine. Turbo switches are pretty rare these days, but if there is a Turbo switch, be sure it's in the on position.

Another possibility is that your hard disk is fragmented. I'm not going to bore you with the details, but on a fragmented hard disk, files are scattered all around instead of in neat, contiguous sections of the disk. A fragmented disk runs more slowly. Fortunately, Windows has a program, called Disk Defragmenter, that solves the problem. (The Windows Help system will tell you how to use it or you can just run the Windows Maintenance Wizard, which will automatically run Disk Defragmenter for you.) In Windows 98, the Disk Defragmenter program has the added advantage of making your programs run faster by moving your most frequently run programs to a section of the disk that is accessed first. The good news is that this is automatic. Just run Disk Defragmenter on a regular basis and everything runs faster.

Another option is to get a Utility program like Norton Utilities or First Aid (see Chapter 58), which automatically analyzes your computer to look for and fix problems that can affect its performance.

If your problem isn't listed here, and you just can't figure out what to do, remember to check your online help and the Troubleshooting section in the user's guide that came with your program for more tips. Also remember that the computer community is there to help you out. Online tech support, user groups, your local computer guru, and if it comes to it, professional computer repair technicians can all help you figure out how to get unstuck. Chapter 5 has a rundown of those resources.

Shutting Down

39 *You don't necessarily have to shut down your computer. Most of today's computers go into a power-saving Standby mode automatically when they've been idle for a while. When you press a special button (or in some cases click on the mouse button or press any key), the computer will wake up.*

Sometimes, though, you'll want to shut down your computer completely. If you don't have the power-saver mode on your PC, you'll probably want to do it every night, just to save electricity. Sometimes you'll need to shut down your computer because it has crashed—it freezes up and just won't do anything. And sometimes you'll want to shut down just because your computer starts acting strange. Often, shutting down and booting up from scratch will solve problems you're having with Windows or your software. In fact, I restart my computer at least once or twice a day just to clear things out. It's not supposed to be necessary, but it only takes a few seconds, doesn't do any harm, and seems to make the machine run faster and better.

When you do shut down your computer, don't just flip the switch. Instead, use the Shut Down command in the Start menu. That allows Windows to do all its housekeeping before it turns itself off. It makes sure your work is saved and it closes all open files and empties its memory in an orderly way.

After an Improper Shutdown, Run ScanDisk

Sometimes your computer will crash or lose power suddenly, so you won't have a chance to shut down properly using the Shut Down command. When that happens, you'll see a message when you turn your computer back on telling you that your computer was shut down improperly and that Windows is running ScanDisk. That's just a safeguard to make sure everything is still in order with your filing system. Just let it run, and then use your computer as usual. If ScanDisk doesn't run automatically, it's a good idea to run it yourself in those conditions. You'll find it in the Start menu under Programs, Accessories, and System Tools.

When you choose Shut Down, Windows will display a dialog box giving you several options. Standby puts it into the power-saving mode I just described. Shut Down puts your PC through the entire Shut Down process, and when you want to use it again, it will need to go through its whole reboot process again. Restart shuts your computer

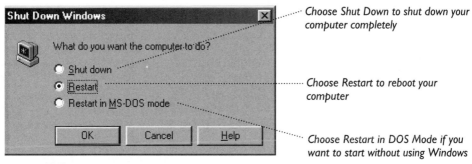

Choose Shut Down to shut down your computer completely

Choose Restart to reboot your computer

Choose Restart in DOS Mode if you want to start without using Windows

When you choose Shut Down, Windows lets you choose just how far down you want to shut.

down completely and then immediately reboots it. (This is the one to use to solve those mysterious problems I was talking about.)

Restarting in MS-DOS mode shuts down the computer and then restarts it without loading Windows. The screen that comes up only displays the MS-DOS prompt. (As I described way back in Chapter 4, MS-DOS is an the old-fashioned operating system that the PC used before Windows was invented.) People who really know their way around computers might use this in order to try to circumvent a problem caused by Windows itself, but you'll probably never use it unless you're on the phone with a tech support person who's trying to troubleshoot a problem for you.

Congratulations. You've just completed a basic course on Windows. You know your way around the desktop, know how to manage your file system, and have learned basic tricks for working with applications. Windows is an incredibly rich system, with lots of capabilities, lots of different ways to do almost any task, and lots of ways to customize it. You'll probably be discovering new features in it for years to come (I still do, every day). But you already have the skills to do your own exploring. Just pull down all the menus in your applications and try the commands and right-click on different objects and see what options come up in the menus that appear. You'll be an expert in no time.

In the next section, I'll take you through one of the most exciting things about PCs these days—the ability to use your PC to explore the Internet. If you have a fairly recent version of Windows, you've got everything you need to start the adventure.

Let's go.

Exploring the Internet

four

Getting Online

40 *Thanks to the Internet and America Online (AOL), today's PCs are no longer just personal computers, they're personal communicators, too. When you're connected via this vast, global network, you can communicate with others throughout the world while sitting at your computer.*

Getting on the Internet gives you access to a whole world of people, activities, and information. Here are just a few of the things you can do:

- Shop, browse catalogs, or just learn about what companies have to offer. You can buy almost anything online or do product research before buying locally.
- Do research for homework, business, or personal interests. You'll find information on just about everything you need to know, from personal health matters to corporate earnings.
- Get advice. Participate in discussion groups about health matters, computer tips, or any other subject that interests you. Create a support group to help you kick bad habits or learn new skills.
- Read newspapers and magazines, or search the archives of back issues of publications for information you need. When news breaks, you can check out the local newspapers from the part of the world where the story is happening.
- Get free software for your computer. You can get demonstration versions and updates for commercial programs, shareware and public domain software, and clip art and other graphics files.
- Plan a trip. Find out air and rail schedules, locate out-of-the-way hotels, find out what's going on in the cities you'll visit, research restaurants, read the local paper, and, of course, get the weather report.
- Find a job. Lots of webites are dedicated to helping you find work. Read the want ads from newspapers around the world or visit a site devoted to helping job seekers.
- Find out about people. Visit celebrity websites, or look up an old friend from high school. You can find listed phone numbers without even knowing where someone lives.
- Keep in touch with all your friends. More and more people, from community workers to grandparents, have e-mail, the quickest and cheapest way to share greetings and information with friends and acquaintances around the world.
- Meet new friends. Chat online with people around the world.

If you have Windows 98, you have lots of built-in software and desktop tools that make getting around on the Internet surprisingly easy. And it's not much harder in Windows 95. This section will describe how you'll use them. But first, let's make sure you've got everything you need to get online.

A Modem

If you read Chapter 18, you know that you'll need some kind of device to connect your PC to the Internet: a modem that connects you to a regular phone line or, for some lucky people, a high-speed connection offered by a cable or phone company. If you're using a computer that's hooked up to a network at your office, you don't need to worry about it; your office's computer staff will doubtless already have taken care of getting your network connected to the Internet. (And if they haven't, ask them why not.)

Most PCs these days come with built-in modems. Look at the back of your machine. See Chapter 18 for more about them, including my advice as to what kind to buy, if you don't have one.

An Internet Service Provider

Once you have your modem, you'll also need an **Inernet Service Provider (ISP)**, a service that takes care of all the networking arcana that makes it possible to connect one computer (yours) to the network of networks that make up the Internet. You don't need to know how all this is done. You'll hear about **TCP/IP** (the **communication protocol** used to send messages across the Net) and **domain name services**, but

Surfer Beware

You can find information on almost any topic on the Net. But remember, just because something is posted there doesn't mean that it's true, responsible, or reliable.

This is an important thing to remember for anyone looking for information on the Internet. The Net is a great place to search for information, but take everything you read there with a grain of salt. As in any other medium, you need to consider the source and look for backup evidence before you send away for a new miracle drug or invest your life savings into a pension plan you read about there.

The "anything goes" nature of Web publishing is also important for parents to remember. The Web includes sites that have content that is sexually explicit, hateful, and otherwise inappropriate for kids. There are special software programs that can help keep your kids away from adult websites and chat areas, but no technology is a substitute for good parenting and safety education. Visit www.safekids.com, my own website about protecting kids online, for more information about keeping your kids safe in cyberspace.

Connect to the
Internet

Set Up The
Microsoft ...

You'll find several ways to get online right on the Windows desktop. Double-click on the
Connect to the Internet icon or the Set Up The Microsoft Network icon to sign up with an
ISP. Double-click on the Online Services folder to find even more services.

you don't need to know anything about them; they're all part of the
plumbing that your ISP takes care of.

This service costs something, of course, but not too much. Most
ISPs charge between $15 and $22 per month for unlimited access to
the Internet, and many offer a variety of pricing plans to suit your own
budget and use of the Net. Again, if you're using a computer that's connected to an office network, you're off the hook here; you'll just use the
ISP used by the rest of your office.

When you install Windows, you'll find several ways to sign up with
an ISP right on your desktop. One of the icons there will be labeled
Connect to the Internet, and if you double-click on it, you'll be taken
through a process that signs you up with a national ISP that contracts
with Microsoft to provide that service. The same thing happens when
you click on the Set Up The Microsoft Network icon. Open the Online
Services folder, and you'll find icons for AOL and other Internet Service
Providers. (See the box on the next page for more about AOL.) To sign
on, just double-click on the icon and follow the process it takes you
through. Before you start, make sure your modem is turned on and
your credit card is ready when you begin the sign-up process. (All these
services will bill their fees directly to your credit card each month.)

Signing On With AOL

One popular way to get access to the Internet is through AOL (America Online). AOL is an **online service**, a special kind of ISP that provides its own software and lots of special content and services to its customers, as well as access to the Internet. AOL is especially well known for its chat areas, where people meet other people online.

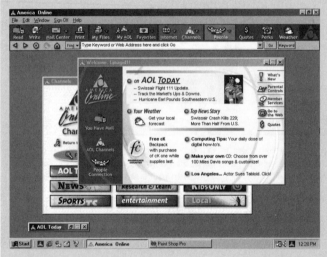

AOL uses special software and offers its own special content as well as access to the Internet.

Signing on with AOL is one of the easiest way to get online (there's an icon on the Windows desktop that helps you sign up). If you're a parent, an advantage is that AOL offers built-in controls for the kinds of content your children can access online. The AOL staff can't police every aspect of their service, but they can track down people who break their rules of etiquette—something that's impossible to do (without an FBI warrant) on the larger, anarchic Internet. You can also choose whether or not to let your kids onto the Internet itself, and if you do, what sites you'll allow them to visit.

The service offers local phone access from just about everywhere in the United States and from major cities in England, France, Japan, and several other countries. If you travel, it's a good way to always have access without having to make a long-distance call.

Although AOL offers access to the Internet, it's not exactly the same as being on the Internet through a standard ISP. The service is designed to take advantage of the company's own tools, and although it's possible to use standard Internet software on AOL, it's not always easy. If you like AOL's software (and many people do), that's no drawback, but the information in the next chapters about Internet Explorer and Outlook Express won't apply to you; you'll need to turn to AOL (or one of the many books available about AOL) for help.

By the way, if you do get on AOL, pay me a visit. I have my own area on the service that you can get to at keyword "LarryMagid."

National Internet Service Providers

The table below gives information about several ISPs that offer service throughout the United States. The last column lists some of the special characteristics of each. Note that in addition to connection to the Internet, some of the ISPs, such as CompuServe and MSN, also offer special content to their members.

Service Name	Phone	Web Address	Notes
AOL	800-227-6364	www.aol.com	Most popular online service
AT&T WorldNet	800-967-5363	www.att.com	Discounted for AT&T long-distance customers
CompuServe	800-739-6699	www.compuserve.com	Has an hourly pricing plan; good national and international access; lots of exclusive forums
Earthlink Network	800-395-8425	www.earthlink.com	Has a discount deal for Sprint long-distance customers
MCI Internet	800-476-7283	www.mci.com	Discounted for MCI long-distance customers
Microsoft Network	800-386-5550	www.msn.com	Offers special content
Prodigy Internet	800-213-0992	www.prodigy.com	Good national access
PSINet	800-774-3031	www.psinet.com	Good national access
UUNET	800-488-6384	www.uunet.com	Good national and international access

These are easy ways to set up a contract with an ISP, but you can also choose your own provider. (You might find a better deal that way.) Most local and long-distance phone companies operate as ISPs. You can also find services through your local Yellow Pages or newspapers. For leads, ask any friends who are already online who they use and how they like their service. If you travel a lot, you might want to consider one of the national ISPs (see the box above for details), which offer connections via a local call from just about anywhere in the United States and sometimes from other countries as well.

Any ISP you sign up with will tell you everything you need to know to connect your computer to the Net, including numbers and other information you'll need to type into special dialog boxes in Windows and in your Internet software.

After you sign up with an ISP and config-ure your software to sign onto your ISP's net-work, your Internet software should take care of signing on automatically, every time you do something that requires an Internet connec-tion, like going to a website or sending e-mail (things I describe how to do in the next few chapters).

Internet Application Software

Once you're online, you're going to need soft-ware for surfing the Web, sending e-mail, chatting, and doing everything else you'll want to do. Your main tools for that are included with Windows. Internet Explorer gives you access to the World Wide Web and everything it holds, and Outlook Express is the tool for e-mail and newsgroups. I'll describe those programs next.

Internet Servers and Clients

Once you begin working with the Internet, you'll probably hear the terms **server** and **client** a lot. A server is a computer (or software on a computer) that manages the files sent over a network: A Web server manages Web pages, an e-mail server manages e-mail mes-sages, a news server manages news-groups, and so on. A client is a com-puter (or software on a computer) with which Internet users (like you) get access to those services. When you're on the Internet, your PC is a client computer, and the Internet software I'll talk about in the next few chapters is all client software.

Internet Explorer and the World Wide Web

41

When most people think of the Internet, they think of the World Wide Web. The Internet has existed for decades, but it became a household word after the Web was invented and Mosaic, the first graphical Web browser, made it possible to post text, images, and lots of other media online. That was in 1993, and since then, people have used the Web to post information about products and services, pet projects, and even their children's birthday parties online. In just a few years, the Web has become an incredible source of information of all kinds.

To use the Web, all you need is a connection to the Internet and a Web **browser**—an application designed to display Web pages and help you navigate around the Web. One of the most popular Web browsers, Internet Explorer, comes with every copy of Windows, so you're ready to go.

Launching Internet Explorer

Microsoft figures you're going to want to use the Internet a lot, so it put lots of different ways to launch Internet Explorer right on the Windows desktop.

As you learned in the last chapter, the icon labeled Connect to the Internet is an easy way to get signed up with an ISP. After you use it, the icon's name changes to Internet Explorer, and double-clicking on it will launch the program, connect you to your ISP (if you're not already connected), and take you to a special Web page that Microsoft designed as a handy launching pad for your exploration of the Web.

Connect to the Internet

Internet Explorer

Double-clicking on the Connect to the Internet icon will set you up with an ISP. After that's done, the icon changes into the icon for Internet Explorer, the Web browser that comes with Windows.

You can also launch Internet Explorer by clicking on the Internet Explorer icon in the taskbar's Quick Launch Toolbar, by selecting it from the Programs list in the Start menu, or by using one of the many Web access features included on the Windows desktop (see the box "Web Features on the Windows Desktop" on the next page).

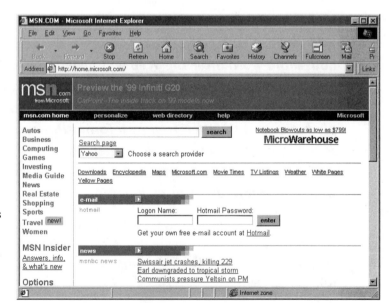

The Microsoft home page is a launch pad for exploring the Web. It might not look like this when you log on—one of the things about the Web is that its content is always changing.

Web Features on the Windows Desktop

Once you learn about surfing the Web with Internet Explorer, you'll start to see how many features of the Windows desktop tie in to the browser. Many of the features of Internet Explorer I talk about in this chapter are echoed on the Windows desktop and have the same effect. (In fact, a Department of Justice antitrust case against Microsoft is questioning the legality of integrating the browser and the desktop so closely.) The illustration below shows many of the features on the Windows desktop that you can use to surf the Web. Using any of them will launch Internet Explorer, and you'll be on your way.

Go menu The Go menu can take you to the Microsoft Search page, your home page, or Microsoft's Channel Guide as well as to folders in your own file system.

Favorites menu You can access your Favorites list from the Favorites menu in any folder window or from the Favorites command in the Start menu.

Address bar Typing a URL in this box launches Internet Explorer and takes you to that website. You can also launch Internet Explorer by choosing the program or an Internet address you've already visited from the drop-down menu. Typing a Windows path here opens the folder window you name.

Links toolbar Appears when you select Toolbars, then Links from the View menu of any folder window.

Explorer bar Choose Explorer from a folder window's View menu to show this bar, which provides links to Search engines, Channels, your History list, or your Favorites, depending on your choice from the submenu.

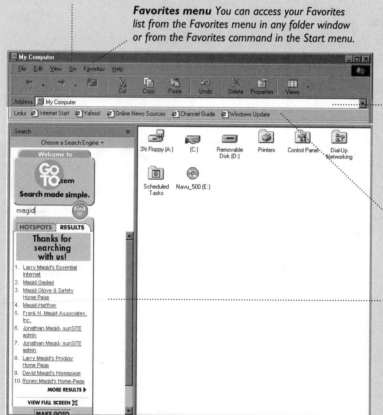

You can access sites on the Web directly from your Windows desktop. Using any of them will launch Internet Explorer.

Explorer Isn't the Only Browser

In this section, I'm going to focus on Internet Explorer because that's the Web browser that comes with Windows, but you should know that Internet Explorer isn't the only Web browser you can use to surf the Web. Netscape Navigator, another popular browser, is also free. Different Web browsers support different kinds of Web page programming, so a given Web page may look and act a little different in different browsers, and each browser has features that might make you prefer one to the other. If you're interested in checking out Navigator, visit Netscape's home page at home.netscape.com; you can download it there. Netscape Navigator is also available bundled with an e-mail program and other Internet software in a version (also free) called Netscape Communicator.

Using Hyperlinks

The thing that sets the Web apart from any other Internet service is its use of **hyperlinks**. Hyperlinks let you move from one Web page to another just by clicking on the link.

Looking at a Web page, you should be able to spot the hyperlinks easily. Hyperlinked text is usually, but not always, set in blue, under-

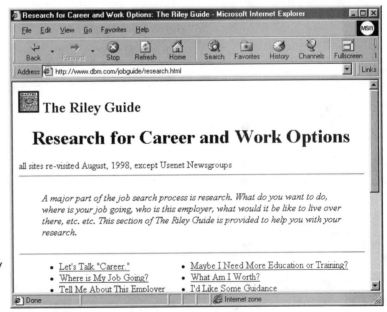

If you see text that's set in a different color from surrounding text, it's probably a hyperlink. What it links to will usually be clear from the highlighted text.

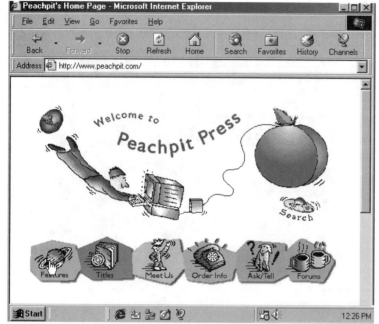

Graphics can also be used as hyperlinks. To spot a hyperlinked graphic, watch your mouse pointer. It turns into a pointing hand when it rolls over a live graphic.

lined text. I say not always because Web page designers can choose different colors for hyperlinks and they can choose not to have them underlined on screen. Designers know enough to make their hyperlinks obvious, though, so the hyperlinks are usually set in some obvious contrasting color. If you're not sure if something is a hyperlink, point at it with your mouse pointer. When the pointer rolls over a hyperlink, the pointer changes from an arrow to a pointing hand.

On-screen graphics can also act as hyperlinks. When graphics are used as hyperlinks, the rollover trick still works. If you roll over a graphic with your mouse pointer and the pointer turns into a hand, that graphic is a hyperlink.

Web page designers can get even trickier with hyperlinks, giving you extra clues or information with more elaborate rollover effects. Sometimes, when you roll your mouse over a hyperlink, the text or graphic will change color or shape. You might even hear a sound. Don't be startled. These are all just ways to get your attention and get you to click.

Web Page Sampler

No matter what you're looking for, you'll probably find it on the Web. The sites shown here offer homework help for kids, up-to-the-minute sports news, information about cancer treatments and clinical trials, help with travel plans, discount prices on just about any book in print, help with finding a job, and a buyers' guide to new cars.

www.startribune.com

espn.sportzone.com

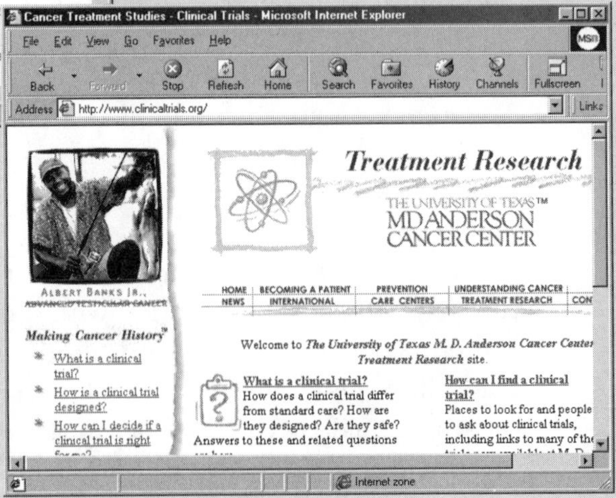

www.clinicaltrials.org

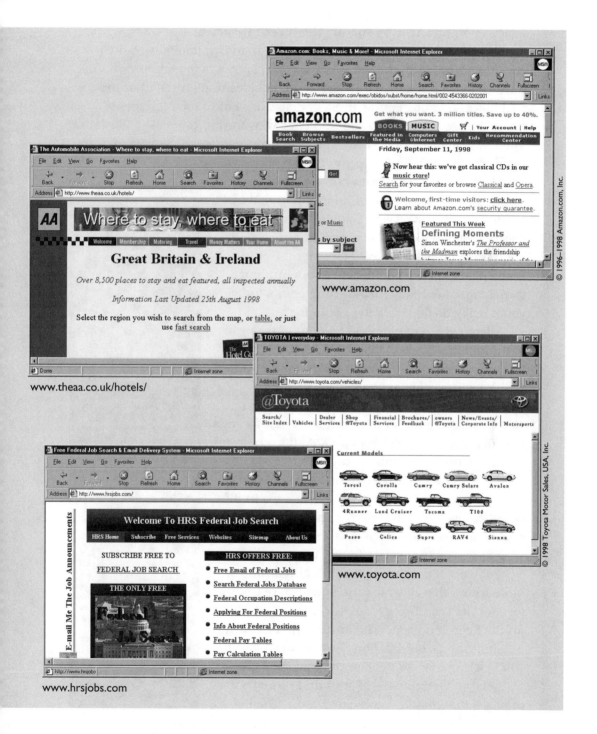

www.amazon.com

www.theaa.co.uk/hotels/

www.toyota.com

www.hrsjobs.com

Finding What You Want on the Web: Internet Portals

By the middle of 1998, the Web had more than two million websites, covering topics from the lyrics of obscure pop songs to computer hardware catalogs to the latest research on diabetes to pictures from the wedding of a happy couple in Saskatchawan, not to mention lots of X-rated material. How do you find your way around this vast collection? The key is a **portal site**—a website designed to organize the vast array of topics on the Web and help you find the ones you're interested in.

Most portal sites let you customize the page you see to show the kind of information that's of particular interest to you, usually including sports scores, stock quotes, and other news, in addition to links to other Web content. Getting all that updated personal information is fun, but these pages are really just starting points for what you'll really do on the Web—exploring.

Microsoft's home page—the one it takes you to automatically when you start Internet Explorer—is one example of a portal page. Other well-known portals are *Yahoo, Excite, Lycos, AltaVisa, InfoSeek, Snap, AOL.com* and *Netscape Netcenter.* There are even portal sites just for kids like *Yahooligans* or *Ask Jeeves for Kids.* (I keep an up-to-date listing of portals on my website, at www.larrysworld.com/searching.html.) All these sites offer easy access to a variety of sites in different categories, plus, most important, a **search engine**, which is a service that searches the entire Web for pages that relate to any topic you name.

To use a search engine, you just type one or more words that describe the topic you're looking for into the search page's text box and then click on the Search button. (The button will be called different things on different Search pages, but it will be clear enough.) The search engine software will refer to its database of sites and return a list of pages that match your search term. The list is

Resources

AltaVista
www.altavista.digital.com

AOL
www.aol.com

Ask Jeeves for Kids
www.ajkids.com

Excite
www.excite.com

InfoSeek
www.infoseek.com

Lycos
www.lycos.com

Infoseek
www.infoseek.com

Mirosoft
home.microsoft.com

Netscape Netcenter
www.netscape.com

Snap
www.snap.com

Yahoo
www.yahoo.com

Yahooligans
www.yahooligans.com

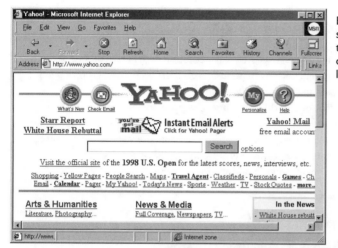

Every portal site features a search engine that you can use to find what you're looking for on the Web. Yahoo is currently the Web's most popular.

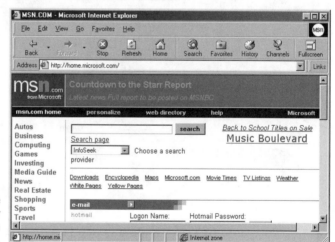

Clicking the Search button in the Internet Explorer toolbar or in any folder window displays a list of search links in an Explorer pane.

hyperlinked, so you can begin exploring by just clicking on the names of pages that interest you.

There's an even easier way to do an Internet search. Type the words describing your search in the Address Bar in Internet Explorer or in a folder window. The words you type will automatically be sent to a search engine, which will return a list of matching sites.

The first few times you use a search engine, you may be startled to see a result that says something like, "We found 332,714 pages that matched your search," along with a list of links to all those hundreds of thousands of pages, including many that have nothing to do with the

Changing Your Home Page

Microsoft takes you to its own portal page not only because it's a handy spot, but because by doing that it automatically gets millions of people to go there every day, giving it a great opportunity to sell advertising and promote their own products. After you've been on the Web awhile, you may find that one of the other portal pages works better for you than Microsoft's portal page. Or you may decide that you'd rather see your favorite newspaper, your mom's Web site, or even nothing at all when you start up Internet Explorer. You can change the page shown at startup using the Internet Options dialog box (which you get by choosing Internet Options from Internet Explorer's View menu).

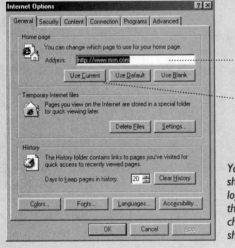

Type the address of the page you want to see at startup here

Click here to choose the page you're currently viewing

You can change the default home page page shown at startup using the Internet Options dialog box. Just type in a new address, or use one of the buttons to choose the current page, to change back to the Microsoft home page, or show a blank window at startup.

topic you're interested in. Most search engines use special algorithms to determine which pages are most likely the ones you're after, and though they list every page they find, they put the most likely matches at the top. You can also make your searches more exact by doing a little studying up on the quirks of each search engine. Most of the portal pages offer tips for effective searching which you should be sure to read. For tips on searching check out Larry's Concise Guide to the Internet at www.larrysworld.com/primer.htm, or if you really want to know everything there is to know about searching, get a copy of *Search Engines for the World Wide Web : Visual QuickStart Guide* by Alfred and Emily Glossbrenner. (It's published by Peachpit Press—the same people who published this book—but even if it weren't I'd still recommend it.)

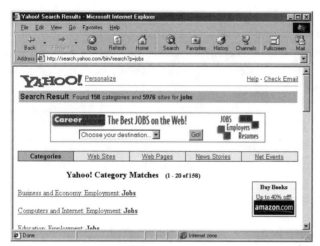

Search engines can return a list of every page they find that fits your search criteria. Typing keywords into the Address Bar of Internet Explorer or a folder window will find related websites.

Internet Explorer's Navigation Controls

Following hyperlinks is an exciting way to move around the Web, but sometimes you'll want to go to a particular site you've heard about or return to a page you've seen before and you don't have a hyperlink to take you there. That's when you use the browser's navigation controls, which you'll find in the browser window's toolbars.

Takes you to the last Web page you visited. If you click on the downward-pointing arrow, you'll see a list of the last pages you visited.

Provides links to useful pages. You can drag a page from the browser window to the Links toolbar to create a shortcut to that page.

Takes you to the page you just backed up from. Click on the arrow for a menu of pages.

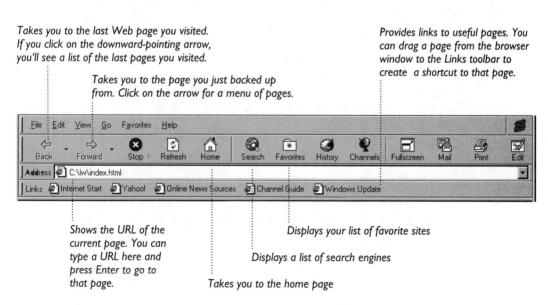

Shows the URL of the current page. You can type a URL here and press Enter to go to that page.

Displays your list of favorite sites

Displays a list of search engines

Takes you to the home page

Internet Explorer's toolbars offer lots of ways to move around the Web.

When you click on Search, Favorites, History, or Channels, Internet Explorer opens an Explorer Bar in which it displays the chosen information. Clicking on an item in the Explorer Bar takes you to the named page. (The same thing happens if you click those buttons in a folder window on your desktop.)

Typing a Web address in the Address Bar and pressing the Enter key on your keyboard takes you directly to that address. If you see an address you want to visit in an advertisement or in this book, or if friends tell you about Web sites they think you'll like, that's how you get there.

Web Addresses

You can't read a newspaper or even watch a TV program these days without seeing a Web address. Every page on the Web has a unique address, referred to as a **URL** (sometimes pronounced "earl") or Universal Resource Locator. Typing that address in the browser's (or folder window's) Address Bar will take you there.

The first part of a URL is always *http://*, but you don't have to type those characters in most browers, so people giving you a Web address often leave that part off. (In case you're wondering, http stands for "hypertext transfer protocol." You already know what hypertext means, so you can probably figure out how they wound up with that term.) The next part of an address, often, is www (standing for "World Wide Web"). These characters are optional in the latest browers, too, so an increasing number of people don't mention them, either.

The next part of the address, though, the **domain name**, is important. The domain name is in two parts. The first part is usually the organization's name or an abbreviation of it: something like bankamerica, latimes, ucla, etc. The next part of it is the kind of domain, called the **top level domain**. If the website is for a company, it's .com (for commercial). For educational organizations it's .edu. Military organization use .mil, and government agencies use .gov. Organizations are usually .org. So http://www.ibm.com is IBM's website. UCLA's is http://www.ucla.edu. The President of the United States's website is http://www.whitehouse.gov. As I finish this book, a group of Internet experts and government officials from around the globe are meeting to talk about coming up with even more domain types, like .inf for "information," .frm for "firm," and so on. There are also domain names associated with countries, like .uk for United Kingdom and .ca for Canada.

When you type in a URL, it's sometimes necessary to type it in exactly as it's given to you, with the same use of uppercase and lowercase characters. If you get an error message or end up at the wrong Web site, check the address carefully; chances are, the problem is just a typo.

Coming Back for More

As you explore the Web, sooner or later you're going to find a few different sites that you're going to want to go back to again and again. That's what the Favorites list was created for.

If you find a site you like and want to make sure you can get back to it, click on Internet Explorer's Favorites menu and choose Add to Favorites. Windows will display a dialog box offering you the option of subscribing to the page and letting you type a descriptive name for it.

No matter what option you choose in this box (as long as you click OK), Windows will add the site to your Favorites list so that you can return to it simply by clicking on its name in the list. Subscribing, though, creates an even tighter link.

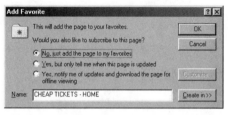

When you find a site you like, you can add it to your Favorites list or subscribe to it using the Add to Favorites dialog box.

If the first button is selected, the site will just be added to your Favorites list. If you select the second button, Windows will monitor the page for changes, and when a change is made, it will add a red star to the icon next to the page name on your Favorites list.

If you choose the third button, Windows will not only notify you of a change, it will download the website's pages to your hard disk so that you can read them at your leisure. If you choose this option, Windows will display a Wizard that takes you through the process of choosing a notification method (the red star or by e-mail), a schedule on which it should check the site for changes, and other options.

To see your list of Favorites, click Internet Explorer's Favorites button or choose Favorites from the Start menu. Then just click on the site's name in the list to go to it.

Now you know enough to get you started exploring the Web. However, this introduction is far from a complete inventory of everything you can do on the Web or in Internet Explorer. When you're more comfortable with your PC and with the Web, you'll want to start exploring Internet Explorer's menus, where you'll find controls for customizing your browser according to your own habits and preferences, ways to save files on your hard disk, and help files that will tell you how to manage it all.

Sending E-mail With Outlook Express

42

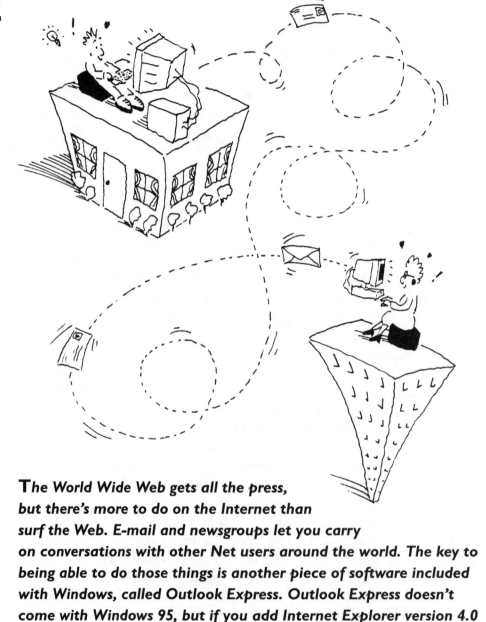

The World Wide Web gets all the press, but there's more to do on the Internet than surf the Web. E-mail and newsgroups let you carry on conversations with other Net users around the world. The key to being able to do those things is another piece of software included with Windows, called Outlook Express. Outlook Express doesn't come with Windows 95, but if you add Internet Explorer version 4.0 or higher to Windows 95, you also get Outlook Express.

Outlook Express is a junior version of a more complex program called Outlook, which you get along with Microsoft Office, a popular software suite I describe in Chapter 49 and that might even have been included on your computer when you bought it. I'll talk about the extra features you get in the commercial version of Outlook later, in Chapter 53. Here, I'll focus on using Outlook Express for e-mail. I describe its use for newsgroups in the next chapter.

Starting Outlook Express

Like Internet Explorer, Outlook Express has an icon right on the Windows desktop and a button in the taskbar's Quick Launch toolbar. (It's the icon that looks like an envelope.) You can double-click on the icon or click on the button to launch the program. You'll also find Outlook Express in the Programs list in your Start menu (it's in the Internet Explorer submenu). And if Internet Explorer is open onscreen, clicking the Mail icon in its toolbar opens Outlook Express.

Any of these methods will open the Outlook Express window and (unless you've changed your preferences) log onto the Internet.

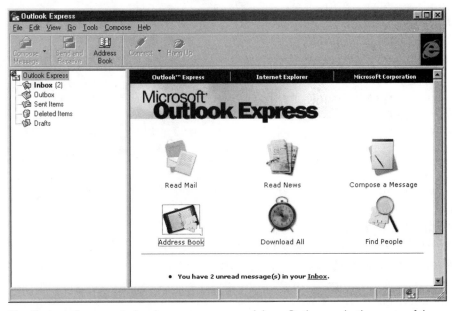

The Outlook Express window lets you access your Inbox, Outbox, and other parts of the program by double-clicking on the icons in the main pane. You can see individual messages using the hierarchical listing in the left-hand pane.

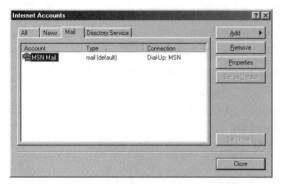

Before you can send or receive e-mail, you need to supply information about your e-mail address and ISP in Outlook Express's Accounts dialog box. When you click the Add button ...

(The program might display a couple of dialog boxes asking you for setup information before it opens the main window. If it does, just click OK in the dialog boxes without making any changes for right now. Their use will be clear after I run through some introductory information.)

Before you actually send or receive e-mail with Outlook Express, you'll need to provide information about your e-mail address and ISP. That information goes into the Accounts dialog box, which you get to by choosing Accounts from Outlook Express's Tools menu. Click the Add button,

and a wizard will help you through the setup process. Before you start, though, make sure you have the information you need from your ISP. (If clear instructions didn't come with your account, just call your ISP and say you want the information you need to set up your e-mail account in Outlook Express.) Don't worry: You only need to do this once. After you complete this setup process, Outlook Express will use this information automatically.

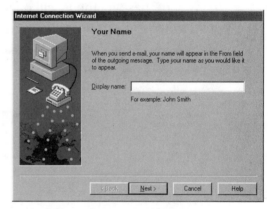

... the Internet Connection Wizard will lead you through the configuration steps.

Sending E-mail

If everyone you know doesn't have an e-mail address yet, they probably will before too long. Soon enough, e-mail addresses will be as common as a telephone numbers, and communication via e-mail is already a lot more common than letter writing.

To write a message to someone, click on the Compose Message button in Outlook Express's toolbar. Sending a message is as easy as

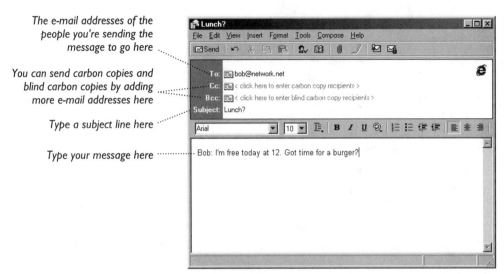

The e-mail addresses of the people you're sending the message to go here

You can send carbon copies and blind carbon copies by adding more e-mail addresses here

Type a subject line here

Type your message here

You write your e-mail messages in Outlook Express's New Message window.

typing it in, adding an address in the To: field, identifying the subject in the Subject field, and clicking the Send button. You can use the Cut, Copy, and Paste functions I described in Chapter 32 to compose and edit your messages.

You can add formatting—text styles like bold, italic, and special fonts—and graphics to your messages using the formatting toolbar. Before you do that, though, you should be aware that some e-mail services can't read all that fancy formatting, so many of your correspondents will still either get the plain-text message (without formatting), or worse, a file that's a lot harder to read than a plain-text version because it contains a lot of untranslated formatting code.

Before you send your message, you can have Outlook Express check your spelling for you. Just choose Spelling from the Tools menu, and the program will check all the words in your message against a built-in dictionary and call to your attention any words it doesn't recognize. You'll have the chance to accept the spelling as is, correct it on the spot, or if you don't know the correct spelling, ask the program to display a list of words from its dictionary that might be the one you're after.

Your message can be as long or short as you want it to be. You can even attach files from other programs to your Outlook Express messages. To do that, just drag the icon of the file from a folder window into the Outlook Express message window and the file will be sent along with your message when you click Send. (Another way to attach files is to select File Attachment from Outlook Express's Insert menu and then browse for the file you wish to attach.)

If you're logged on to the Internet, Outlook Express will send the message immediately when you click Send. If you're not logged on, the message will be sent to your Outbox, where it will stay until you sign on to the Net again. Once it's sent, the message will travel over the Internet to the Inbox of the addressee, where it will stay until that person logs on, whether that's in a couple of minutes or several weeks later. On your end, the message will move automatically from the Outbox to the Sent Mail folder, creating a record of your correspondence.

Checking Mail

Sending messages is only half the fun, of course. The other half is reading messages you get from others. For that, you use Outlook Express's Inbox. You get there by double-clicking on the Read Mail icon or on the Inbox item in the hierarchical list in the main Outlook Express window.

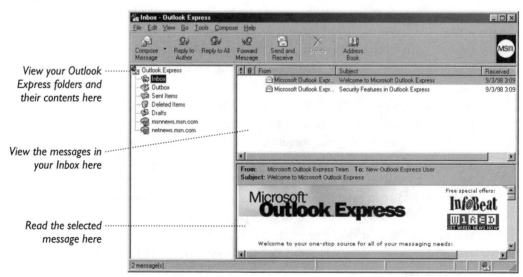

View your Outlook Express folders and their contents here

View the messages in your Inbox here

Read the selected message here

The Inbox windows includes panes for choosing the message you want to view, for seeing message you've received, and for reading the currently selected message.

To find out whether you have any messages, click the Send and Receive button in the window's toolbar. Outlook Express will check your ISP's mail server for messages addresssed to you and send them on to your computer, saving them on your PC's hard disk. (You need to be on the Internet to do this, so if you're not already signed on, Outlook Express will log on automatically.) At the same time, it will check your Outbox for any unsent messages and send them. Any new messages appear in the message list (the top pane), showing the name of the sender and the message's subject line. The message at the top of the list will be selected, and its contents will appear in the Preview pane (below the list).

Sometimes, of course, there won't be any messages at all, but that will change quickly once you tell your friends about your new e-mail account and send them messages to reply to.

To read a message, just scroll through its contents in the Preview pane. To view the other messages, click on their entries in the message list. After you've clicked on a message in the message list to read it, its entry, which starts out in bold type, will change to regular Roman type to indicate that it has been read; the icon next to it will also change, from a closed envelope to an open one. You can delete your messages (before or after you read them) by selecting them in the message list and clicking the Delete button in the toolbar. (You can select multiple messages to delete by holding down the Shift key while clicking on any messages after the first one.)

You can reply to a message from the Inbox by clicking the Reply to Author or Reply to All buttons. (Which one you should click depends on whether you want what you write to go just to the person who sent the message or to everyone else listed in the To: or CC: field of the original message.) Clicking on either button opens the New Message window with the sender's address in the To: field, the original subject line (prefaced with Re:) repeated in the New Message window's subject line, and the text of the message you received quoted in the message pane. (It is s customary, when replying to e-mail, to include the message you're replying to so that there's no confusion about what you're talking about.)

You can also forward any message you receive to anyone else's address by clicking the Forward Message button. Again, the text of

When you reply to a message, the New Message dialog box will include the text of the message you're replying to.

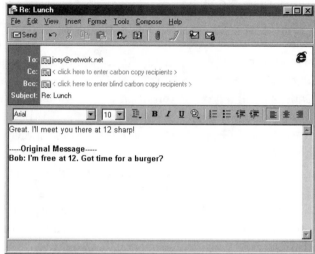

the original message will be quoted in the message pane, where you can also type any additional comments.

You can delete messages by selecting them and pressing the Del key or clicking on the X in the Outlook Express toolbar. Deleting a message doesn't actually erase it; it just moves it to the Deleted Items folder. It works like the Recycle Bin. You can recover a deleted message by double-clicking on the Deleted Items icon and dragging the message back to your Inbox. When you're running low on space and are really sure you don't need those files, just right-click on the Deleted Items folder and select Empty Folder.

You can read and delete messages in the Preview window, but you can do even more if you double-click on the message's entry in the message list. That opens the message in a new window with its own, more detailed menus and toolbars; there you can do things like print the message or copy part or all of it to the Clipboard so you can paste it into another program.

The Address Book

Once you get started, you'll probably work up a roster of regular correspondents to whom you'll send e-mail frequently, maybe several times
a day. Under ordinary circumstances, that would mean typing the
same addresses over and over—and risking the typos that will send
your messages to the wrong recipient or right back to your own Inbox
with an error message. To save the time and effort, Outlook Express
includes an address book, where you can keep e-mail addresses (and
lots of other information) for your friends and colleagues.

When someone writes you an e-mail message, you can easily add
their information to the address book by right-clicking on their name
and selecting Add to Contacts. By the way, you're not limited to just
their e-mail address. You can also add their postal address, phone
number, fax number, and any notes you might care to include.

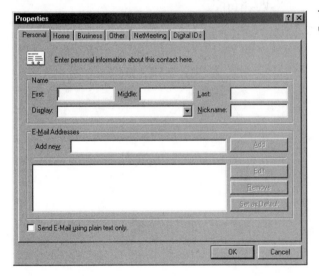

The address book holds commonly
used addresses.

Joining Newsgroups With Outlook Express

43

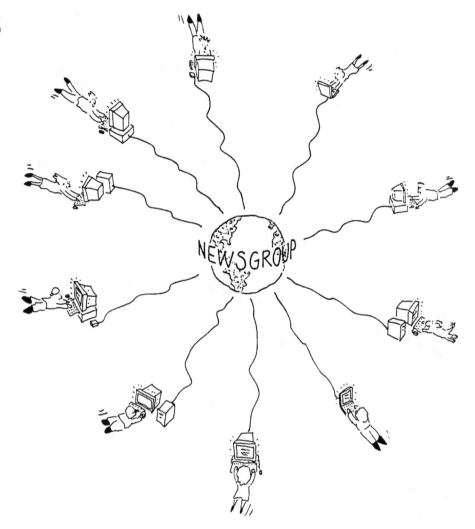

Almost everyone who uses the Internet uses the Web and e-mail. But before there was the Web, there were newsgroups. Newsgroups don't necessarily have anything to do with the kind of news you read in a newspaper—they're electronic bulletin boards, or "forums," where you can exchange messages with people around the world on any number of topics.

Unlike with chat rooms, newsgroup discussions don't take place "live" or in "real time." Messages you send to newsgroups are posted where others can read and respond to them. When you log on later, you can read the responses. Like a lively party, newsgroups can have lots of separate discussions going on at the same time. Over time, you get to know the other participants, creating a virtual community online.

In newsgroups you can meet people from around the world who share any special interest you can name, from traffic rules to, well, some pretty personal stuff that we won't go into in this G-rated book. And if you don't find a newsgroup on a topic you're looking for, you can start one yourself.

While you were exploring Outlook Express's e-mail features, you probably noticed that one of the categories listed on its main page was News. That's your entry into the world of newsgroups. If you used the Internet Connection Wizard (described in Chapter 43) to set up your e-mail, you're all set up for newsgroups as well. If you didn't enter a news server, call your ISP or visit its website and get the needed info and type it in according to your ISP's instructions.

What's Available

To open Outlook Express's News Reader, click on the News Reader icon in Outlook Express's main window or on the News folder in the hierarchical list. You can also launch the News Reader from within Internet Explorer by clicking the Mail icon and selecting Read News.

Outlook Express will display a dialog box asking, first, if you want to download a list of newsgroups (click Yes). If you're not already connected to the Net, it will then ask you if you want create a connection (click Yes again).

There are thousands of newsgroups, so this initial download could take a while. Go take a break, and wait for the list to download.

It's also possible to access newsgroups via the Web using a website called Deja News (www.dejanews.com). Deja News has a sophisticated search engine that makes it easy to find anything you want by keyword. Deja News has all newsgroups and postings indexed by word so that you could, for example, use it to search for a particular person's name or a piece of software and have it locate messages that include those words in every possible newsgroup.

Reading and Subscribing to Newsgroups

The list of newsgroups displayed in your Newsgroup dialog box is hard to make sense of at first. You'll see a list of weird words starting with A that probably don't mean much to you, and that list scrolls—a long way—all the way through Z. The method of naming newsgroups takes a little getting used to, but there is a wierd method to it (see the box "The Art of Newsgroup Naming" on the next page.)

Now, before you go on, I have to warn you that there are newsgroups about just about every subject you can imagine—including some that can be disturbing to both children and adults. If someone can think it, draw it, photograph it, or say it, it's probably in a newsgroup somewhere. As you read through the list, expect to be shocked as well as amused by the variety of topics people find to discuss.

One way to find newsgroups you like is to just start scrolling through the list until you find one that looks interesting. If you have a particular topic in mind, though, a quicker way is to type a term in the text field at the top of the dialog box. Try something like "games" for instance. Outlook Express will change the list of newsgroups to display only the ones that have "games" in their name. This isn't a foolproof method—there may be a newsgroup that has the name of a particular game, but not the word "games" in it, for instance. Take a few shots at it, though, and see what you get.

When you've found a newsgroup that looks interesting, double-click on its name in the list. This will open a dialog box you'll be familiar with: It has a three-pane arrangement like the one you used to read your e-mail. Here, though, the message list shows messages posted to the newsgroup (with unread messages, again, in boldface type). The name of the newsgroup is shown under the News and More category in the hierarchical list. And the text from the selected message (probably the first one in the list) is displayed in the Preview pane.

Outlook Express's search feature helps you find newsgroups that relate to a particular subject.

The Art of Newsgroup Naming

The list of newsgroups will make more sense to you once you learn a couple rules for newsgroup names.

The first thing to know is that all newsgroups are sorted into a few main categories. When someone creates a new newsgroup (and anybody can), they first figure out what category the topic belongs to. These are the main categories:

alt
Short for Alternative, it is the unofficial category that is used by people to create newsgroups that don't fit neatly into any of the other categories. It can be anything from someone's favorite TV program or a website for left-handed French speakers from Cincinnati. Just about everything goes in the alt category, including newsgroups that contain sexually explicit messages and photographs.

comp
Contains topics related to computers.

sci
Contains messages related to the sciences.

rec
Has topics about recreation, including sports, hobbies, the arts, and movies.

soc
Social issues and socializing.

news
Contains announcements and news about the Internet.

misc
Contains anything that doesn't fit into the other categories.

All newsgroup names start with a category name, followed by a period and one or more subcategory identifiers. For instance, a newsgroup about Web page design is called comp.infosystems.www.authoring.site-design, and a group for Star Trek fans is called rec.arts.startrek.

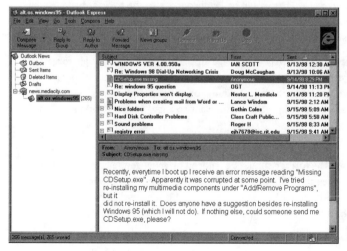

Outlook Express's News Reader window is organized like the e-mail Inbox.

To the left of the list of messages, in the hierarchical list, you'll see little plus signs that mark topics that have subtopics. Click on one to show the subitems—messages posted in response to the original message. In e-mail speak, the related messages form a newsgroup **thread**.

You can read the messages in a newsgroup just as you read e-mail messages—by clicking on any posting you want to read. You can double-click on the message to open it in a new window. And you can respond to the message by clicking the Respond to Author or Respond to Group buttons in the Inbox toolbar. When you're reading a newsgroup message, clicking Respond to Group creates a new message addressed to the newsgroup address. (Your message will be a new entry in the thread you're responding to.) Clicking Respond to Author creates a new message addressed just to the author of the original message. Although sending a message only to the author is antithetical to the idea of newsgroups, which are designed as a place for public discussion, it's something you may want to do once in a while. You can forward the message to someone else (as an e-mail) by clicking on Forward.

Keep on Topic:
The Etiquette of Newsgroups and Chat Sessions

If you went to a meeting that was focused on putting up stop signs in your community, you probably wouldn't stand up to talk about food quality at local restaurants or what you thought of the latest Steven Spielberg movie. That would be inappropriate to the topic at hand. And if someone says something you disagree with, you'd state your opinion and argue against their points without trying to insult that person's intelligence or integrity.

Yet even though most people behave civilly in public, a surprising number of people forget their manners when they go online. When you're online, you're still talking to real people who have real feelings, even if you can't see them, hear them, or even know their real names. Just as you want to show proper etiquette in real life, you want to show proper "netiquette" in the virtual world.

Bad manners in cyberspace run the gamut from people who are mildly annoying to those guilty of criminal harassment. The former should be ignored or given gentle reminders. In my experience, many shape up once they realize the error of their ways. Those who deliberately harass can be brought to the attention of whoever operates the service they're using. If what they're doing is bad enough, they can be warned, kicked off the system, and, in some cases, prosecuted.

Of course, your postings to newsgroups don't have to be limited to responses to other people's messages. You can post your own opinions, questions, jokes, you name it, by clicking on Compose. If you're currently viewing a newsgroup, Outlook Express will automaticaly insert the newsgroup address in the To: field. When you finish composing your message, type a subject, click Send, and the next time you download the newsgroup, you'll see your message there.

When you're done reading the postings of one newsgroup and want to browse through another, you can return to the list of newsgroups by clicking on the News and More icon in the hierarchical list or on the Newsgroups button in the News Reader toolbar.

If you find a newsgroup you think you'll want to return to, you'll want to subscribe to it. To do this, right-click on the newsgroup name in the hierarchical list and choose Suscribe To This Newsgroup from the menu that appears. That tells Outlook Express to keep the newsgroup listed in the hierarchical list until you unsubscribe from it (by choosing Unsubscribe From This List from the same menu).

Here are some guidelines for keeping things friendly.

- Avoid sarcasm, unless you're sure it will work, and think very carefully before using e-mail to express anger. With e-mail, once it's sent, it's gone. If you're posting a message in a public forum, remember it will be read by a wide variety of people.

- Be careful about your use of irony or even some forms of humor, which can be misinterpreted. Unlike face-to-face meetings or phone conversations, there are no visual or oral clues to provide a sense of what is going on.

- Exercise good taste. An Internet mail account is not a license to abuse or insult people.

- Be succinct and considerate of the recipient's time. E-mail messages, newsgroup postings and chat comments work best if they're short and to the point.

- Stay on the topic. Messages that stray too far afield can be annoying.

- Be aware that e-mail, newsgroup messages, and chat comments can be archived and may be looked at later or forwarded to others. Don't say anything online that you wouldn't say in a public forum.

- Don't "cry wolf." Avoid marking a message "Urgent" or "Priority" unless it really is. Employ capital letters sparingly. Using them for an entire message is perceived by many as SHOUTING.

Internet Channels and Active Desktop

44 So *far I've spend most of this book telling you how to use Windows features. This chapter is dedicated to explaining how not to use some. Microsoft, in its unending desire to pile more and more features into Windows, has created a couple that I think are more annoying than useful. They are Active Desktop and the Internet Explorer Channel Bar—ways of adding Web content right to your desktop.*

The Channel Bar

Channels are special websites designed to provide constantly updated information directly to your desktop. When I wrote this chapter, a vertical bar, called the Internet Explorer Channel Bar, appeared on the desktop by default, displaying buttons for a handful of special **channels**. In theory, the Channel Bar is a feature that lets uses add their favorite Internet sites directly to the desktop. In practice, it's a way for Microsoft to promote itself and its business partners. The channel providers in the Channel Bar paid Microsoft for the privilege of having their icon on your desktop. A lot of people have complained about the Channel Bar for a variety of reasons: It slows down the PC a bit, it represents an unfair advantage to Microsoft's business partners, it puts advertising on users' desktops, and it's just not that useful. As a result, I've heard reports that Microsoft may eliminate the Channel Bar, so it's possible that you may not even have one.

If you do have a Channel Bar on your desktop, my best advice is to simply remove it. There are several other ways to easily get back to your favorite websites without it. To delete it, right-click anywhere on the desktop. Click on Properties and then click on the Web tab. In the box in the center of your screen will be a place where you can uncheck Internet Explorer Channel Bar. Do so, click OK, and it's gone. (To bring back the Channel Bar you would use the same procedure

The Channel Bar lists a selection of Internet channels.

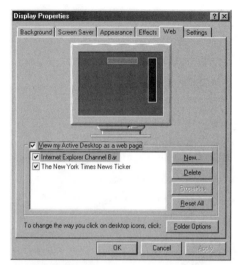

You can activate and deactivate channels and the Channel Bar by selecting or deselecting them in the Web panel of the Desktop Properties dialog box.

but place a checkmark next to Internet Explorer Channel Bar.)

If you want to see what channels are about, there are a couple of ways to access them. If you have the Channel Bar on your desktop, just click one of its buttons. If you don't, click the Channel's icon in your taskbar's Quick Launch Toolbar. That brings up the Channel Guide, from which you can select among a variety of channels to view. (That is, unless Microsoft has discontinued channels altogether by the time you read this.)

Each channel you visit will usually offer one or more subscription options. You click on a button to activate a channel subscription. (The channel provider determines which options are available.)

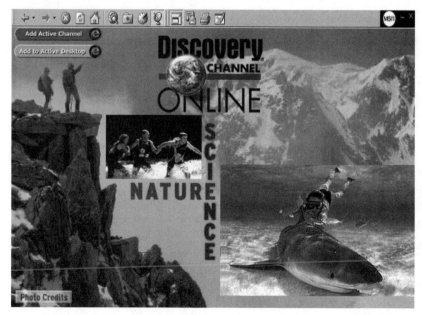

Internet channels are displayed in a browser that uses most of the same navigation controls as Internet Explorer, but looks a bit different. Every channel includes buttons that let you subscribe.

Add to the Channel Bar	Subscribing with this button will add a new button for this channel to your channel bar.
Add to Active Desktop	Subscribing with this button will add the channel's content right to your Windows desktop
Use as Screensaver	Subscribing with this button will turn the channel into a screensaver, meaning the channel will take over your screen whenever your computer is idle for awhile. (See Chapter 36 for more on screensavers.)

Viewing Your Desktop as a Web Page

You may have already noticed an option that shows up when you right-click on the desktop or in a folder window's View menu, offering you the option of viewing your desktop "As a Web Page." If you (or whoever sold you your computer) hasn't changed Windows' default settings, that option is selected, and you've been viewing your desktop as a Web page this whole time.

The View as Web Page command has a different effect depending on whether you're at the desktop or inside one of the folders. When you're looking at a folder window, viewing it as Web page gives you some useful features, including the ability to preview what's in a file by just single-clicking on its icon in the folder. On the Windows desktop you might not notice much of a difference (especially if you took my advice and turned off the Internet Channel Bar).

Why does Microsoft call this feature View As Web Page? (After all, it doesn't really make your views look any more

Right-clicking on the desktop brings up this menu, from which you can choose Active Desktop and then View as Web Page to activate (or deactivate) the Active Desktop features. In folder windows, you can choose View As Web Page from the Folder Options command in the View menu, for an entirely different set of effects.

like a Web page than they did before.) It's because when it's selected, Windows actually rewrites its underlying code as HTML, the language used to display content on the Web. This doesn't make a lot of difference in the way the desktop looks to you, but it does change the way it works, and it makes lots of extra features possible—including Active Desktop and the Channel Bar. It also makes it possible for expert users to customize the desktop so it does look like a Web page, but I'll spare you the details because it's an advanced (and largely useless) feature.

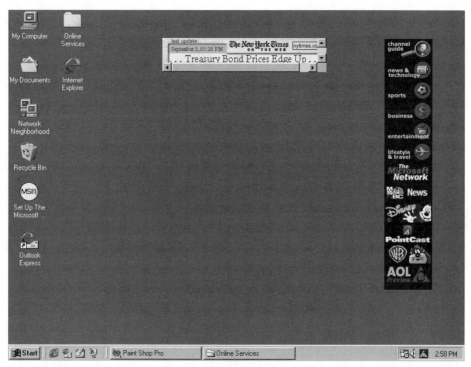

Adding a channel to Active Desktop puts the channel contents right on your Windows desktop. As long as you're connected to the Internet, the content will be updated regularly.

Active Desktop

Active Desktop is the ability to display active Web content on the Windows desktop. If you read about channels, just above, you've already seen one aspect of Active Desktop—channels can be designed to work as news tickers or other content embedded right into your desktop background.

So far, you've seen how to add channels to your desktop by clicking a button on the channels' site, but it's a crapshoot as to whether any given channel will have the Active Desktop option. To find channels specifically created for Active Desktop, make sure you're viewing your desktop as a Web page (see the box on the previous page), and make sure you're signed on to the Internet. Then right-click on the desktop, select Active Desktop, and then Customize My Desktop. In the Desktop Properties dialog box that appears, select the Web tab and click on the New button. That will bring you to a special Microsoft Web page that offers options for Active Desktop items. You can click on any item you want and follow the instructions to have it appear on your screen. I have to warn you though, this is one of the most buggy parts of Windows 98. In my experience, it works about a quarter of the time, so if you have trouble, don't blame yourself. It's not your fault!

My advice is, give this feature a pass, too. If you're like me, you'll rarely see your desktop anyway—mine is usually covered by Microsoft Word or whatever other program I'm using. And I find information constantly flowing across my screen too distracting. If I want to get the latest news, I can always visit a website!

Now that you've learned the basics of Internet Explorer and Outlook Express, you and your PC are on the Net, ready to explore the world of information you'll find there.

You've also finished your basic introduction to Windows, and you're ready to start thinking about what other software you need—application sofware that will help you with everything else you'll want to do on your computer, whether that's running a business, writing a novel, delving into a little digital artwork, or tutoring your kids. In Part 5, I'll go through what you already have and what more you might need in the way of application software, along with advice about what to look for in each category.

How Much Software Do You Need?

45 *You'll be able to find programs to take care of pretty much everything you want to use your PC for—business correspondence, working out your budgets, touching up photographs, writing music, getting access to information on the Internet, you name it. And once you get used to working with a few basic pieces of software and start hunting through magazines, catalogs, and websites, you'll find all sorts of games, utilities, and accessory software that you won't want to do without.*

Although there are an enormous number of programs to choose from, you'll find that most of them fall into a few categories, described below, which take care of most of the work you'll do on the computer.

Software Categories

Category	What It's For
Word processing and desktop publishing	Writing and formatting documents
Spreadsheet	Working with numbers
Personal information management	Tracking names, addresses, appointments, and other personal information
Financial management	Managing budgets, investments, and taxes
Presentation software	Creating graphics slide shows to accompany business presentations
Graphics	Working with photographs and illustrations
Database management	Tracking lots of information
Utilities	Managing the computer itself
Entertainment	Stuff to do in all your spare time
Children's software	Having fun and learning skills
Reference software	Lots of information at your fingertips

These are the main categories of application software—software you use to get things done on your PC. (The term is used to differentiate those kinds of programs from the operating system software, which is Windows itself.) There are lots of applications that don't fall into these categories, too—programs that handle specialized tasks like accounting, type design, or music composition, for instance. Another group helps professionals, from video store owners to landscape gardeners, run their businesses. The categories named in the box are the kinds for general use, though, and those are the ones I'll be covering in this section.

I'll go through each category, one at a time, from the most commonly used to the most specialized. For each category, I'll tell you more about what that kind of software does and I'll make recommendations for what to look for and what to buy. First, though, I'll go through a few introductory chapters explaining how to choose, buy, and install software for your PC.

Software You Already Have

46 **A** *set of simple application programs come preinstalled with Windows, including a word processor, a couple of graphics programs, games, and utilities. In many cases, you might find that the free programs you already have are sufficient for your needs, and you won't need to buy anything else in that category.*

To find out what you already have, click on the Start button and select Programs from the Start menu. The list of programs will include Internet Explorer (which you've already worked with), a group called Accessories that holds the programs that come with Windows, and any other software the PC maker, your dealer, or anyone who has used the computer before you has installed there. The list might be somewhat different for Windows 95, but it should still include an Accessories group and all the other installed programs.

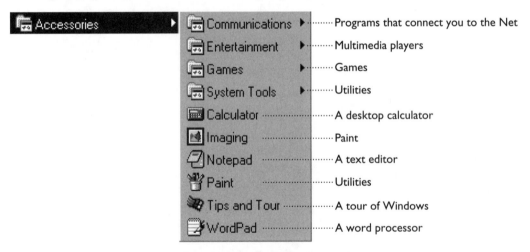

A set of simple application programs that comes free with Windows is installed in the Accessories program group. The Programs list will also include Internet Explorer and any other programs installed on your PC. (The Windows 98 menu is shown here.)

I'll talk more about many of these programs when I describe the categories they belong to in the chapters that follow. Others you'll want to explore by yourself after you've become more familiar with Windows. Open 'em all and try 'em out.

The Windows Setup pane in the Add/Remove Programs Control Panel lists all the programs that come with Windows. Double-click on the category name to view the programs within it. Put a checkmark next to the programs you want to install.

In reality, the programs you see here are just the tip of the iceberg. Windows comes with scores of programs buried throughout your system. If you're curious to see the entire range, open the Add/Remove Programs Control Panel tool and Click on the Windows Setup tab. (To find find Add/Remove Programs, click on the Start Button, then on Settings, and then on Control Panels. Double-click on Add/Remove Programs to open it.)

You'll see a list of programs and program categories. Not all the programs you see here will be installed on your computer, but they all come on the Windows installation CD. (A checkmark next to a category name means that at least one program in that category has already been installed.) To see the programs in each category, click on the icon next to the category name; another window will open, showing more programs. (Again, a checkmark next to a program name means it has been installed.) To find out about any of these programs, you can look in the Windows Help system. (Click the Start button and then Help, as you learned in Chapter 30.)

You can install any programs that haven't been installed yet by clicking on the empty box next to their names to put a checkmark there. Click the box next to any program you want to install, then click OK, and follow the instructions on the screen. Make sure you have your Windows installation CD-ROM ready; you may be asked to insert it.

How to Choose Software

47

I'M SHOPPING FOR WORD PROCESSING SOFTWARE. HOW'S YOURS?

A REAL DOG — MY HIGHEST RATING!

There are tens of thousands of application programs available for Windows 95 and Windows 98, not to mention the older programs written for Windows 3.1 and MS-DOS that still work on today's PCs. With so many choices, how do you know which ones are for you?

Matching the list of features on the back of the box to your wish list is just one way. But programs differ in how easy they are to use, whether or not the company that makes them will give you technical support if you need it, how reliable the program is (will it crash a lot? does it have bugs that make it work in unexpected ways?), and a lot of other factors. It's a good idea to do research on a product before you buy it.

Here are some things to consider before you choose a software package.

What Is Everyone Else Using?

In almost every software category, there are one, or at most two, run-away best-sellers. The best-selling program isn't necessarily the best one on the market, or the best one for your own needs, but it is an important signpost if you need a place to start looking.

Sometimes best-sellers get to be best-sellers because they were the first on the market and they got a head start on the others or because the publisher has a lot of marketing money to throw behind them. Programs usually gain popularity, though, through word of mouth—people who have tried the program praise it to other users who go out and buy it themselves. One advantage to owning a best-seller is that there will be lots of help available—from friends or colleagues who know the program and from books that are always available about the most popular programs. Another advantage is that you can easily share files with colleagues who are using the same program. Although it's often possible to share files between different programs (as I explained in Chapter 31), it's always easiest when the person who needs your file is using the same software you are using.

What Do Your Friends Like?

If you know some other people who have a PC, ask them what they use and how they like it. People who have used a program for a while can give you insights into how a program works that you wouldn't have thought to ask about. A program might have a lot of important features, but it might also have a really annoying way of organizing its commands or dialog boxes. Or it could have other problems that might make it a bad choice. Ask everyone you know what they would recommend. You'll probably quickly find one or two top choices. One cautionary note: People often prefer the program they learned first. That doesn't mean it's bad, but it doesn't necessarily mean that it's the best, either.

What Do the Dealers Suggest?

People who sell software may or may not know a lot about the products they sell, but asking them is worth a shot. After all, they have day-to-day contact with users of all sorts of software, and they know if a lot of customers are happy or unhappy with certain products. Many computer dealers, including mail-order companies, are happy to advise you on your purchases. After all, they want satisfied customers. Having said that, though, don't forget that Latin phrase, *caveat emptor*—let the buyer beware. Look hard enough and you're bound to find some software dealers who don't know what they're talking about. Don't let the dealer talk you into something you don't think you want.

Which Programs Offer Free Support?

Try to buy software published by a company that offers free telephone support, and it's even better if it offers a toll-free number to call. Believe me, it's something you'll use. These days a lot of companies offer free support only for the first 90 days or so. If that's the case, it's an incentive to take the software out of its package and try it out right away, because after the free support period is up, you'll have to start paying for the developer's help.

What Do Reviewers Say?

Every computer magazine puts new products through rigorous tests and publishes the results. By all means, take advantage of this resource. If the program isn't covered in a current issue, check the back issues in a library or on the Internet. Most computer magazines provide free access to online reviews. (See Chapter 5 for a rundown of the leading computer magazines and what they cover.)

What Do You Use at Work?

If you use a program at work and want to take work home (as if anybody really *wants* to do that), then it makes sense to have the same program at home that you have at the office. You might want to check with whomever is in charge of the computer systems at work about how to get copies of the software for use at home. In some cases, companies can get it for you for free (legally) or may buy it for you or pass on the company discount. It doesn't hurt to ask.

Does It Do Everything You Need—But Not Too Much More?

In almost every category of software, you can find two kinds of programs—so-called high-end or industrial-strength programs designed for professionals and low-end programs designed for more casual

Try Before You Buy:
Shareware, Freeware, and Demo Software

In many cases, you can actually try out software before you buy it. A whole category of software, called **shareware**, is based on this idea. Shareware is distributed on the honor system. You can get a copy for free, but you're expected to "register" and pay for the program if you find it useful. The registration fee for most shareware programs ranges from as little as $5 to more than $150, with the median being about $50—in most cases, far less than the cost of similar commercial programs.

In some cases, shareware programs are slightly disabled until you register, as an extra incentive for you to pay up. A shareware database program, for example, may limit you to a hundred or so listings, whereas the full-featured version has no such limit. Other shareware programs have all the features but keep displaying notices asking you to register each time you start them. When you pay the registration fee, you get a version that doesn't nag.

Another category of software, **public domain software** or **freeware**, really is free. No one even asks you to pay for these programs, but they're often great, and sometimes indispensable. In some cases, these programs were developed at government expense; it's your tax dollars at work, so take advantage of them.

Recently, commercial software publishers have also bought into the try-before-you-buy idea, offering demonstration versions of software that you can order from them or download from their websites. In some cases, demo programs are designed to work for only a certain period of time—usually about 30 days—after which you can purchase the program by forking over a credit card number. Another strategy of software companies is to partially disable the program so you get an idea of how it works but can't truly use it. This might include printing something obnoxious on each document you create with the program or not letting you save files, print, or perform other essential tasks.

Often, you can try out software for free by using a **beta version**, software that isn't quite ready to release (it probably still has a few bugs and might not have every feature the final version will have). Companies often distribute beta software for free so they can get user feedback that will help them finalize the software. Being a "beta tester" does put you on the leading edge but, if something goes wrong, you'll soon find out why they also call it the "bleeding edge"—the software might crash your computer. Usually, beta software works for only a limited period of time, after which you'll need to buy the final, commercial version, if you want it.

When I recommend a piece of software in this section, look for the website address in the Resources box. That's where you can look for demo and beta versions of the software for download. You can also find demo software, public domain software, and shareware from a variety of general software sites, such as www. download.com, www.shareware.com, www.hotfiles.com, and www.filemine.com.

users. If you're using a word processor only to write letters, you don't need all the fancy formatting capabilities you'd want if you were planning to use it for a home business or to publish a newsletter. The low-end programs are not only often a lot less expensive than the high-end ones, but they're usually easier to learn and use and they take up a lot less memory and storage space than the industrial-strength programs. For each category of software I discuss in this section, I'll usually recommend an industrial-strength program and a less-expensive, "everyday-strength" one.

Is It Priced Right?

Of course, cost nearly always counts. And in almost every category, you can find software that is both excellent and reasonably priced.

Will It Run on Your Computer?

Every box of software and many software reviews will list the program's minimum **system requirements**—the hardware and software you'll need to run the program. These days, most computers are equipped to run most software, but some programs require more memory, more disk space, or a faster CPU than you have. Be sure to check before you buy.

If the box says you need Windows 95 and you have Windows 98, don't worry—the software should run fine. If the box says Macintosh, though, worry: Look for the Windows version instead. Some boxes say "Win/Mac," which means there are actually two copies of the program on the CD-ROM—one for Windows and another for Macintosh.

Where to Get Software

48

You can get software from all sorts of sources, some of them surprising. The software marketplace ranges from software specialty stores you can find in any business district, to websites on the Internet or AOL, to thriving mail-order companies. You can also buy software directly from the publisher.

Depending on where you buy, you can save hundreds of dollars on a piece of software, get money-back guarantees, and even get free upgrades. It pays to shop around. I'll run through the list of major options here.

The Software Publisher

Usually, when software is reviewed or mentioned in a magazine, the publication also provides the phone number of the software publisher, as if that were where you should buy the product. I give phone numbers and website addresses for software publishers in this book, too, because they are good sources for finding out about the product's features and requirements. You can also usually buy the product from the publisher, but don't assume that that's where you'll get the best price. Some publishers insist on selling their programs at full list price so they won't undercut their retailers. Others offer a reasonable discount. Some software companies don't sell their products directly at all, but they will refer you to a local dealer if you contact them.

Specialty Stores

If you shop around, you can find good deals and good service at computer specialty stores such as **CompUSA** or office supply stores such as **Staples**, **OfficeMax**, *or* **Office Depot**. The best have knowledgeable staffs, good prices, and enlightened return policies. The worst, of course, have none of those things.

Mail Order

Like hardware, you can buy software via mail order. Mail-order prices are sometimes less expensive than you'll find in stores, and many mail-order companies also offer money-back guarantees. The best way to find a mail-order house is to look in practically any computer magazine. You can't miss their ads. Leading mail-order houses include **Egghead**, **PC Warehouse**, **PC Connection**, and **PC Zone** (some of the same companies that sell hardware, as I mentioned in Chapter 7). If you call them, they'll send you a catalog.

Online

Most mail-order companies have also set up shop on the Internet. This can be a convenient way to shop because you can often get more information about a product online than you can in a catalog. Sometimes you can also see sample screens before you buy, and you can send e-mail to the dealer if you have any questions or comments. Other mail-order houses let you download your new software right over the Net. **BuyDirect.Com** lets you download the software directly from the software publisher, after you provide a credit card number, and **Parsons Technology** sells and downloads a wide variety of software directly from its website.

AOL users can find software vendors in the Computing Channel (keyword: Computing). You can also find out information, get demo versions, and, often, purchase software from software

Resources

CompUSA
800-266-7872
www.compusa.com

Office Depot
888-284-3638
www.officedepot.com

OfficeMax
800-788-8080
www.officemax.com

Staples
800-333-3330
www.staples.com

Resources

Egghead
800-344-4323
www.egghead.com

PC Connection
800-800-0005
www.pcconnection.com

PC Warehouse
800-727-8673
www.pcwarehouse.com

PC Zone
800-258-8088
www.pczone.com

Resources

BuyDirect.Com
www.buydirect.com

Parsons Technology
www.parsonstech.com

company websites. The Web is also the best source for shareware and public domain software (see the box "Try Before You Buy: Shareware, Freeware, and Demo Software" on page 251).

The Five-Finger Discount

You've paid all this money for your computer and now you find out that you have to buy your software, too. You could easily spend more for the software than you did for the computer. Is it really necessary? After all, the guy next door offered to give you a copy of a program that would otherwise cost you about $300. It would be as simple as borrowing his CD. You don't get the manuals, but for about $20, you can buy a book that will teach you the program.

Should you accept the gift? Legally, you shouldn't. Commercial software is copyrighted, which means it's illegal for its users to distribute copies. (The same issues apply to making copies of music and movies.) Copyrights protect the people who own the rights to the software and the creative people who make it. Creating a piece of software is an expensive business, and the practice of illegally copying software deprives companies of the revenue they have earned.

Copying software illegally is called software **piracy**, and many software companies vigorously defend their copyrights. According to the legal department of the Software Publishers Association (a trade organization that monitors the illegal use of software), it tends to go after businesses that buy a single copy of a program and distribute it throughout the organization. It also investigates claims that people are illegally reselling their programs.

If you have "borrowed" your neighbor's disks, chances are you won't be wakened from a sound sleep one night by the FBI pounding on your door. But there are good reasons besides legal and moral considerations to buy your own copies of software. What happens if you run into a serious problem and can't get help from the software company? What if there's a bug in the program that you'll never learn about because you're not on the list of registered owners? I wouldn't dream of trusting my tax records or business information to a program that I didn't legally own. I could be in big trouble if something went wrong with the program and the company's tech support department wouldn't help because I'm not a registered owner.

Rules for Buying Software

Don't Pay the Full Retail Price

Software publishers generally establish a "suggested retail price" that often has relatively little to do with what you actually pay for programs in the real world. Prices of popular programs are often heavily discounted, sometimes 50 percent or more. Check the ads in the computer magazines or call or visit the website of one of the mail-order houses to see what the street price really is. The prices I quote for software in this book are, whenever possible, the typical "street price" at the time the book was written. These prices change all the time, though, so call a couple of software dealers to get some current prices before you buy.

Be Sure You're Getting the Right Version

Every piece of software goes through several versions as its manufacturer adds features and fixes bugs. The version number follows the product name, as in "Microsoft Word 7.0" or "Quicken 99" (where it is noted by the year the version was released).

I have seen ads for software at extremely attractive prices, but when I call or visit the dealer, I discover that the software is out of date. Make sure you know the latest version number before you order software. (You can find out with a quick call to the software company or a visit to the company's website.) There's nothing wrong with using an older version of software if you don't need the new features, but if you're not getting the latest version, you should be getting a substantial discount as well as an opportunity to upgrade to the new version at a reduced price.

Try to Get a Money-Back Guarantee

It's not easy, but if you call around, you might be able to find a dealer who will give you a full refund if you're not happy with a software program. Many stores refuse to accept returns because they think people are buying programs, making copies, and then returning the original as a way of "stealing" the software. Fortunately, some dealers have more enlightened policies. Don't accept a guarantee that's limited to replacing a defective disk. If the program doesn't work right, chances are that the problem isn't the disk or CD, but rather bugs in the program, an incompatibility with your system, or documentation that's too poorly written for you to understand.

Buy With a Credit Card

Even if the company you buy from has a good return policy, it's always best to buy computer products with a credit card. Most bank cards offer a dispute clause that allows you to get a refund on a product you're unhappy with, and some now double the warranty for products purchased with the card. It also makes refunds easy if a return is necessary.

Software Suites:
Cheaper by the Half-Dozen

49

One of the most popular ways to buy software is to buy a software "suite," a set of programs from a single publisher, packaged together in a single box.

Buying programs in a suite often results in an incredibly steep discount. For instance, you can get Microsoft Word (a word processor), Microsoft Excel (a spreadsheet), Microsoft PowerPoint (a presentation program), and Microsoft Outlook (a personal information manager) all together in **Microsoft Office**, one of the suites Microsoft offers, for about $450. If you bought each of those programs separately, you would pay hundreds more. Often, the entire suite will also come on a single CD-ROM, which makes them easier to install.

Software suites come in all sorts of categories. Office suites, like Microsoft Office, Lotus's *SmartSuite*, and Corel's *WordPerfect Suite*, contain a core set of applications for businesses: a word processor, a spreadsheet, a presentation program, and a personal information manager. Other types of suites group tools that are specialized for other tasks. Corel offers a suite called *Graphics Pack II*, for example, that includes a set of illustration and page layout programs. When you're shopping for a program, check out what types of suites the publisher offers. For a relatively small additional price, you might be able to get a whole set of programs instead of just the one you were shopping for.

Microsoft Office, which combines a set of programs almost everyone needs at an attractive price, is by far the most popular software suite. It comes in four editions. The basic set I talked about above contains

Why Just About Everyone Uses Microsoft Software

In the next several chapters, as I go through the most popular categories of software, including word processors, spreadsheets, and personal information managers, you'll notice that I'm going to mention Microsoft products a lot. They're the best-sellers in each of those categories, and they are often the products I recommend, too.

There's no easy explanation as to why Microsoft dominates the software market. One reason, though, is that as the company that provides the operating system, Microsoft has tight relations with PC makers, making it likely to have its software bundled with PCs. Microsoft also has a lot of money to spend on marketing, advertising, and public relations.

Another reason is that Microsoft Office is an incredibly popular suite for business software buyers. Most offices whose employees use PCs use Microsoft Office for their basic software, making the programs in Microsoft Office the best-sellers in each of their categories. And when you're talking about software, success breeds success. People will usually recommend the program they use to other people (if the program is any good at all), so the people who use Microsoft products at work are a built-in PR machine for Microsoft, and the circle keeps on growing.

Finally, Microsoft makes good programs. The company may not always get its products right the first time (a lot of Microsoft products aren't that good when they're first shipped), but eventually, it gets them right. One reason Microsoft Office became so popular is that its spreadsheet, Microsoft Excel, blew away every other program in its class, and Microsoft Word was one of the best in its category, too. For office software managers, then, the opportunity to get Word and Excel, plus a whole set of other programs that work with them for a good price in the Office suite was a no-brainer. They snapped it up and now Microsoft rules every category covered by the Office suite.

Word, Excel, PowerPoint, and Outlook for about $450. **Microsoft Office Professional Edition** adds Microsoft Access (a database management program) and Bookshelf Basics (a set of reference books on CD-ROM) for about $525. And **Microsoft Office Small Business Edition** includes Word, Excel, and Outlook, plus Microsoft Publisher (a simple page layout program), Small Business Financial Manager (as you guessed, a financial management program), Internet Explorer (which you probably already have, as I explained in Chapter 41), and Expedia Streets 98 (a map-making program for U.S. cities), all for $450.

Another Microsoft suite, called **Microsoft Home Essentials**, is designed for home users and costs about $100. It includes Microsoft Word, Microsoft Encarta (a multimedia encyclopedia on CD-ROM), Microsoft Money (financial management), Microsoft Greetings Workshop, and Microsoft Works, an **integrated program** that contains functions of a word processor, database manager, and spreadsheet.

One of these suites (usually one from Microsoft) often comes bundled with computers. Look through the CD that came with your system and peruse the Programs list in the Start menu. A software suite may already be installed.

Resources

Graphics Pack II, WordPerfect Suite
Corel
800-772-6735
www.corel.com

Microsoft Office, Microsoft Home Essentials
Microsoft
800-426-9400
www.microsoft.com

SmartSuite
Lotus Development
800-343-5414
www.lotus.com

Installing and Uninstalling Software

50 *When you get a new program, your first task is to install it on your system. "Install" is an ominous-sounding term. It evokes images of a service person with a truck, a set of tools, and specialized skills. Installing programs is generally quite easy, though, made simple by the special installation program most applications come with.*

Usually, an install program for an application program creates new folders, copies the application files from the original floppies or CD-ROM to your hard disk, and makes any necessary changes to your Windows configuration. (For programs, such as reference software or games, that are designed to be run off the CD-ROM, the installation program won't copy all the files over, but will install just a few files that help Windows run the program.) The installation program prompts you for the information it needs to configure the software so that it works on your machine. In many cases, the install program runs automatically when you first insert the CD-ROM.

Using an Install Program

If the install program doesn't run automatically, it's easy enough to run it yourself. Look on the CD-ROM or floppy disk for a program called something like Setup.exe or Install.exe. Double-click on it, and follow any instructions that appear.

Setup.exe

Most programs come with an Install or Setup program that automatically puts the program files where they belong on your hard drive. Its icon usually looks like this—a box to be unpacked. Double-clicking on it will start the process.

If you can't find an install program, use the Install/Remove program that comes with Windows. To use it, open the Control Panel (using the Settings command in the Start menu or by opening My Computer) and double-click on the Add/Remove Programs icon. Then click the Install button and follow the instructions on the screen. The Add/Remove Programs system will look for any installation programs on your CD-ROM drive or floppy disk and do the work for you.

The READ.ME File

Sometimes the installation program will create a file on your hard disk called README or README.TXT. This file includes information that the programmers found out about too late to include in the manual. Here you'll find any late-breaking news about additional features, features that work differently from the way the manual describes them, and any known bugs or incompatibilities with other software or hardware. You might not understand most of the information in the READ.ME file (no one does), but it's a good idea to scan through it anyway, just in case there's something that's important to you.

To open the README file, just double-click on it. Usually the file is in ASCII (plain text) format, so WordPad or some other program on your disk will open it automatically. If that doesn't work, open it with any word processing program.

Uninstalling

If you have a program that you don't want any more, don't just erase the files. That will get rid of the program itself, but it won't remove the program from the Windows **registry**, a system that allocates memory and other resources to programs and information about programs. To take that information out of the registry, you need to follow a special uninstall process.

The proper way to go about uninstalling a program is to use the Add/Remove Programs tool. Open the Control Panel (using the Settings command in the Start menu or by opening My Computer) and double-click on the Add/Remove Programs icon. Then select the program you want to remove from the list that pops up. A Wizard will lead you through the rest of the procedure; all you have to do is answer the questions it asks and do what it tells you to do. (In some cases, it will ask if it's OK to restart the computer. Say Yes.) That should remove all the program files as well as the program's record in the registry.

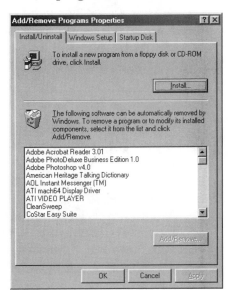

The Add/Remove Programs tool in the Windows Control Panel can safely remove programs from your hard disk.

If for some reason the program you want to remove doesn't show up in the Add/Remove Control Panel, you'll have to delete the files manually. It's not the neatest way, but it's the best you can do without a special utility. (See Chapter 60 for more on utilities that can help you clean up the files left behind.)

Sometimes Windows tells you that it hasn't quite completed the uninstall and that you have to remove some items yourself. Usually that means that it couldn't erase the folder that contains the program files. Remember I told you never to delete program folder? Well, this is an exception. Go ahead and delete the folder—but first make sure you're deleting the right one. When in doubt, leave it alone. It might waste a small amount of disk space, but that's better than disabling your computer or another software program by getting rid of the wrong files.

Some Reasons to Register Your Software

When you open a box of software, most likely a registration card will fall out. It's usually a postcard that asks you to fill in your name and address, along with some other information that will be useful to the software company's marketing department, and return it to the company. They're like the warranty cards you get with many consumer items. I don't know if it makes any sense to register your new toaster, but it is a good idea to register your software.

Sometimes you can register the software online via the Internet. Just fill out the questionnaire on the screen and let the modem send it off for you.

Registering software makes you eligible for benefits that you can't get any other way. To begin with, registering makes you eligible for a free upgrade if serious bugs are found in the program. Second, registered users receive information on program updates and generally get a discount on new releases. Some companies require you to be registered in order to use their telephone support lines.

All you have to do to register is fill out the form or enter the information on the screen. If you don't want to fill in the marketing information, just leave it blank. Your name and address will still make it into the database.

Word Processing: Writing Made Easy

51

Basically, a word processing program turns a PC into a very advanced electronic typewriter. It not only provides tools that make it easier to write and edit your words, but it also makes it easy to dress them up.

Word processors let you format your text with a variety of typefaces, add graphics, and set your work in sophisticated layouts. With a word processor, you type, edit, and design your work on screen, rather than on paper. When you're done, you print it. And with a high-quality ink jet or laser printer, your final document can look as if it were professionally printed.

Best of all, a word processing system lets you make changes to your work with amazing ease. Word processors let you delete, insert, copy, and move text whenever you get a new idea, and this will change the way you write. It takes the anxiety out of committing something to paper because you know that you can keep what you like and easily change what you don't.

Word processing programs can also check your spelling, and some can help you find the right word with a built-in thesaurus. The best word processors make it easy to automatically create parts of documents, like tables of contents and indexes, that would otherwise take days to create, check, and recheck. And an electronic index or table of contents generated by a word processing program can be automatically updated when you change the text.

Scorecard: Word Processors

Most Popular	Microsoft Word (Microsoft)
Low-Cost Alternative	WordPad (comes with Windows)
	Microsoft Works (Microsoft)
Recommendation	
Everyday strength	Microsoft Word (Microsoft)
Industrial strength	Microsoft Word (Microsoft)
	Word Pro (Lotus Development)
	WordPerfect (Corel)

Another advantage to using a word processing program is that it makes collaboration easy. Material that is in electronic form can be easily transmitted over a network or via modem to co-workers and can be edited by whoever needs to work with the document next. A word processing document, with a little bit of special formatting, can even be posted to a website to share with the rest of the world.

WordPad: The Word Processor You Already Own

WordPad, which comes with Windows 95 and Windows 98, has everything you'll need to be able to write letters, memos, and reports. The program lets you change fonts (see the box "Using Fonts" on the next page), insert graphics from other Windows programs, and print very attractive documents. The only really important feature missing is a spell checker, which is something I can't do without anymore. WordPad is OK for starters, and even if you decide you need something else later on, practicing with WordPad will give you an opportunity to get used to

Working in a word processor is like working with a typewriter that has a lot of whizbang features. You type on screen instead of on paper.

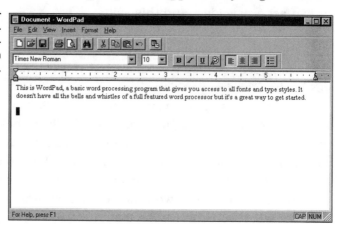

Using Fonts

Fonts are what determine how type looks on screen and printed out in documents. Windows comes with lots of them, and you'll often get extra fonts when you buy some kinds of software. Greeting card programs or desktop publishing applications, for example, often come with hundreds of extra fonts.

When you install Windows or any program that comes with fonts, the installation program will install the fonts where they belong on your system, which is in the Fonts folder inside the Windows Directory on your hard disk. A Fonts tool in the Control Panel folder helps you view, install, and uninstall others. (Choose Settings and then Control Panel from the Start menu, then double-click on the Fonts icon.) Once fonts are installed, they can be applied to text though menu commands in almost any program.

Unless you're a graphic designer or are intent on a certain look for your documents, the batch you already have is probably more than enough for your needs. If you really get interested in experimenting with different designs, though, you can buy extra fonts quite reasonably. Leading font vendors include, Bitstream (800-522-3668, 617-497-6222, www.bitstream.com) and Letraset (201-845-6100, www.letraset.com). You can also purchase fonts designed for other languages. Davka Corp. (800-621-8227, 312-465-4070, www.davka.com), for example, sells Hebrew fonts. DataCal Corp. (800-223-0123, 602-813-3100, www.datcal.com) offers fonts in several languages, including Japanese and Russian.

word processing. Most other Windows word processors can import WordPad documents, so sharing files with other programs is no problem. Also, WordPad can read and write Microsoft Word files.

Notepad: A Simple Text Editor

Windows also comes with Notepad, which, like WordPad, can be used to edit text. The difference between Notepad and WordPad is that Notepad can only be used to edit plain ASCII text files. You can't add formatting, and you can't use it to edit Word files.

Microsoft Word and Microsoft Works

There is no more powerful word processor I know of than *Microsoft Word*.

If you buy Word alone, it will set you back around $300, but you can get it much more inexpensively in a suite. *Microsoft Home Essentials* (which I described in Chapter 49) includes Word and a bunch of other useful programs for home users for about $100. In fact, for the price of the Home Essentials package, you get two word processors. *Microsoft Works*,

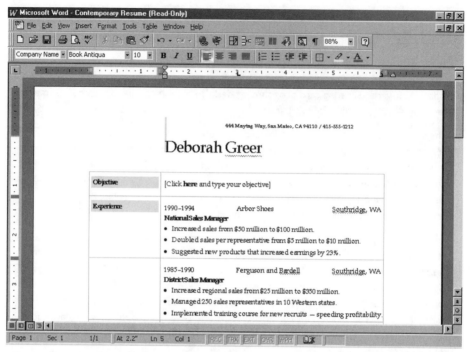

Microsoft Word, part of every Microsoft suite, is the most popular word processor and one of the most powerful.

also included in the suite, has a very good word processing component. Some people might even like the Works word processor better than Word because, although it has enough features for most people, it is less difficult to learn.

The two other leading Windows word processing programs are **Word Pro** from Lotus Development and **WordPerfect for Windows** from Corel. (They're part of the suites available from Lotus and Corel, which I described in Chapter 49.) They're both quite good, and Word Pro is especially good for groups of people who work together on documents because it has features especially designed to help keep control of versions. WordPerfect for Windows is a good choice for people who use WordPerfect at the office. (WordPerfect is still popular in law offices, though its market share has shrunk over the years.)

Resources

Microsoft Word, Microsoft Works
Microsoft
800-426-9400
www.microsoft.com

WordPerfect for Windows
Corel
800-772-6735
www.corel.com

Word Pro
Lotus Development
800-343-5414
www.lotus.com

What's All This About Desktop Publishing?

With a good word processor and a laser printer, you can easily create documents that, just a few years ago, would have been possible only by using professional typesetting and printing. In fact, PC software for creating documents has gotten so good that it has pretty much put professional typesetters out of business. Now, professional graphic designers do their work on PCs and Macintoshes.

These professionals typically use page layout or **desktop publishing** software such as Adobe's *PageMaker* (800-833-6687; 650-961-4400; www.adobe.com) and *QuarkXPress* (800-788-7835, www.quark.com). These powerful programs offer all the tools for typographic refinements and four-color printing that designers need for the most sophisticated color publications. Other programs, such as *Corel Ventura* (800-772-6735, 613-728-8200, www.corel.com) specialize in helping publishers of books, technical manuals, and other long documents in which creating regular formats, complicated tables, and indexes are the most challenging tasks.

Although professional publishers will turn to these page layout programs, most people will find that high-end word processing programs such as Microsoft Word, Lotus Word Pro, and WordPerfect offer all the design flourishes they're likely to need. In fact, the top-of-the-line word processors offer a lot of the same capabilities, including multicolumn (newspaper-like) layouts and the ability to import color graphics and wrap text around them. Although these programs don't provide the kind of free-form layouts and color separation for professional printing that page layout programs specialize in, they can easily handle most day-to-day documents, and even pretty fancy newsletters.

If you find you're pushing the boundaries of your word processing program and you want to try something a bit fancier, consider looking into a page layout program designed for nonprofessionals. Programs like *Microsoft Publisher* (800-426-9400, www.microsoft.com/publisher/) and SPC/Serif Software's *Page Plus* (800-489-6703, www.serif.com) offer many of the same features of the professional-level packages, at a much lower price. They're also easier to master than the professional programs.

What to Look for in a Word Processor

• **automatic index generator** Lets you tag certain words in your document for inclusion in the index, then creates the index, with page numbers, from those words. If the page breaks change while you edit, the page numbers in the index are automatically updated.

• **automatic footnotes** Automatically numbers footnotes and places them at the bottom of the proper page, or at the end of the document if that's what you prefer.

• **automatic table of contents** Looks for all the headings in your document and puts them together as a table of contents, complete with page numbers.

• **equation formatting** Some word processors are better than others at creating good-looking equations (the kinds that have all sorts of fractions within fractions). If you create technical documents, make sure your word processor handles equations well.

• **envelope and label formatting** Any word processor can print on envelopes and label stock, but making it easy is another matter. Look for a program that automatically formats an address for standard envelopes and labels.

file management from within the application The better word processors have advanced text searching features for locating files. Most can sort files by date as well as by name.

graphics support Virtually all Windows word processing programs let you insert a picture from a graphics program into your document.

• **grammar checker** These tools check your documents for proper syntax and grammar. It's not an exact science, but it could be helpful.

• **macros** A macro is a keyboard shortcut. Using a macro feature, you could distill commonly used text into a single keystroke. For example, I've set up the key combination Ctrl-L to type Sincerely, Lawrence J. Magid at the bottom of my letters. You can also use macros to set into motion an entire sequence of commands by issuing a single keystroke.

• mail merge The most common use for mail merge is merging a form letter with a list of names and addresses to personalize a business mailing. You've seen this at work in junk mail that addresses you by name—you know, "Congratulations, Mr. Marion Connecticut, you may already have won a valuable prize."

multicolumn formatting Some word processors enable you to set up multiple columns per page, as in a newspaper.

• outlining Gives you an overview of your document by letting you collapse it down so that you see just the headings or just the first lines of each paragraph.

saving in different formats If you're sharing your documents with anyone—a secretary, an editor, a boss, a graphics department—you'll have to make sure you can give them the document in a file format they can read with their own program. (See Chapter 31 for more on formats commonly used to share word processing files.)

spell checking Checks every word in your document against an electronic dictionary. If a word isn't in the dictionary, it will ask you if you want to change it or add the word to your dictionary. It may also offer other possible spellings for the word. Some programs, such as Microsoft Word, have automatic spell checking that highlights misspelled words as you type.

• style sheets This feature allows you to change the appearance of all or part of a document by selecting a menu item or issuing one or two keystrokes. A style is a preset format that, once created, can be used over again.

• text searches across documents Some word processors let you search all the documents on your hard drive to find those that contain certain words or phrases.

• thesaurus If you want to vary the words you use in your writing (always a good idea), you can look up alternative words in a built-in thesaurus. You can just highlight the word, activate the thesaurus, and the word processor will give you a list of other words that mean the same thing.

Spreadsheets: Working With Numbers

52

If you work with numbers at all, you're probably a candidate for a spreadsheet program. A spreadsheet is like a giant piece of electronic ledger paper. You enter numbers into a grid of rows and columns and then perform calculations on them.

It's a simple concept, but an extremely powerful piece of software. When you revise a figure or modify a formula, all the numbers affected by the change are revised as well. Most spreadsheets can also turn your numbers into a bar chart or a pie chart for a quick visual summary of what the numbers mean. Spreadsheets can include text as well as numbers, and most offer text-formatting capabilities so you can also create good-looking reports from them.

Spreadsheets are amazingly versatile programs. They're used by accountants at multinational corporations to do budgets and sales forecasts, but they're also useful for simpler tasks, like quickly

Scorecard: Spreadsheets

Most Popular	Microsoft Excel (Microsoft)
Recommendation	
Everyday strength	Microsoft Works (Microsoft)
Industrial strength	Microsoft Excel (Microsoft)
	1-2-3 (Lotus Development)
	Quattro Pro (Corel)

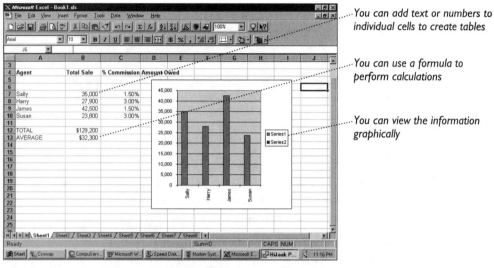

A spreadsheet document is modeled on a piece of ledger paper, with rows and columns that make it easy to create tables. In each "cell" (the box that results from an intersection of a row and a column), you can enter numbers, text, or a formula that performs a calculation on other cells.

adding up a set of personal expenses. Even a beginner can quickly master the few commands necessary for simple tasks.

The most popular full-featured spreadsheet program is **Microsoft Excel**, the spreadsheet program included in Microsoft Office. Excel is easy to use, and it offers all the features anyone could ever need. Many common formulas can be implemented by clicking an on-screen button that writes the formula for you. To add up a row of numbers, for example, you simply place your insertion point at the bottom of the column you want to add and click the Sum button.

Lotus 1-2-3 and Corel's **Quattro Pro**, the spreadsheets included in Lotus's and Corel's office suites, respectively, also have more features than you'll ever need, but each has a slightly different set. If you're considering springing for a high-end spreadsheet program, I suggest you read reviews in computer magazines that exhaustively test and compare all the

What to Look for in a Spreadsheet

• *indicates a feature found in industrial-strength programs*

• **ability to link spreadsheets** This feature lets you pull data from multiple spreadsheets for your calculations. For example, you could create one spreadsheet documenting sales for each month of the year, and then create a summary spreadsheet that pulls the data from the monthly spreadsheets to calculate yearly totals.

• **automatic formula writing** Formulas tell a spreadsheet what cells you want added, multiplied, or otherwise operated on. Once you get the hang of them, they're not too hard to put together, but the syntax can be somewhat complicated. Some programs, such as Microsoft Excel, let you select just the cells you want to work on; then you click a button that indicates the operation you want to use, and the program writes the formula for you.

graphics Most spreadsheets include the ability to generate business graphics such as pie charts and bar graphs from your spreadsheet data.

import and export other formats Most spreadsheets can read and save to ASCII, Excel, and Lotus 1-2-3 formats. The ability to save to leading formats is important not only for sharing data, but also in case you want to change to another program later and want to take all your old models with you. You can invest a lot of time in working out problems, and it would be a shame to lose that work if you should change spreadsheet programs down the line.

• **lots of useful functions** Functions are little programs built into the spreadsheet that automatically calculate the numbers. Any spreadsheets will have basic ones, like SUM (which adds a row of numbers), but from there they can get pretty wild. If you're interested in really putting your spreadsheet program to work, automating accounts payable for your business and such, check out what it offers in the way of advanced functions.

• **macros** A macro capability lets you create your own programs within the spreadsheet, to automate updates and reports, for instance.

text formatting In order to use a spreadsheet for presentations, you'll need some control over how the text looks, especially the ability to italicize and boldface words and to pick appropriate typefaces.

features of a few such programs. It could be that one program will have just the tool you're looking for.

If you're not ready to spring for an office suite and don't need an industrial-strength spreadsheet, I suggest you try the spreadsheet in *Microsoft Works,* which is included with Microsoft's inexpensive Home Essentials suite. That's the one I use because it's faster and easier to use than Excel, and it has all the features most people will ever want.

Personal Information Managers: Your Electronic Secretary

EVOLUTION of the PERSONAL INFO MANAGER

ROCK

ZONK
BIG CAVE

PAPER

ANN
ARTHUR
BILL
BYRON

ROLODEX®

JILL

PC

CARL

JAN

DATA-SPECS™
(COMING SOON!)

53

Not everyone needs to computerize his or her personal data, but storing all your phone numbers, addresses, and e-mail addresses on your computer can alleviate the problem of shuffling through piles of papers to find notes or hunting for your address book to find a phone number. What's more, you'll have a convenient place to enter information that you know you'll need later. Personal information managers, or "PIMs" as they are sometimes called, also have a calendar and typically have extra features like a "to-do" manager or a place to keep track of your expenses.

Structured PIMs

Most PIMs have predefined fields for basic information—name, phone number, and so on—although many allow you to change the fields as well.

Such "structured PIMs" are ideal for anyone who wants control over how their information is displayed and printed. Data kept in a structured PIM can easily be sorted or formatted for mailing labels, phone directories, and other purposes.

Sound familiar? You've already worked with such features in Outlook Express and its address book for e-mail. Outlook Express has no calendar-management functions, so it's not really a full-fledged PIM, but its address book can be used to keep track of phone numbers, street addresses, and other tidbits.

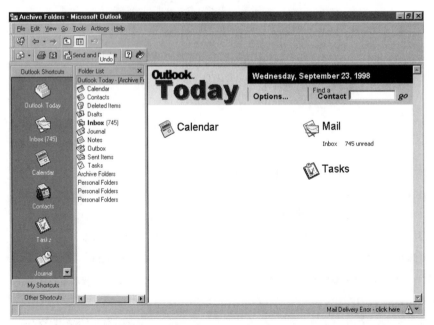

Personal information managers, like Outlook, shown here, take care of your contact list and schedule.

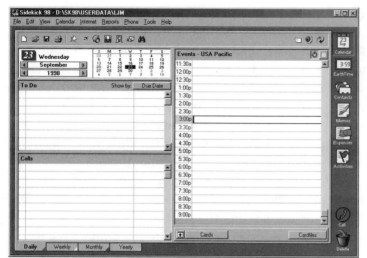

Sidekick, a popular PIM from Starfish Software, offers modules for your expenses and meals as well as contacts and appointments.

The leading structured PIM is Outlook Express's bigger cousin, **Microsoft Outlook**, which is included with Microsoft Office. Like Outlook Express, it handles e-mail and has an address book, but the address book is much more sophisticated, with lots of ways to search and plenty of ways to customize it. Also, Outlook has a calendar and a to-do list, so you can use it to organize your entire life.

Organizer from Lotus and **SideKick** from Starfish Software are two other leaders in the field. They both have the same combination of address book, calendar, and to-do list, but they lack Outlook's integrated e-mail—the feature that makes Outlook my favorite.

If what you want is a program that creates great looking and easy-to-print calendars—and also happens to have an address book—then consider **Calendar Creator** from The Learning Company ($59). It has more than 5,000 clip art images so you can spiff up your calendar print-outs. The scheduling and contact management features let you work with multiple calendars, attach alarms to appointments, and link names of people from your address book to events in your calendar.

Resources

Calendar Creator
The Learning Company
617-494-1200
www.learningco.com

Organizer
Lotus Development
800-343-5414
www.lotus.com

Microsoft Outlook, Microsoft Office
Microsoft
800-426-9400
www.microsoft.com

SideKick
Starfish Software
888-782-7347
www.starfish.com

Contact Managers

One category of PIM, called **contact management software**, is designed for salespeople and others who need to keep track not only of addresses but also of information about the calls they make to the people on their list. *ACT* from Symantec and *Goldmine* from Goldmine Software (about $90 each) help users organize contact and scheduling data, which can be shared with colleagues over a network.

Goldmine is a champ at contact management. While you're looking at contact information you can also take notes about conversations, schedule meetings, or enter a reminder to call the person back. You can even send the contact a fax, write a letter using your word processing program, or send an e-mail, using the software built into Goldmine. All incoming and outgoing messages are linked to the contact record.

ACT is the best-seller in the category. You can use its calendar and contact management features to set up meetings, schedule phone calls, and coordinate activities for you or a work group. Like Goldmine, it links all activities, notes, and calendar items to the appropriate person's contact record. Though ACT doesn't have built-in e-mail, it does have links to other e-mail programs, so you can send and receive mail without leaving the program.

ACT lets you attach documents (such as spreadsheets or word processing files) to a contact record, so you can quickly access the file while you are interacting with the person it pertains to. A set of 70 predefined fields and 10 prebuilt layouts get you up and running quickly, but you still have plenty of control; you can add you own fields or modify the layouts to your own tastes. One nice feature finds and removes duplicate entries from your database.

Resources

ACT
Symantec
800-441-7234
www.symantec.com

Goldmine
GoldMine Software Corp.
800-654-3526
www.goldminesw.com

Unstructured PIMs

A drawback of structured PIMs is that all your information must fit into predefined categories. If you have free-form information or notes, you must plan ahead to be sure to predefine a space for that data. For my purposes, that's a bit awkward. I take a lot of notes on the phone and want a very quick way to enter—and later find—random bits of information. That's when an unstructured PIM comes in handy.

Info Select from Micro Logic Software (about $100) is a free-form personal information manager that lets you enter information in whatever order you choose, without the constraints of designated fields. Even though the program lets you enter data randomly, you can add a category name that lets you sort your data, just like a more structured database.

Resources

Info Select
Micro Logic Software
800-342-5930
www.miclog.com

What to Look For in a Personal Information Manager

• *indicates a feature found in industrial-strength programs*

address book Most PIMs have a convenient place to keep addresses and phone numbers. You should be able to search on any field (first name, last name, etc.) or look at an entire listing.

calendar and appointment book Most PIMs have some kind of calendar and appointment book.

export formats You should be able to export and import data in other formats so you're not stuck with the program if you decide to try another one.

• **group scheduling** High-end PIMs (such as Lotus Organizer) can be used to schedule meetings around other people's calendars, accessed over a local area network.

integrated e-mail Some PIMs now integrate e-mail, which is handy because it lets you keep your e-mail addresses stored with your other contact information.

moving and copying data You should be able to easily move or copy data between parts of the program.

multiple views of calendar You should be able to view the calendar a day, week, month, or year at a time. The month- and week-at-a-glance views should display your appointments on the calendar.

telephone dialing Dialing the phone isn't exactly my idea of an onerous chore, but if the program can do it for you (via a modem), why not? Most PIMs will do this.

universal search You should be able to search for any data across all modules. Enter someone's name, and you should find his or her address, phone number, and any appointments you have scheduled with that person.

Financial Software: Running Your Budget Like a Business

54

Your computer can't make you wealthy, but it can help you manage the money you already have. After all, computation—what most of us haven't done since grade school, and what computers do best—is what finances are all about. Financial management packages are relatively inexpensive, and they can save lots of trouble.

Organize Your Finances

Quicken, from Intuit, is one of the best-selling programs of all time for the PC. It's an inexpensive, all-around personal finance program that helps you pay your bills and keep track of various accounts, including stocks and mutual funds, and see how you're doing at managing your money for retirement and other financial goals. Another program with similar features is **Microsoft Money** from Microsoft. The prices on these programs vary slightly, but they are typically about $35 to $50. You'll pay more for the "deluxe" versions, which add some multimedia files providing extra help and financial advice but really don't have all that much more functionality.

Both programs let you keep track of income and expenses. Each has a "check-book" metaphor, allowing you to pay a bill by filling out an on-screen form that looks like a check. The programs keep

track of your income and expenses in a register that, not surprisingly, looks like a check register. You can print out reports detailing things like each expense category and income source.

Now that American Express and many banks that issue Visa and MasterCard accounts issue electronic statements, these programs can

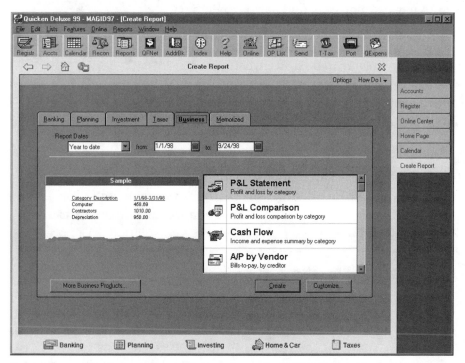

Quicken, one of the best-selling programs of all time for the PC, helps you manage every aspect of your finances.

also manage your credit cards. I get all my credit card statements online these days, letting me record all the expenses in Quicken automatically—a real time saver at tax time. You can also use Quicken and Money to manage your investment accounts with certain brokers, including Fidelity and Schwab.

Both programs also let you connect to the Internet to pay bills electronically. You enter the information in the program, and instead of printing the check, the software transmits the check order over the Internet. I know what you're thinking—you don't want your personal financial information going through the Internet. Well, I can't tell you that anything is 100 percent safe, but I've been doing online banking for years and I never worry about security. The odds of someone stealing my information over the Internet are probably lower than someone stealing my wallet. One nice thing about electronic banking is that it can handle recurring payments automatically. I've set up the program to pay my mortgage and car payments every month.

Before you get excited about home banking, check with your bank and investment brokers to be sure they work with Quicken or Money. If not, you could do what I did, and change banks.

Resources

Microsoft Money
Microsoft
800-426-9400
www.microsoft.com

Quicken
Intuit
800-446-8848
www.quicken.com

Tax Preparation Software: Making Tax Time Less Taxing

There are lots of advantages to using a computer to do your taxes. First of all, the software does all the math for you, eliminating the chance for human error in your calculations. Tax preparation programs can also automatically sort and add all of those receipts you've been keeping in shoe boxes. Once they're entered in the program, the program keeps them all in their proper categories.

Garbage In/Garbage Out

The IRS doesn't mind you using a tax preparation program. In fact, IRS officials have told me that the agency likes it when people use tax preparation software because it tends to cut down on errors. Nevertheless, it's important to remember that the tax payer, not the tax preparation software company, is responsible for any errors in a return.

Another useful feature is that tax programs include all the forms most taxpayers need. You don't have to get forms from the IRS or even search around your desk. You just bring them up on the screen, fill them out, and then print them and send them in. (You can even use tax programs to file your returns electronically, but that requires using and paying a small fee to another company.) The programs carry forward data from each form and schedule to the appropriate line of the 1040. And if you use a personal finance program such as Quicken or Microsoft Money to keep track of your finances during the year, you can import the tax data into any of these programs.

While such programs can't give you the kind of strategic advice you can get from a good tax professional, they do come with lots of detailed information about each tax form, which will help you better understand which deductions you're entitled to and how to enter them on the forms.

The leading tax preparation programs are *TurboTax* from Intuit and *TaxCut* from Block Financial Software; both are about $40. I can't recommend one program over the other because each developer upgrades the software annually to try to outdo the competition. TurboTax and TaxCut are almost always the top two in reviews, so I'd go for either of them. And don't think you can get away with buying tax software just once. You have to buy a new copy every year.

Resources

TaxCut
Block Financial Software
800-235-4060
www.taxcut.com

TurboTax
Intuit
800-224-0991
www.turbotax.com

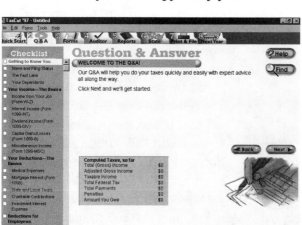

TaxCut's Q&A feature leads you through a set of questions that helps determine what forms you should file.

Presentation Software: Making a Professional Impression

55

Want to make a splash and impress your boss and colleagues? Your computer can help.

Desktop presentation software is designed to help you create visual aids for business presentations. These programs can help you create sophisticated slides and overhead transparencies or colorful screens that you can display on a computer while you talk. (Sales and marketing professionals often bring along notebook computers on which they can display their presentation when they visit clients.) Some packages even let you create "multimedia" presentations that include animation, video, and sound.

The leading presentation program, by far, is *Microsoft PowerPoint*. The most obvious reason it's so popular is because it is included in Microsoft Office. Other presentation programs include *Persuasion* from Adobe, *Freelance Graphics for Windows* from Lotus Development, and *Harvard Graphics* from SPC/Serif Software. Each of the

Scorecard: Presentation Software

Most Popular	PowerPoint (Microsoft)
Recommendation	PowerPoint (Microsoft)
	Persuasion (Adobe)
	Harvard Graphics (SPC/Serif Software)
	Freelance Graphics (Lotus Development)

products has its strengths and, frankly, there is no compelling reason to use Microsoft PowerPoint over another program unless you got it for free or as part of the suite.

PowerPoint, like the competitive products, is quite easy to use. I give a fair amount of presentations and am amazed at how quickly I can put one together using one of PowerPoint's templates. Just follow the wizard to set up an attractive design and enter your own text and graphics to complete your slide show.

You can use the program to create overhead transparencies, but many presentation programs' features work best when you give your presentation from the computer; in live presentations, you can add effects like animations and special transitions. Since I usually give my own presentations on the computer, I can even make last-minute changes to the presentation on my notebook PC just before I'm about to go on stage. The other thing I do is post my presentations to the Internet so that audience members or people who didn't make it to the live presentation can access it later. The program's HTML export feature makes it quick and easy to create Web-ready files, although you still have to upload them to a website.

Resources

Freelance Graphics for Windows
Lotus Development
800-343-5414
www.lotus.com

Harvard Graphics
SPC/Serif Software
800-557-3743
www.serif.com

Microsoft PowerPoint
Microsoft
800-426-9400
www.microsoft.com

Persuasion
Adobe
800-628-2320
www.adobe.com

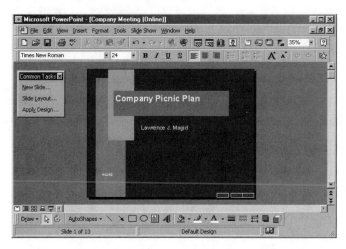

PowerPoint's templates make it easy to set up a colorful presentation.

What to Look For in a Presentation Program

• *Indicates a feature available in industrial-strength programs*

• **ability to create graphics from spreadsheet data** For business presentations, a program's ability to create pie charts or other graphs from raw data is important. And in this day and age, two-dimensional charts won't do. You'll want to present your information in three dimensions.

• **ability to define your own bullets** Bulleted lists are used a lot in business presentations. The ability to use interesting bullets—arrows, your company logo, smiling faces—is an important factor in creating interesting slides.

ability to import common graphics formats Likewise, you should be able to import the graphics you've created in another program. This is useful for things like company logos and other business graphics that you want to include in your slides.

• **animation** Animation effects can range from blinking or moving arrows to zooms to the on-screen assembly of a technical drawing.

• **audio support** Some programs allow you to include audio clips for use in computer-based presentations.

• **ease of use** Most people who use presentation programs do so on an occasional basis. As a result, it's important to find a program that's easy to learn and easy to use.

export to the Web Most presentation programs can now save presentations as HTML files, which means they can be posted on a website. That way your presentation can be seen by people who weren't able to attend your presentation in person.

• **outliner** Many new programs allow you to view your presentation as an outline. You can then "expand" the outline to see what topics are covered in each slide and move headings to rearrange the presentation.

• **run-time player** A run-time player is a limited version of the presentation software, which you can put on a disk and distribute to clients along with your presentation so that they can run the presentation on their own computers.

templates Templates, or preformatted slides and screens, can make it easy to create a professional-looking presentation. The type, borders, and colors are already chosen. You just add your own text.

• **varied transitions** You can add life to an on-screen presentation by varying the way one slide is replaced by the next on screen. Many programs offer dissolves, wipes, explosions, and other dynamic transitions.

Graphics: Working With Pictures

56

For a lot of people, the notion of computer graphics implies the slick, special-effects animation used in TV advertisements and science-fiction movies. Well, all that is possible, but a lot of more modest effects are possible, too.

Graphics tools for PCs have become pretty specialized. There are separate tools for retouching scanned or digital photos, designing personalized greeting cards, creating business diagrams, modeling in 3-D, and planning building projects. In many of these categories, the field offers programs for both professional graphic artists and novices. The consumer-level products have more than enough features for most users, so in the overview of graphics software I'll supply in this chapter, I'll talk briefly about the professional-level applications, but mostly I'll recommend the more affordable, less ambitious ones.

Drawing Programs

The most popular drawing program for Windows, **CorelDraw**, works with both object (drawing-style) and bit-mapped (paint-style) graphics. CorelDraw, which costs about $400, is one of the programs I recommend for people who are really serious about creating professional-level drawings. It's big and complicated.

Scorecard: Drawing Programs

Most Popular	
Everyday strength	Windows Draw (Micrografx)
Industrial strength	CorelDraw (Corel)
Recommendation	Windows Draw (Micrografx)

Windows Draw from Micrografx is a much easier to use, affordable (about $50), yet solid program for the masses. The latest version comes with photo-editing software, a free-form drawing tool, clip art, and software for editing Web pages.

AutoSketch from Autodesk is a $99 precision drawing program for simple business drawings. It's ideal for people who make occasional product design drawings, or diagrams, and it contains features for creating organizational charts and flow charts.

Visio ($149) from Visio Corp, is a more specialized package. Billed as an "intelligent drawing package for nonartists," it provides a collection of stencils and "SmartShapes" designed to make it easier to create organizational charts, office layouts, flowcharts, and engineering drawings. A $349 version of Visio called **Visio Technical** makes creating and sharing 2-D drawings and technical schematics easier and more efficient than using traditional CAD programs.

Resources

AutoSketch
Autodesk
800-228-3601
www.autodesk.com

CorelDraw
Corel
800-836-3729
www.corel.com

Visio, Visio Technical
Visio Corp.
800-248-4746
www.visio.com

Windows Draw
Micrografx
800-733-3729
www.micrografx.com

What to Look For in a Drawing Program

• indicates a feature available in industrial-strength programs

a good set of drawing tools Drawing programs come with a set of basic shapes to draw with, including rectangles, circles, lines, and polygons. The more the merrier.

• Bezier curves The more advanced drawing packages work with Bezier curves, which allow you to shape forms with mathematical precision.

clip art Most packages come with a large selection of clip art to use in your own work.

fills Most drawing programs allow you to fill shapes with a variety of patterns and colors.

• flip and rotate These tools allow you to change your drawing's orientation on the page.

font-manipulation tools Creating special effects with type is one of the most popular uses of drawing packages. CorelDraw is particularly good at this, and it comes bundled with a lot of fonts.

good color handling Your drawing program should support the number of colors available on your monitor, plus it should allow you to work in shades of gray. The more advanced programs support color standards, such as Pantone and Trumatch, used by graphics professionals.

text effects In some programs, you can play with text as with any other graphic form, reshaping it and wrapping it around curves.

• 3-D effects Some drawing programs enable you to extrude shapes into three-dimensional forms. More advanced packages offer very sophisticated 3-D effects, including the ability to realistically wrap text and other patterns around 3-D objects.

rulers and grids These tools make your drawings conform to measurements you choose.

support for a variety of file formats There are a ton of graphic file formats. GIF (which stands for Graphic Interchange Format) is used on the World Wide Web and most online services. PCX and BMP are popular Windows formats. TIFF (which stands for Tagged Image File Format) is the most popular format for use in publishing. TIFF can be used on both IBM-compatible machines and Apple Macintoshes, which are popular in the publishing community. The images in this book, for example, are TIFF files that I created on my PC and sent to my editor for use on her Macintosh.

Bit-Mapped and Object-Based Graphics

Graphics programs are often broken into two main categories: those that create **bit-mapped** graphics (sometimes called **paint programs**) and those that create **object-based** or **vector** graphics (often called **drawing programs**).

A bit-mapped graphic program lets you paint with dots. You lay down some red and then some blue over it and you have blue and red images on the screen. You run your eraser through the middle and everything it passes over is erased. It's a lot like painting with real paint. "Bitmap" is a technical term describing the format in which the images are saved—as a map of "bits" that describe the color of each dot that makes up the image.

Paint programs create graphics with a collection of individual dots, resulting in softer-edged pictures.

With an object-based drawing program, you create a graphic with objects: boxes, circles, curves, and other shapes. Object-based graphics are easy to edit. The program organizes the information that makes up a picture as a set of objects that can be moved, colored, and edited separately. These days, a lot of drawing programs also offer 3-D effects.

Drawing programs compile collections of shapes, or objects, into complex graphics. You can edit each object separately.

Paint and Photo Editing Programs

Paint programs not only let you create graphics with tools supplied in the program itself but also let you work with photographs, drawings, and other bit-mapped artwork created with a digital camera or scanned into the computer (see Chapter 20 for more on digital cameras and scanners). In fact, most digital cameras and scanners come with a paint program.

Windows comes with a simple painting program called Paint. It isn't particularly sophisticated by computer graphics standards, but it's pretty handy. You can use it to paint freehand or to draw with circle, square, rectangle, and line tools, and it works in color, grayscale, or black and white.

If you're shopping for something new, check out *Paint Shop Pro*, a $99 program from Jasc Software. It includes plenty of image manipulation tools for both novices and expert users and you can import and export a wide range of file formats.

Adobe, which publishes Adobe Photoshop (described on page 291), the editing program of choice for graphics professionals, also makes a program for the rest of us called *PhotoDeluxe*. This $50 program is designed to clean up scanned snapshots, a job for which it has lots of special tools, like red-eye and scratch removal and the ability to correct color, sharpness, brightness, and contrast. It also has features and templates you can use to create greeting cards, banners, calendars and other projects. PhotoDeluxe's special-effects options are particularly fun. The Art option, for example, lets you make your photo look old-fashioned or give it the feel of an impressionist painting.

To my mind, the $49 *Microsoft Picture It* is even easier to use than PhotoDeluxe. Picture It lets you

bring in and manipulate multiple images to create a collage. You can add fancy text to any project, and a Paint and Color Effects button lets you paint anything on an image. Picture It also includes plenty of special effects as well as automatic tools for cleaning up photos—a Fix Red Eye command, for example, and others that let you create cutouts of people and other objects.

What to Look For in a
Paint or Image-Manipulation Program

• indicates a feature available in industrial-strength programs

a good selection of brushes The more brushes you have, the more effects you can create. Look for a feature that lets you create your own custom brushes.

a good set of tools Particularly look for a rubber-stamp tool, which lets you copy a part of your image and duplicate it in another part of the picture, and an eye dropper or sampling tool, which lets you pick up colors from one part of the picture to use in another.

• color separation If you will be printing your images professionally, your paint program should offer automatic color separation of its files.

• filters Most image programs give you a set of "filters" that let you sharpen, blur, and add special effects to your image.

• good font support Some paint programs include extra fonts in addition to the ability to handle type creatively.

• gamma correction Professional-level programs have a gamma-correction tool, which allows you to change the overall brightness and contrast in your image.

good color support Your program should work with at least 16 colors (256 for professional work or photographic slides) or in grayscale.

photo retouching tools for scanned images Paint programs should be able to work with scanned and digital photographs.

scanning from within the program Many graphic programs support the TWAIN scanning protocol, which means you can control most scanners from within the program. This saves having to exit the program and run the scanner separately.

support for TIFF and PCX TIFF is the standard format for bit-mapped files. PCX is a standard Windows format.

undo When you're working with bit-mapped images, where changes are made dot by dot, a good undo feature is important.

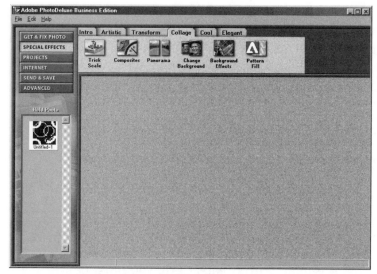

Adobe PhotoDeluxe offers a wide variety of effects, from simple photo-editing features like scratch removal to special effects like playing with a picture's scale or filling images with colorful patterns.

Adobe's **Photoshop** is the granddaddy of photo manipulation tools— the tool of choice for professional graphic artists. It's so sophisticated, in fact, that it has pretty much replaced an entire industry of specialized photo-retouching equipment. If you really want to get into the far reaches of what's possible with photo manipulation and paint effects on the PC, you should take a look at it. It not only has sophisticated tools of its own for every aspect of photo retouching and special effects, but it is also supported by a whole raft of "plug-ins"—software tools from other publishers that work with Photoshop to add additional special effects and other capabilities. It also comes with a hefty price tag (around $900, list, though you can get it for about $600), and humongous memory and storage requirements.

Greeting Card Software

For most of us, the closest we'll come to a career in the graphic arts is designing our own greeting cards for special occasions. Now a whole category of popular software has popped up to let us do just that.

First, let me admit that on the occasions when I have used my PC to custom-design a card for my wife, Patti, she always thanks me, but I've noticed that she doesn't get as excited as when I write a note by hand or purchase a printed card. When asked, she admits that she thinks printed cards look better and handwritten notes seem more thoughtful.

Professionally printed greeting cards do look better. But with the correct software, a good inkjet printer, and high-quality card stock, you can do a pretty good job with a PC. With home computer–generated cards, you can create a more personal greeting and even add photographs. And they're great for procrastinators like me who remember they need a card after it's too late to go to the store.

The leading greeting card programs for Windows are **Micrografx CreateaCard** ($49.95), **Print Shop Signature Greetings** ($19.95) from Broderbund, and **Greetings Workshop** from Microsoft ($39 for the one-disk product; $50 for the two-disk deluxe version).

All three programs come with a wide selection of graphics, designs, sayings, and other elements that let you assemble a greeting card for just about any occasion. Each program also lets you import your own graphics—including photos—and enter your own text. All also allow you to send your greeting by e-mail. With CreateaCard, you must be signed on to the Internet to send a card. But once you're on, all the software you need is built into the program. The card arrives at its destination as a stand-alone program that the recipient just clicks to view. The catch is that the recipient must have a Windows machine, and because files can be pretty big, they might take a while to send and download. Personally, I'd rather not have people send me large e-mail files without first asking my permission.

In opening screen of Microsoft's Greetings Workshop, you pick card categories from a display designed like an old country store.

Micrografx CreateaCard lets you choose from among thousands of cards designed by American Greetings and comes with about 5,000 pieces of clip art. It also lets you create signs, awards and certificates, business cards, invitations, stationery, labels, postcards, calendars, gift tags, and stickers.

Microsoft's Greetings Workshop program opens with a "display rack," where you can choose to create a card (designed by Hallmark), announcement, calendar, invitation, poster, banner, sign, award, label, or sticker. If you choose to create a card, you will be asked to select an occasion.

Print Shop Signature Greetings doesn't offer as many types of projects as the other two programs, but it's the easiest one to use and has the cleanest interface. The program's desktop has clearly marked options for creating greeting cards, labels, postcards, and envelopes and for setting up an address book. Once you pick a project, you get to choose the kind of occasion (birthday, holiday, friendship, encouragement, events, and thanks) and are then taken to a screen where you can preview 5,000 available cards and projects.

The Print Shop program comes with 90 fonts, which can be great. But fonts also take up a lot of disk space and can, in some situations, slow down your computer. Unfortunately, the program automatically installs all of the fonts and its "un-install" program doesn't remove them.

Before buying a greeting card program, take stock of what you have. A lot of PCs, printers, and scanners come with greeting card programs, so you may already have one. Also, you can create cards using Microsoft Publisher, Broderbund's Print Shop, and several other general-purpose graphics programs.

If all you want is to send greeting cards via the Web, you don't need to buy anything. Point your browser to www.pcanswer.com/greeting.htm for links to several sites that let you create and send free online greeting cards.

Resources

Greetings Workshop
Microsoft
800-426-9400, 425-882-8080
www.microsoft.com

Micrografx CreateaCard
Micrografx
888-216-9281, 972-234-1769
www.micrografx.com

Print Shop Signature Greetings
Broderbund
800-548-1798
www.broderbund.com

Computer-Aided Design Software

Computer-aided design (CAD) software is used by industrial-design professionals to plan products, buildings, printed circuit boards, and other objects. The professional-level offerings are incredibly sophisticated and incredibly expensive. The most popular CAD program for personal computers, **AutoCAD** from Autodesk, costs nearly $4,000. It enables industrial designers to envision their creations in 3-D, from any angle, and in lifelike settings. If you're about to invest millions of dollars in product development, it's worth it … but I'm assuming you aren't.

Of course, you don't have to spend thousands to get basic CAD tools. In fact, for only $35, you can get **KeyCad Deluxe** from the Learning Company, which offers the tools you need to draft, design, plan, or layout just about any project. Features include more than 5,000 symbols, multiple palletes and toolbars, 3-D rendering and animation, and a set of easy-to-use drafting and dimensioning tools.

The same kind of visualization aids are also available for more specialized uses. The **3D Home** series (about $30) from Broderbund includes programs that handle both interior design and house design. Each easy-to-use package comes with a library of architectural shapes, structural details, plants, and furniture. If you want it all, check out **3D Home Design Suite** (about $80), which includes modules for designing an entire home, home interiors, and landscape. The really cool thing about these programs is the ability they give you to play "what if" games with your design. Making changes on a PC screen is a lot easier—and far cheaper— than making changes after the contractor has started work.

If you want to redesign your backyard, consider **Sierra Complete LandDesigner**, a computer-aided design program for landscapes. Sierra also makes **3D Deck**, which, as its name suggests, helps you design a deck for your yard.

Resources

AutoCAD
Autodesk
800-964-6432
www.autodesk.com

KeyCad Deluxe
The Learning Company
800-826-0706
www.learningco.com

Sierra Complete LandDesigner,
 3D Deck
Sierra
800 757-7707
www.sierra.com

3D Home series
Broderbund
800-548-1798
www.broderbund.com

Clip Art

Clip art is a collection of precooked graphics that you can use in your own publications. It's for people who don't want to (or can't) draw but want to spice up their documents with appropriate art. Clip art comes in many different styles, from cartoons and brightly colored icons to sophisticated photography.

Broderbund's Click Art collections offer hundreds of pieces of high-quality clip art on CD-ROM. The image shown here is from the Fine Arts disc.

You get a batch of clip art with many graphics programs. You can buy high-quality clip art from companies like Broderbund, or you can download appropriate pieces one by one from the Web. One site I use a lot, called Art Today (www.arttoday.com), lets you download all the clip art you want for a membership fee of $29 a year. Clip Art Now (www.clipartnow.com) offers images for $5 apiece. Most clip art sites and sellers offer the art in a variety of formats. When you're downloading, make sure you get the art in a Windows-compatible format that you can use with your image-editing and word processing or greeting card software. Popular formats are BMP for bitmapped art and WMF for object-based drawings.

The Art Today website features a searchable database of clip art in all sorts of styles. A membership allowing you to download an unlimited number of pieces costs $29 per year.

Microsoft's Clip Gallery offers object graphics, photos, sounds, and animation files free for Microsoft Office users.

Clip art often comes with applications. This folder holds art files, such as the car shown at left, that come with Microsoft Office.

Database Management: Organizing (Lots of) Information

57

YOU'RE SAYIN' YOU CAN SEARCH THROUGH THOUSANDS OF RECORDS IN A MATTER OF SECONDS? SHOW ME.

OKAY, I'LL FIND THE NAMES OF EVERY HONEST POLITICIAN IN THE COUNTRY...

WOW, LIKE NEEDLES IN A HAYSTACK!

To thoroughly cover database management programs in a book like this would be like reviewing 18-wheel trucks in Car and Driver magazine. Frankly, if you're reading this book and need to manage large amounts of data, what you really need is a consultant who can help you set up a database. Nevertheless, I'm going to talk a little about the genre, just so you know what people are talking about.

Database management programs are used for all kinds of tasks. Customer mailing lists are one common use. So are personnel records, inventories, and people's CD collections. Database software enables you to keep track of lots of information and easily pull out just the pieces of information you need in the form of database "reports." It also lets you sort the information in different ways. For example, let's say you have put your personal address book into a database. You can tell the database program to arrange the names in the address

book in alphabetical order and print out the list. Alternatively, you can tell the database to arrange them in Zip code order and print the list that way.

The more powerful database programs, like Microsoft Access, are called relational database programs because they can relate, or connect, information from several database files. Simpler ones are called flat-file database programs. The more powerful database programs also include their own programming languages, which allow you to create a customized program that includes data entry forms for a specific purpose, such as entering sales for an inventory database or entering customer queries for a product database.

Working with a database program requires a certain amount of organization. It's not rocket science, but it doesn't exactly come naturally, either. Usually, it requires that you do a pretty complete analysis of all

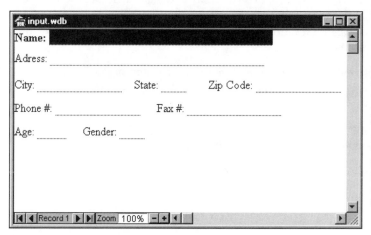

There are usually two kinds of screens in a database program: data entry forms (like the one shown here) and reports. Once the information is entered, you can sort it any way you like, calling up reports that list just the people who live in Oregon, or who bought a product that cost more than $100, for instance.

What to Look for in a Database Management Program

• indicates a feature found in industrial-strength programs

ability to handle a variety of data types, including graphics and multimedia files
People don't live by words and numbers alone. A database program should also be able to handle pictures, drawings, and even video and audio files.

• ability to link files This feature, which usually defines a relational database, allows you to draw reports from a number of different database files.

easy addition, modification, and deletion of fields Make sure your database program lets you add, modify, and delete fields in already-created databases.

easy data entry Entering data should be a piece of cake. All commands should be obvious to anyone looking at the screen.

easy report creation The best database programs let you create forms by using a mouse to select possible fields from a palette. It goes downhill from there to programs that make you write a program to create even the simplest form.

integration with the Internet These days Internet connectivity is a requirement for just about all kinds of software. A database management program should be able to export its files so they can be viewed over the Internet. It should even be possible to create a live Internet database that users can update from a remote location.

• programming language If you want to create a database program tailored to your own business, you'll need a programming language.

saving in different formats Most full-strength databases will save in dBase or ASCII format. (dBase was once the best-selling database program, and its file format is still used.) Other formats to look for are standard spreadsheet formats such as Lotus 1-2-3's WKS format and Microsoft Excel's XLS format.

simple setup If you want to get right to work with a database program, you'll need one that's easy to set up. Most have some kind of point-and-click setup routine, but even some of those programs can be daunting.

Web support features Many databases not only export to websites but some, including FileMaker Pro, can be used to manage data that people enter *from* a website.

the ways you'll be using the database in the future so that you can set up the proper **fields**. Fields are different categories of information, and you'll need separate fields for every way you intend to sort (arrange) the data. In a mailing list, for example, you would have one field for name, another for street address, another for phone number, and so on. (A collection of fields that makes up one entry is called a "record" in database lingo.) If you intend to sort the mailing list by Zip code or state, though, you'll need a separate field for that data, and not lump it in a general "street address" field. Fortunately, you don't have to anticipate every field you might possibly need down the road because virtually all database programs allow you to add new fields (or get rid of fields you don't want) at any time.

If you need a database program, you can usually get away with a very simple database program like the one built into **Microsoft Works** (available by itself or as part of the Microsoft Home Essentials suite I talked about in Chapter 49). The Works database handles up to 32,000 items—probably more than adequate for keeping track of your CD collection, insurance records, or just about any other personal data you can think of. Although the Works database has more than enough features for my needs, that wouldn't be the case if I ran the subscription department of a large magazine or handled the inventory for a chain of stores.

Microsoft Access, which comes with Microsoft Office Professional Edition, is the most popular database program, probably because it is from Microsoft and because people get it automatically when they buy Office Professional Edition. It can do practically everything, but getting it to do *anything* can be a hassle. I prefer **FileMaker Pro** from FileMaker Corp. It's a lot easier to use and is actually just about as powerful as Access.

There are plenty of shareware database programs you can download for free and then pay for if you decide to keep them. **Instabase** from EzeNet ($29.95) is a basic program that enables you to store phone numbers and add hot links to any e-mail or Web address in the database.

Resources

Instabase
EzeNet
416-482-3037
www.instabase.com

Microsoft Access, Microsoft Works
Microsoft
800-426-9400
www.microsoft.com

File Maker Pro
File Maker Corp.
800-986-2249
www.filemaker.com

Utility Software:
Computer Housekeeping

58

The category of utilities *is rather general, and the word can mean a lot of different things, but in general it means software that helps your computer operate more efficiently or more safely.*

There are all sorts of utility programs. In this chapter, I'll run through what I consider the most important, which fall into four categories:

- **General utilities**, which help protect your data from possible corruption and rescue it if it has been damaged.
- **Antivirus software**, which checks for harmful **viruses** on your machine.
- **Uninstall** software, which removes unwanted programs from your hard disk.
- **Backup** software, which automates the process of backing up your data.

Utilities You Already Own

Windows 95 and Windows 98 include a backup program called ScanDisk that checks for and corrects possible problems on your hard disk, and Disk Defragmenter, which makes your computer run faster by rearranging the clusters where data is stored on the hard disk. Windows 98 also comes with a program called Disk Cleanup, which removes unnecessary files from your hard disk, and the Maintenance Wizard, which automates the process of running all of those tasks. Both Windows 95 and Windows 98 have a compression program, called Drive Space, that allows you to increase the number of files you can store on a computer by compressing the files on your hard drive. And finally, Windows 98 has Drive Converter (Fat32) that can increase the capacity of your hard drive by changing the way files are stored.

Scorecard: Utility Software

General Utilities

Best-seller	Norton Utilities (Symantec)
Recommended	Norton Utilities (Symantec)
	ScanDisk and Disk Defragmenter (come with Windows)
	Maintenance Wizard (comes with Windows 98)

Antivirus

Best-seller	Norton Anti-Virus (Symantec)
Recommended	Norton Anti-Virus (Symantec)

Uninstaller

Best-seller	Norton Uninstall (Symantec)
Recommended	CleanSweep Deluxe (Quarterdeck)

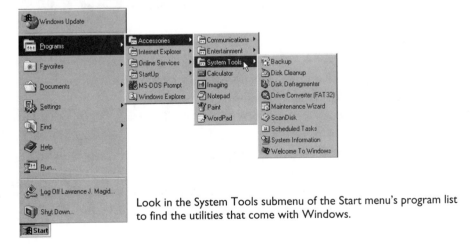

Look in the System Tools submenu of the Start menu's program list to find the utilities that come with Windows.

The utilities that come with Windows supply a lot of important features, but you still might want to check out the commercial offerings. The commercial toolmakers stay in business by staying one step ahead of Microsoft's features and by offering features, such as virus protection, that Windows doesn't include.

General Housekeeping

If you're looking for a good overall program that handles just about anything that can go wrong with a PC, then you can't go wrong with **Norton Utilities**. It has a number of different utilities that let you manage files and improve overall PC performance. Its Disk Doctor program is similar to Microsoft's ScanDisk but is able to work in the background, keeping watch on your machine as you use it so that it finds problems before they affect your computer's performance.

Network Associates offers a somewhat less ambitious but easier to use program called **First Aid**, which is designed to reduce problems, warn you in advance of potential hard drive failure, protect you from system crashes, and recover your data if something goes wrong. First Aid also has limited virus protection and a "one-button check-up" that checks your entire system for possible problems. The program's strength is that it doesn't ask you for a lot of information. It just goes off and checks your system, and if it finds any problems, it fixes them with a minimum of human interaction.

Resources

Norton Utilities
Symantec
800-441-7234
www.symantec.com

First Aid
Network Associates
800-764-3337
www.networkassociate.com

Disk Cleanup

The Add/Remove Programs tool that comes with Windows is pretty good, but it doesn't work with all programs. Occasionally you may find that a program doesn't show up on the program list or can't be completely removed by that tool. The way to be sure that you're really removing your software is to use an "uninstall" utility. These utilities monitor your actions when you install programs and keep track of everything that is done. Then, when you remove a program, they just reverse the process.

Resources

CleanSweep
Quarterdeck
310-309-3700
www.quarterdeck.com

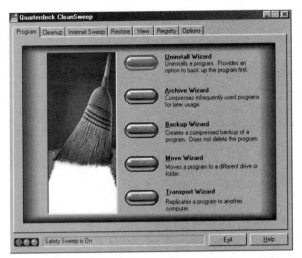

Quarterdeck's CleanSweep safely removes programs and other files from your system.

There are a number of good uninstall utilities on the market, but my favorite is *CleanSweep* from Quarterdeck. CleanSweep not only removes unwanted programs but gets rid of the pesky files that sometimes get downloaded from the Internet. It's safe and very fast.

Antivirus Software: An Ounce of Prevention

Antivirus software helps safeguard your computer against destructive programs, called **viruses**, that are sometimes planted on floppy disks and networks. If you get a virus, your computer could undergo damage that ranges from the annoying to the disastrous (see the box "How Bad Can a Computer Virus Be?" on the next page.)

A virus-protection program scans your hard disk and memory for known viruses and if it finds one, removes it. These programs can also load software into memory to protect your computer by continually checking for possible infections. Windows doesn't come with antivirus software, so you'll need to buy some. The most popular commercial antivirus program is *Norton Anti-Virus* from Symantec ($50) and *ViruScan* from Network Associates ($39), and they're both good.

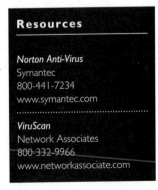

Resources

Norton Anti-Virus
Symantec
800-441-7234
www.symantec.com

ViruScan
Network Associates
800-332-9966
www.networkassociate.com

How Bad Can a Computer Virus Be?

Viruses are bugs that have been deliberately planted by vandals who are out to destroy other people's property. A virus gets into your computer by infecting a program or a floppy disk. Most viruses attach themselves to programs and are activated as soon as the infected program is run. Some viruses aren't carried by programs but are spread by floppy disks. All it takes to be infected with such a virus is for you to turn on your computer while an infected floppy is in a drive or run an infected file on your computer. The virus copies itself to your computer's memory and infects any other disks in the computer, including your hard disk. Another, more common kind of virus is one that is built into a macro—a little program—that runs inside Word or Excel.

Before I go on, let me give you a word of assurance. Although viruses are a real threat, they're not as common as some people claim. I use an enormous number of programs and I download software from the Internet regularly. I've been using a computer almost every day for about 20 years. Yet I've only twice caught a virus, and I was able to detect it and get rid of it before it did any damage. There is a good chance you'll never encounter one. Nevertheless, it's worth taking precautions, just in case. If a virus enters your system, you could lose everything on your hard disk, or you could find that your computer just starts doing crazy things.

New viruses are always being introduced, and it's important to make sure that your virus-protection program can detect all the newest strains. Companies that make virus-protection utilities make new versions of their virus data files available regularly. You can get them by calling the company, you can download them from the Net, or you can get them from your local user group.

Update Utilities

In Chapter 37, you learned about Windows Update, a utility built into Windows 98 that lets you automatically find product enhancements from Microsoft. Windows Update is great for updating Windows and other Microsoft programs, but what about your other software?

CyberMedia has a much more extensive service, called *Oil Change* ($39) that's designed to keep all of your software up to date. It helps resolve problems with programs by making sure that you have the latest version of each (the versions least likely to have bugs). To use Oil Change you must be connected to the Internet and you must have a piece of software that you can download from CyberMedia's website. Of course, you don't need Oil Change to stay current. You could frequent the website of every hardware and software company whose products you use, but Oil Change makes it a lot easier.

Resources

Oil Change
Network Associates
800-572-5939
www.neteworkassociate.com

Entertainment Software: Just for Fun

59

Despite common wisdom, the majority of PC game players aren't kids and teens. Most are adults who have been seduced by the ability of computer games to test their powers of deduction and quick thinking.

Almost everybody who has a computer has a few games on it—even if they're just the games that come with Windows (described on the next page). There's an almost unbelievable variety available. In addition to electronic versions of old standbys like Solitaire and Scrabble, you can get the kinds of interactive games that are possible only on computers, which offer impressive animation and intelligent responses to your actions.

There are quite a few companies—such as Sierra, Origin, Blizzard, and Broderbund—that specialize in computer games, but even companies you might think of as more serious-minded—including Microsoft and IBM—have their own game offerings.

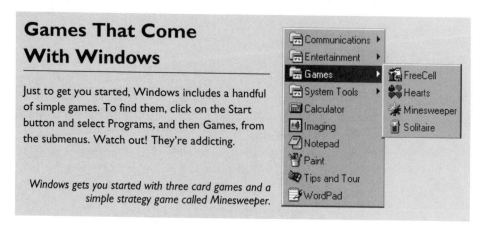

Games That Come With Windows

Just to get you started, Windows includes a handful of simple games. To find them, click on the Start button and select Programs, and then Games, from the submenus. Watch out! They're addicting.

Windows gets you started with three card games and a simple strategy game called Minesweeper.

New titles come out practically every day, and it has become impossible to keep up with everything being published. If I were to write a book on entertainment software, it wouldn't have the word "little" in the title. It would look like an encyclopedia. So in this chapter, I'm going to stick to a few perennial classics and some personal favorites of my family and friends. But, please, don't limit your search to what you see here. Visit your local software store, read the consumer magazines, and find out what your friends enjoy. In fact, entertainment software has become such big business that you'll even find reviews in your local paper and even on TV. Explore and enjoy.

Before I get too far, I have to confess that I'm not the game expert in my family. My son Will, now 12, has been running his own website about games since he was 9 (you can find it at www.gamefun.com), and he helped me write this chapter.

Simulation Games

If you'd rather be flying, Nascar racing, or playing golf than sitting at your computer—but you can't be—simulation games are for you.

Simulation games featuring the excitement of flying a fighter jet or helicopter have been hot sellers ever since *Microsoft Flight*

Prices for Games

In other chapters in this section I include prices, but when it comes to entertainment and children's software, the initial suggested list price has almost no meaning. Prices are constantly fluctuating, and it's not uncommon for a title to be released at, say $39.95, only to have it reduced to $19.99 or $14.99 within a few months. In most cases, you'll find educational titles to be priced in the $20 to $40 range, but the only way to really know the price is to shop around just before you're about to buy.

In Microsoft's Flight Simulator, you choose the plane, airport, and flight conditions. The program provides the visuals and sound effects.

Simulator was introduced in the early 1980s and became the first blockbuster game for the PC. As you fly, the computer throws you into battle-like situations to test your reflexes and strategy. The best such games have truly impressive graphics that make you feel like you're actually flying a plane. Microsoft Flight Simulator is still one of the best. It offers great scenery and realistic flight scenarios from a range of airports including Chicago's Midway and Paris's Charles de Gaulle. You get to choose how much airport traffic to deal with and determine time of day, season, and weather conditions. And you get to choose from a variety of different planes including a single-engine Cessna, a Learjet, and a Sopwith Camel.

Golf fanatics who live in rainy climates or just can't get away from the office will enjoy *Links* from Access Software. The graphics and strategy are based on real courses that were taped and digitized. Links gives you a chance to play some of the leading courses with 360-degree views of the greens. You can buy extra modules to add new courses, including Mauna Kea in Hawaii, Banff Springs in Canada, and many more. (A free trial version is available from the Access website.)

Cheats and Tips

If you ever go online and hang out with gamers, you'll hear the word "cheats." These are codes that gamers pass around to help each other get through the game. Another term to know is "walk-through," which is a book or Internet site that helps you figure out the game. Hang around long enough and you'll get all sorts of tips on how to find your way around a game. So if you're stuck, get online, buy a book, or just ask the nearest teenager.

Links, from Access Software, puts you on the fairways of the world's best golf courses.

The **Wing Commander series** from Origin Systems features space combat simulations. I can't say whether they're realistic because I've never witnessed real space combat, but they *are* just like the space combat scenes that you see in the movies. In fact, the program takes a cinematic approach, using video footage featuring well-known actors such as Malcolm McDowell and Mark Hamill of *Star Wars* fame.

SimCity 3000, from Maxis, is an extremely popular simulation game that lets you create and manage a city. The graphics are terrific and the scenarios quite realistic. I know of one family in which both parents and each of the kids have their own cities. They rush home every night to play the game, and each person waits impatiently for his or her turn. People who use it tend to become addicted after a few minutes, so be careful.

Sierra's **Nascar Racing 2** is based on the races held in Daytona. With superb sound effects, outstanding music, and simulations of actual drivers and their cars, this game is about as realistic as you can get without smelling the rubber.

Resources

Links
Access Software
800-800-4880, 801-359-2900
www.accesssoftware.com

Microsoft Flight Simulator
Microsoft
800-426-9400
www.microsoft.com

Nascar Racing 2
Sierra
800-326-6654
www.sierra.com

SimCity 3000
Maxis/Electronic Arts
800-245-4525
www.maxis.com

Wing Commander series
Origin Systems/Electronic Arts
800-245-4525
www.origin.ea.com

SimCity 3000 is the latest and greatest of the popular Sim games from Maxis. As absolute ruler, you plan the laws, buildings, and events that make up a great city—and live with the consequences.

Fantasy and Role Playing

Fantasy adventure games put you in settings like an ogre's castle or a labyrinth, where you use your native wit and quick reflexes to find the right paths, choose the right weapons, and team up with the right allies to win your way to the treasure or rescue the princess. Some of the situations can get incredibly complicated. If you make the wrong choice, you can die a bloody death. But don't worry—you get a chance to learn from your mistakes: Just enter the game again, making different choices at crucial points.

Ultima Online from Origin is a game with a twist. You buy the software on a CD-ROM, but you play it online with other people by hooking into the Internet. (Lots of CD-ROM games have an Internet component now, but this is the first I know of that *requires* an Internet connection.) The CD comes with 30 days of free online play; after that, you pay $9.95 a month to compete. You start out solo, with some money, basic armor, weapons, but with no home or magic. Dragons, monsters, and demons are creeping outside the city gates. Be careful out there.

Resources

Final Fantasy VII
Eidos Interactive
800-617-8737
www.eidosinteractive.com

Leisure Suit Larry
Sierra/Cendant Software
800-757-7707
www.sierra.com

Ultima Online
Origin Systems/Electronic Arts
800-245-4524
www.ultimaonline.com

The imaginative graphics and game-playing of the Final Fantasy series have made it a favorite.

Final Fantasy VII, long a favorite for the Sony PlayStation, is now available for PCs from Eidos Interactive. Your goal, as is often the case with role-playing games, is to save the Earth. When you start out, the villain is a large company that governs the world, but the plot soon gets twisted and assumptions change. The story line and graphics keep you glued to your PC.

If your taste tends to be less romantic, you have your choice of plenty of other roles to play. How about *Leisure Suit Larry*, in the eponymous game from Sierra? It features a character you might call a sexist pig, but that would be giving him too much credit. In this self-mocking series of games, Larry, the hero, is on a quest for true love—or at least a little companionship.

Strategy Games

Ever wonder what it would be like to conquer a country or save the world? You can find out by playing a strategy game, using your wits to deploy your forces against your enemy. These games test your abilities to think clearly and devise winning strategies.

Starcraft, a popular game from Blizzard, is set in the distant future, where a band of exiles fight for survival on the edge of the galaxy. You're the military leader, in control of any of three unique species, and your job is to organize your resources and prepare for battle. You can also play Starcraft with multiple players, with opponents at your side or on the Internet.

Total Annihilation from Cavedog is a futuristic strategy game with great sound effects and excellent 3-D graphics. An imperialistic society believes all of its citizens should be "patterned," that is, their consciousness should be transferred to machines. Others believe that patterning is an atrocity. You can fight for either side as "the Commander." You're armed with a light laser and a "d-gun" that will disintegrate anything it touches.

Myst, from Broderbund, the best-selling computer game in history, is a fanciful adventure game in which you explore a beautifully rendered series of worlds and solve puzzles. It's a gorgeous product with a

Games Call for Some Serious Hardware

You can play most games on today's standard PCs, but to get the full effect of the sounds and graphics, you need souped up sound and graphics cards. (See Chapter 10 for more on sound equipment and Chapter 15 for more on graphics adapters.) That means that a serious PC-gaming habit—and they've been known to develop—can get a lot more expensive than the prices of the games might suggest.

Myst's evocative landscapes and involving storyline have made it the best-selling computer game of all time.

slow, dreamlike pace. Unlike many computer games, it appeals to both women and men and is a great program for families to play together. Myst's sequel, **Riven**, takes place in a "deceptively beautiful world torn apart by age-old conflicts ... where secrets lie hidden at every turn ... and nothing is as it seems." You explore it in a quest to discover the secrets of the land and its inhabitants.

Although no longer on the best-seller lists, **King's Quest** games, which have been on the market since 1984, are now considered classics, and the way I look at it, if they were fun then, they'll be fun now. There are now seven in the series, and they are all available on a single CD-ROM for $30.

Resources

King's Quest
Sierra/Cendant Software
800-757-7707
www.sierra.com

Myst, Riven
Broderbund Software
800-521-6263
www.broderbund.com

Starcraft
Blizzard Entertainment
800-953-7669
www.blizzard.com

Total Annihilation
Cavedog
888-477-9369
www.cavedog.com

Arcade Games

Computer arcade games offer the kind of reflex-testing sport you'd find in a coin-operated video arcade.

I'm a sucker for pinball machines, and with the PC, I can play all day without having to part with a single quarter. You don't get the feel of the plunger and the vibration of the ball bouncing around, but you do see all the sights and hear all the sounds of a real pinball game. There are lots of pinball software games, but the *3-D Ultra Pinball* series

In the King's Quest series, from Sierra, you become an adventurer in search of lost treasure and romance.

from Sierra is one of the best. Each game has its own theme; for a really ghoulish experience, try **3-D Ultra Pinball 2: Creep Night**.

Resources

3-D Ultra Pinball series
Sierra/Cendant Software
800-757-7707
www.sierra.com

TV Quiz Shows

I can't think of a lot of programs to put in this category, but **You Don't Know Jack**, from Berkeley Systems, is so good that I have to mention it, and since I can't find a category for it, I'll create one.

You Don't Know Jack is my 14-year-old daughter Katherine's favorite game. The program (there are several editions) pits you against a friend, the computer, or folks out on the Internet in a wacky and fun quiz show. You can earn (or lose) plenty of virtual money, but win or lose it's a hoot. In addition to the CD-ROM version, there is a version called "You Don't Know Jack: The Netshow" on the Internet that you can play for free. In this version you'll play against folks all over the world, and as you play, you can carry on a little chat in a window on the screen. You'll find it on the Web at www.berkeleysytems .com. While the Net version is great, the CD-ROM is faster and more fun. It really feels like a TV quiz show.

Resources

You Don't Know Jack
Berkeley Systems
800-344-5541
www.berkeleysystems.com

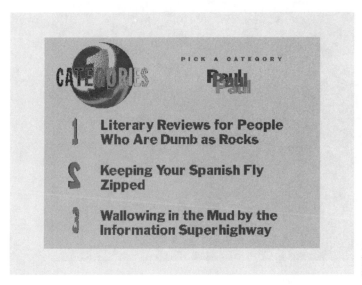

In You Don't Know Jack, you test your IQ against the CD-ROM or against other players on the Net.

Action/Adventure

A sequel to Quake, the most popular 3-D animation game, **Quake II** has gotten stellar reviews from just about everyone who has played it. After landing on an alien surface you and your small army must shut down the alien's war machine. You have a series of complex missions, and one false move could alert security, flood an entire passageway, or worse. Once you get hooked on Quake, you'll want **Quake II Mission Pack: The Reckoning**, which, for about $15, extends the game play with an entirely new mission.

I'm not a big fan of blood and guts, but if you're going to do it, you may as well do it right. **Doom II: Hell on Earth** is the clear leader in this field. Use your chain saw to hack away at soldiers from hell and engage in bloody hand-to-hand combat. This game is definitely R-rated: We're talking major violence here. It can be played by one or many players at a time, and you can even compete over a local area network.

Other popular games in this category include **Star Wars Jedi Knight** from LucasArts (one of a whole series of Star Wars games) and **Wofenstein 3D** from Activision.

Resources

Star Wars Jedi Knight
LucasArts Entertainment
888-532-4263
www.lucasarts.com

Descent
Interplay
800-468-3775
www.interplay.com

Doom II, Quake II, Wofenstein 3D
id Software
800-434-2637
www.idsoftware.com

In Quake II, it's you and your gang against an army of aliens.

Game Packs

A number of software distributors are selling multigame packs that include five or even ten CDs for between $25 and $50. What you typically get are older programs that, at some point, may have been classics.

Don't expect all the titles to be great, but if you get two or three good ones, you've gotten your money's worth. And an advantage of older programs is that they don't require state-of-the-art hardware.

The Best of Microsoft Entertainment Pack comes with 13 of the most popular Microsoft games for Windows including Tetris, Golf, Taipei, Pipe Dream, FreeCell, Tut's Tomb, Rodent's Revenge, Tri-Peaks, Ski Free, Chip's Challenge, Jezzball, Dr. Black Jack, and Tetravex. *Microsoft's Arcade* comes with five classic Atari games: Asteroids, Battlezone, Centipede, Missile Command, and Tempest. And Mindscape's *Game Pack III* includes Chessmaster 2100, Robot Tank, Beyond the Black Hole, Life and Death, Gin King/Cribbage King, Checkers, Loopz, Puzzle Gallery, and Life.

Resources

Game Pack III
Mindscape
415-895-2000
www.mindscape.com

Microsoft Game Packs
Microsoft
800-426-9400
www.microsoft.com

Game-Oriented Web Sites

There are plenty of games you can play over the Internet and game-related sites are popping up (and sometimes closing) all the time. Here are some of leading ones. For more go to Yahoo and search for "interactive Web games."

Site	Web Address	Notes
GameFun	www.gamefun.com	Game information for kids, including links to games you can play over the Net
GamePower	www.gamepower.com	Reviews, demos, and cheats
GameSpot	www.gamespot.com	Games and reviews
Happy Puppy	www.happypuppy.com	Demos, freeware, and shareware downloads
Imagine Games Network	www.imaginegames.com	Demos, gaming news, and games you can play online

Kids' Stuff

Games for children are covered in the next chapter, but some of those kids' programs could just as well be for adults. Check out the Carmen Sandiego series from Broderbund. I listed it in the kids section, but adults love it too.

Children's Software: Learning and Playing

60

WATCH THIS, TOMMY: IN ONE KEYSTROKE, I TAKE CONTROL OF THE UNIVERSE _AND_ GET A FIVE DOLLAR BUMP IN MY ALLOWANCE!

This book is for adults. That's because kids don't need a computer book; they take to computers naturally.

My two kids, Katherine, who's 14, and Will, 12, have both been playing with computers since before they could walk or talk. During the first year or two they were content to pound on the keyboard. For the next couple of years, they enjoyed watching the letters form and seeing their names on the screen. As they reached prekindergarten age, my kids and I began to experiment with children's software, and many of the programs I review here are their favorites. As they reach their teen years, of course, they are the ones who start telling me what software to buy, and not only in this category. It's like music, movies, and anything else: They have their ears to the ground.

KidDesk Internet Safe from Edmark provides an easy-to-work-with interface for kids while keeping them away from your files and inappropriate sites on the Internet.

Keeping Your Kids (and Your Stuff) Out of Harm's Way

KidDesk, from Edmark, has been around for years as the leading tool for creating a kid-friendly computer desktop that also keeps kids from accessing mom and dad's programs or data files. Now, like so many other software programs, KidDesk is also an Internet tool.

The newest version, **KidDesk Internet Safe**, not only provides kids with a fun and safe PC desktop but also keeps them from going into inappropriate places on the Internet. KidDesk only lets your kids see the Internet sites you specify (Edmark supplies a list of recommended sites). Children can also run programs set up for them on the KidDesk desktop by clicking on a colorful icon, but they can't run your spreadsheet or do any damage to your files because they have no access to the Windows desktop. By pressing a secret sequence of keys, you put the program into

Resources

CyberPatrol
The Learning Company
617-494-1200
www.cyberpatrol.com

KidDesk Internet Safe
Edmark
800-691-2986
www.edmark.com

NetNanny
NetNanny
800-340-7177
www.netnanny.com

SurfWatch
Surfwatch Software
800-458-6600
www.surfwatch.com

"adult mode," where you can add or delete icons, access other programs, and make any other changes. The program is appropriate for ages five and up.

There are plenty of other programs that can keep your kids safe on the Internet. Most aren't as much fun as KidDesk, but like KidDesk, they can block access to questionable sites. Such **Internet filters** include *SurfWatch*, *NetNanny*, and *CyberPatrol*, but you can get a complete list of them, as well as other information about keeping kids safe online at my website on the subject, www.safekids.com.

Kid-Style Graphics

KidPix from Broderbund Software isn't quite as old as my kids, but it has been around for quite a few years—and it's still one of the best children's creativity programs on the market. It lets children create their own artwork, and it is a lot easier to use than painting programs designed for adults are. It offers lots of goodies, including sounds, predrawn images, and plenty of special effects—you can actually hear the paint gurgle as it's poured from the can, and the pencil makes a faint scratching sound as you drag it around the screen. When you select a letter or number, the program reads it aloud in either English or Spanish. There are now several versions of KidPix on the market, including *KidPix Studio Deluxe*, which lets children create their own animations. The KidPix series is appropriate for kids from about age four till—well, I'm still fond of it.

Parental Control Is Important

Having said that your kids are probably going to start knowing more than you do about software, let's not forget who's in charge. A lot of software on the market includes violence, nudity, sexism, profane language, and other material that may not be appropriate for your children. Some software companies have adopted a voluntary rating system. One such system, adopted by Recreational Software Advisory Council (www.RSAC.org), provides information on the level of violence, sexuality, language, and other factors. As with all rating systems, these should be used as general guidelines. I strongly advise parents to play games with their children to find out if they meet your own criteria for what's appropriate.

Resources

KidPix, KidPix Studio Deluxe
Broderbund Software
800-521-6263
www.broderbund.com

Rules for Online Safety for Children

I've spent a lot of time over the past two years working on policies that will teach kids to use the Internet safely. My website on the subject, at www.safekids.com, has a lot of information that I think parents will find helpful, as well as lists of sites I think are particularly good for kids of different ages.

Although there have been some highly publicized cases of abuse involving computers, reported cases are relatively infrequent. Of course, like most crimes against children, many cases go unreported, especially if the child is engaged in an activity that he or she does not want to discuss with a parent. The fact that crimes are being committed online, however, is not a reason to avoid using these services. To tell children to stop using these services would be like telling them to forgo attending college because students are sometimes victimized on campus.

A better strategy would be for children to learn how to be "street smart" in order to better safeguard themselves in any potentially dangerous situation.

Although children and teenagers need a certain amount of privacy, they also need parental involvement and supervision in their daily lives. The same general parenting skills that apply to the "real world" also apply to the online world. Teach your kids the following rules:

- I will not give out personal information such as my address, telephone number, parents' work address or telephone number, or the name and location of my school without my parents' permission.

- I will tell my parents right away if I come across any information that makes me feel uncomfortable.

- I will never agree to get together with someone I "meet" online without first checking with my parents. If my parents agree to the meeting, I will be sure that it is in a public place and bring my mother or father along.

- I will never send a person my picture or anything else without first checking with my parents.

- I will not respond to any messages that are mean or in any way make me feel uncomfortable. It is not my fault if I get a message like that. If I do I will tell my parents right away so that they can contact the online service.

- I will talk with my parents so that we can set up rules for going online. We will decide upon the time of day that I can be online, the length of time I can be online, and appropriate areas for me to visit. I will not access other areas or break these rules without their permission.

Curious George helps youngsters learn to read in the Curious George Young Readers' Series from Houghton Mifflin Interactive.

Interactive Stories

Broderbund's *Living Books* series are classics in the genre of interactive stories, bringing stories to life with a variety of pop-up activities. Now it's offering classic stories, too, with an interactive version of *The Cat in the Hat* by Dr. Seuss. Other Living Books titles include *Arthur's Birthday*, *The Berenstain Bears Collection*, *Green Eggs and Ham*, and *Daniel in the Lion's Den*.

When my kids were little, I'd read them stories about the monkey Curious George and the Man with the Yellow Hat. Now there's the *Curious George Young Readers' Series*, from Houghton Mifflin Interactive, which challenges children to build critical thinking and reading skills in what the publisher calls a "magical" environment. In the fourth volume of the series, George becomes a cub reporter at the local newspaper and is assigned to cover a story on his own. Of course, he manages to get into trouble, but that's where the fun starts. Children go through about a dozen activities, helping George complete his assignments while practicing reading, writing, and spelling skills.

Resources

Living Books
Broderbund Software
800-521-6263
www.broderbund.com

Curious George Young Readers' Series
Houghton Mifflin Interactive
800-829-7962
www.hminet.com

Learning Skills in Electronic Playgrounds

Kid Phonics 1 and 2 from Knowledge Adventure teaches children to read by giving them an "auditory experience" that helps them progress from hearing sounds to reading words. Children are encouraged to learn with talking creatures, music, and sound effects.

Knowledge Adventure's **Fisher Price series** of games provides preschoolers through first graders with a number of useful learning tools. Fisher Price Ready for School Toddler, for example, takes children on a colorful journey with 20 activities designed by educators to encourage discovery and stimulate the child's curiosity. Toddlers learn computer skills, ABCs, numbers, shapes, colors, and basic manners.

You're the guest conductor at the Wonder Dome when the theater is zapped by lightning, causing the laser control system to fail. To rescue the show, you have to learn all about light, sound, and electricity. Fortunately you have **Zap** by Edmark, so you can not only learn about light but also fix and create electrical gadgets, create your own laser show, and see sound waves in action. Zap is part of Edmark's Thinkin' Things series. Edmark also publishes **Thinkin' Things Sky Island Mysteries**, which invites children to "wrap your brain around twisty riddles," experiment with language, and lots more. Of course it's educational, but it's fun, too.

MIllie and Bailey Preschool teaches the ABCs and basic writing and math skills to the very young using entertaining games.

Edmark's early learning series includes *Millie and Bailey Preschool*, which includes a series of activities including learning your ABCs with the Talking Letter Machine, learning writing skills with the Make-a-Story tool, and learning math concepts.

Millie's Math House, also from Edmark, is a delightful game that teaches very young children (ages two to six) to recognize sizes, shapes, patterns, and numbers. A mere list of activities—building houses for mice; putting jelly beans on cookies; bouncing an object over ducks, pigs, and Millie herself—doesn't do the program justice. It's the combination of sounds, music, animation, characters, humor, and ease of play that made this an instant classic.

When they were a younger, both my children liked the **Reader Rabbit** series from the Learning Company. For each game, a parent or teacher can set a challenge level for each child, so if a child is good at rhymes but not so good at vowels, the parent can adjust the levels accordingly. If you decide to buy any Learning Company products, I recommend you visit their website (www.learningco.com) and check out the "for parents" section for some pretty good advice on how to make the best use of their software.

Resources

Millie and Bailey Preschool,
Millie's Math House,
Thinkin' Things Sky Island
Mysteries, Zap
Edmark
800-691-2986
www.edmark.com

Fisher Price series
Knowledge Adventure
800-542-4240
www.adventure.com

Reader Rabbit series
The Learning Company
617-494-1200
www.learningco.com

Interactive Games

Freddi Fish and the Case of the Missing Kelp Seeds from Humongous Entertainment is an interactive game for kids age three to seven that stresses problem solving and critical thinking and, by the way, is lots of fun. The program starts out with a report that someone has Grandma Grouper's kelp seeds. She needs the seeds to keep her garden intact and it's up to your young ones to help her out. Freddi, a cute little fish, and her friend Luther go on an undersea adventure in search of the seeds.

Designed for preschoolers, *Putt-Putt Goes to the Moon*, also from Humongous Entertainment, puts your child on an extraterrestrial

Freddi Fish helps Grandma find missing kelp seeds. Cute graphics and Freddi's sweet voice enchant young players.

adventure, searching the moon for the missing rocket parts needed for the return trip to Earth. As with other games from Humongous, children will learn simple problem-solving skills while playing. Putt-Putt, a charming and disarming character, is a great playmate, and the game is full of "hot buttons" that, when clicked, will trigger an animated surprise. It's pretty easy to navigate around the program, making it a good choice for times when you want your child to explore on his or her own. You can now get this program, plus Putt-Putt Joins the Parade and Fatty Bear's Birthday Surprise for on one CD called the **Humongous Classic Collection**.

Another Humongous character, Pajama Sam, "the world's youngest super-hero," is aimed at kids age three to eight. In his second adventure, **Pajama Sam 2: Thunder and Lightning Aren't So Frightening**, Sam visits the World Wide Weather Factory in the sky, where he needs help from your kids as he works to repair Thunder and Lightning's weather-making machines before Mother Nature finds out.

Resources

Freddi Fish and the Case of the Missing Kelp Seeds, Putt-Putt Goes to the Moon, Humongous Classic Collection, Pajama Sam 2: Thunder and Lightning Aren't So Frightening
Humongous Entertainment
800-499-8386
www.humongous.com

Software for Girls

I was cynical at first, but it's hard to argue with success—and a daughter and wife who love Barbie. Mattel Media, the software division of the company that makes Barbie dolls, has proven that it's possible to make a lot of money selling software based on the popular fashion doll. The company doesn't have quite as many software titles as it does versions of Barbie, but there is now an entire line of Barbie-related software titles.

The first in the series, **Barbie Fashion Designer CD-ROM**, astonished the software industry by turning into an almost immediate best-seller when it was introduced. The software helps girls design real outfits for their plastic Barbie dolls and comes with fabric that you can run through a laser or ink jet printer to make real Barbie-size outfits.

I didn't think I'd be a particularly good judge of this program, so I asked my daughter Katherine—who was 12 when it came out—to put it through its paces. Katherine loved it. Even though she was older than the intended target audience, she still had a great time making outfits and watching Barbie model them on the virtual stage.

Now there are even more titles, including **Barbie's Magic Hair Styler**. There is something about this software that brings out Katherine's creativity. It's fun, and it gives her a chance to play with the computer without having to deal with violence, competition, or any of the elements so typically found in computer games. Mattel also publishes **Adventures with Barbie Ocean Discovery**, in which Barbie searches for undersea treasure and helps save undersea animals.

Mattel is now also integrating technology into its dolls. The $89.95 "Talk to Me Barbie" doll comes with a CD-ROM that kids use to program Barbie to say just what they want her to. Barbie comes with her own computer workstation, which is connected to the PC via a serial port. Once everything is connected, the child can teach Barbie her name, her friends' names, and other information.

My daughter grew up reading *American Girl* books, and now girls can play with the **American Girl** software from The Learning Company featuring Felicity, Kirsten, Addy, Samantha, and Molly. Girls can choose their favorite character, make her move and talk, change her costume, and select her props. Kids can even create conversations between characters by creating their own little plays based on the American Girl collection.

Purple Moon is a software company created to make software just for girls between eight and twelve. In one of its products, **Rockett's New School**, a girl can play an eighth grader on the first day in a new school. You meet new kids, get in on the gossip, and do some research to figure out what your next move should be. In another title, **Secret Paths to the Sea**, you join your friends in a girls-only hideaway, then set off on paths that lead past idyllic and adventuresome landscapes, including the Frozen North. Sounds like fun to me, and I'm not even in the target market. And even if you don't buy the software, check out Purple Moon's website at www.purple-moon.com for cool games and projects.

Resources

American Girl
The Learning Company
617-494-1200
www.learningco.com

*Barbie Fashion Designer CD,
 Barbie's Magic Hair Styler,
 Adventures with Barbie Ocean
 Discovery*
Mattel Media
800-524-8697
www.mattelmedia.com

*Rockett's New School,
 Secret Paths to the Sea*
Purple Moon
888-278-7753
www.purple-moon. com

Learning Adventures for Older Kids

Broderbund's **Where Is Carmen Sandiego?** series is very popular educational software for kids ranging from age ten to young adult. There's

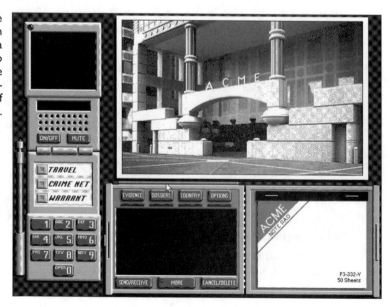

Broderbund's classic Where in the World Is Carmen Sandiego turns you into a supersleuth whose job is to find Carmen wherever she hides. Your handy videophone lets you call the chief to get your instructions.

also a ***Where in the World Is Carmen Sandiego? Junior Detective Edition*** for kids five to eight. In each game, you, the player, are an agent with the San Francisco–based Acme Detective Agency. You're assigned a case and sent on a high-tech, high-flying adventure to find Carmen and her companions. The search entails solving clues to a variety of mysteries.

In some games, like *Where in the World* and *Where in the U.S.A.*, you find Carmen by demonstrating your understanding of geography as well as your deductive skills. In others, you focus on time, culture, or politics. Each game comes with a book of facts and clues. These aren't just game manuals. For instance, *Where in the World* comes with the *World Almanac* and the *Book of Facts*. Where in the U.S.A. comes with *Fodor's U.S.A.* travel guide.

The Blaster series from Knowledge Adventure is an entire line of learning programs starting at age four and going all the way up to high school. For the little ones, there is Math Blaster and Reading Blaster (different versions for ages four to six, six to nine, and nine to twelve). Writing Blaster is for kids nine to twelve years old, and there are algebra, pre-algebra, and geometry programs for kids all the way through middle school and high school. Come to think of it, I'm a bit rusty on *my* geometry.

Resources

Blaster series
Knowledge Adventure
800-545-7677
www.knowledge.com

Where Is Carmen Sandiego series
Broderbund Software
800-521-6263
www.broderbund.com

Reference Software: Knowledge on CD-ROM

61

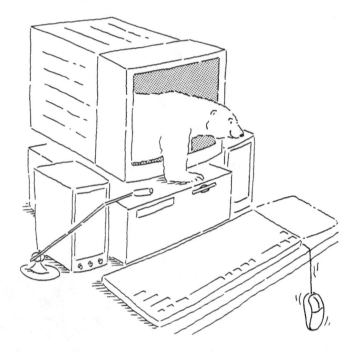

When I wrote the first edition of **The Little PC Book** in 1993, I didn't even have a section on reference works because there weren't enough CD-ROM drives around then to make it a popular category. In the second edition, which came out in 1996, they were emerging as an important category. Now things have changed again, thanks to, you guessed it, the Internet.

A lot of the reference works that used to be distributed on CD-ROM are now being offered online. Unlike CD-ROMs, online references can be updated constantly, so the information there is always current. And for publishers, it's a lot easier to put things on the Web than to press CDs and get them into stores.

Nevertheless, there are still plenty of reference titles coming out on CD-ROM and even a few on DVD.

Whether it's worth owning a CD or DVD reference work versus getting it from the Internet depends on how and how often you plan to use it. If you have only an occasional need to look something up in the encyclopedia and you don't care for lots of animations, graphics, and sound, than you might be better off just using an online resource. But if you need to use it often or really want to take advantage of rich media, it might be worth buying a CD or DVD.

Reference Bookshelves

CD-ROM encyclopedias such as the *Britannica CD, Compton's Interactive Encyclopedia*, the *Grolier Multimedia Encyclopedia*, and *Microsoft Encarta* come on one or two CD-ROMs and for about $50 replace that bulky set of books that was a fixture in so many homes of my parents' generation. Each holds not only the equivalent of 20 or so printed volumes, but also animations, videos, and audio presentations. Microsoft's Encarta in particular has done a phenomenal job of including tons of videos, audios, and animation. I've tried all three of these sets and I don't have a strong preference because they're constantly trying to outdo each other. One year one is better than the others, but the next year they switch places. Frankly, I don't think you can go wrong with any of them.

The home I grew up in didn't just have an encyclopedia. Our bookshelf also held an almanac, a thesaurus, a dictionary, a book of quotations, and an atlas. *Microsoft Bookshelf* has all those tools for $100, and like the CD-ROM encyclopedias, they come to life with pictures, sounds, and animation. The disc also includes The Concise Columbia Encyclopedia.

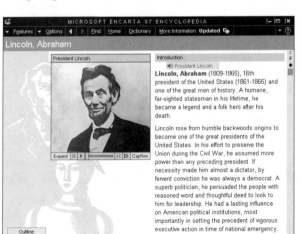

Hyperlinks and sound and video clips enliven each entry in Microsoft's popular Encarta CD-ROM encyclopedia.

Online References

Before you buy an encyclopedia on CD-ROM, check out what's offered on the Web. Try the sites listed here and go to Internet search engines like Yahoo, Excite, or Lycos to see what they have listed, too.

For now, most of these sites are free, though they may be charging for access before long.

General Encyclopedias

Site/Web Address	Comments	Price
Britannica Online www.eb.com	All the articles from the *Encyclopædia Britannica,* plus more—72,000 articles in all for you to search or browse, plus more than 12,000 illustrations and tens of thousands of related Web links, selected by Britannica's editors. Updated continuously.	Free trial. Annual subscription is $85; Monthly subscriptions cost $8.50
Compton's Encyclopedia Online www.comptons.com/index_retail.html	An electronic encyclopedia with the full text from the Compton's CD-ROM and a good sampling of multimedia	Free trial, $29.95 a year
Electronic Library www.elibrary.com	A searchable database that includes access to the full text of many newspapers, radio and TV transcripts, magazine articles, books and other resources.	Free trial, $9.95 a month
Electronic Library's Free Encyclopedia www.encyclopedia.com	More than 17,000 articles from *The Concise Columbia Electronic Encyclopedia, third edition.* The entries are short but it's still quite useful.	Free
Encarta Concise Electronic Encyclopedia encarta.msn.com/find/find.asp	An abridged online version of the *Encarta Encyclopedia.* It contains 16,000 articles; more than 2200 photos, illustrations, maps, charts, and tables; and more than 13,000 Web links.	Free
Funk and Wagnalls www.funkandwagnalls.com	Complete text of the 29-volume *Funk & Wagnalls Multimedia Encyclopedia,* including Hot Topics, Cool Facts, Term Paper Templates, and loads of multimedia.	Was free when I tried it, but they may start charging for access

Site/Web Address	Comments	Price
Grolier Multimedia Encyclopedia Online gme.grolier.com	Includes 35,000 Articles from the *Academic American Encyclopedia,* along with multimedia featuring an atlas, pictures, sounds, flags, and timelines.	Free trial, $60 annual subscription

Specialty Encyclopedias

Site/Web Address	Notes
Better Homes and Gardens Home Improvement Encyclopedia www.bhglive.com/homeimp/	Search more than 1,000 home improvement tips with more than 125 animations
Encyclopedia of Women's History www.teleport.com/~megaines/ women.html	Written by and for K-12 students
Biography.com www.biography.com	Over 20,000 biographies
Internet Movie Database www.imdb.com	Information and reviews about thousands of movies
Frommer's Outspoken Encyclopedia of Travel www.frommers.com	One of the more definitive travel information sources
Nolo's Legal Encyclopedia www.nolo.com/briefs.html	A searchable encyclopedia on major legal topics
Stanford Encyclopedia of Philosophy plato.stanford.edu	An encyclopedia of philosophers and ideas
Internet Mental Health www.mentalhealth.com	An encyclopedia of mental health information

The American Heritage Talking Dictionary can demonstrate the proper pronunciation of its more than 200,000 entries.

Microsoft Encarta Suite DVD—one of the first reference works to come out on DVD—takes advantage of the new medium's increased storage to bundle Microsoft Encarta, Encyclopedia Deluxe Edition, Encarta Virtual Globe, and Microsoft Bookshelf. The DVD version of the encyclopedia has 35 percent more videos (according to Microsoft—I admit that I didn't count them) and offers higher-resolution playback than you get with the CD-ROM.

If you want to learn everything there is to know about the English language, consider the ***American Heritage Talking Dictionary*** from The Learning Company. The CD is based on the printed *American Heritage Dictionary of the English Language,* including over 200,000 definitions, plus geographical and biographical entries and an integrated thesaurus. This dictionary doesn't just show you how to pronounce the words, it pronounces them for you.

Resources

American Heritage Talking Dictionary, Compton's Interactive Encyclopedia
The Learning Company
617-494-1200
www.comptons.com

Britannica CD
Encyclopedia Britannica
800-747-8503
www.eb.com

Grolier Multimedia Encyclopedia
Grolier Electronic Publishing
800-285-4534
www.grolier.com

Microsoft Bookshelf, Microsoft Encarta, Microsoft Encarta Suite DVD
Microsoft
800-426-9400
www.encarta.com

Exploring Your World

The Learning Company, which has recently bought up lots of companies, now competes with itself as the publisher of the two leading

CD-ROM–based atlases. ***Compton's Interactive World Atlas*** and ***3D Atlas*** from its Creative Wonders division both have some pretty eye-catching graphics. Comptons has a good visual interface with easy-to-use icons and a cool "make a map" feature that lets kids (or adults) create a custom map of the area they're looking at. The Creative Wonders 3D Atlas comes with a virtual "fly through" of the Earth, time-lapse multimedia exhibits, and satellite photography of our planet. The Deluxe Traveler's edition includes a *U.S. Street Guide* that provides directions and road maps throughout the United States.

If you think finding your way around a PC is hard, try driving across the country without a map. Of course, you can get a paper map from the auto club or just about any gas station, but if you want to really plan your trip in style, consider a CD-ROM road atlas. There are several to choose from. ***Automap*** from Microsoft is one of the leading programs, but my favorite is ***TripMaker***, which is based on the Rand McNally road atlas of the United States, Canada, and Mexico.

The Rand McNally program includes a "trip guide" that asks about the types of attractions you like to visit and plans your route accordingly. Options include discovering history, urban attractions, and fun for kids.

The maps are useful as an overview, but I wouldn't rely on them for specific driving directions. To begin with, you probably won't have a PC with you while you're traveling. Second, the map doesn't have as much detail as a good state road map. The program does, however, provide

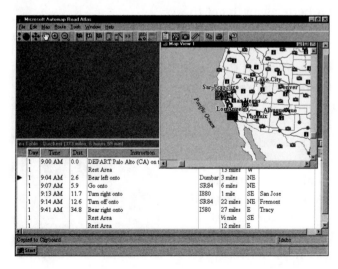

Microsoft's popular Automap provides a map and driving instructions for your next road trip.

you with a reference number to make it easy to find the locations it describes on Rand McNally's printed road atlas.

Another category of map software helps you on the local level. **Rand McNally StreetFinder Deluxe**, for example, lets you find locations by address and generate a local map or driving directions to the area. It also has address-to-address directions from your origin to your destination. It also includes listings of businesses, hotels, and the complete *Mobil Travel Guide.*

Before you spend money on a product like StreetFinder, be aware that there are free street finding tools on the Internet. Lycos (see www. lycos.com/roadmap.html), Yahoo (maps.yahoo.com/py/maps.py) and Excite (city.net/maps/driving/) all offer free driving directions and maps. Also check out *MapQuest* (www.mapquest.com), which gives free driving directions within or between any city in the United States.

Resources

Automap
Microsoft
800-426-9400
www.microsoft.com

Compton's Interactive World Atlas, 3D Atlas
The Learning Company
617-494-1200
www.comptons.com

TripMaker, StreetFinder Deluxe
Rand McNally
800-333-0136, 708-329-8100
www.randmcnally.com

Getting Religion

And last but not least, though I don't expect to see CD versions of the good book prominently displayed in millions of American living rooms, I can't think of a better way to get the word than from an electronic version of the Bible. Not only can you read the text, but you can research the text by subject. In **Comptons Interactive Bible—New International Version**, from The Learning Company, you can also experience multimedia versions of its famous stories. This edition contains the full text of Bible, along with study plans, an extensive concordance, and a historical atlas. Parsons Technology offers the **New Unger's Talking Bible** with definitions and pronunciations of 6,700 names, places, and objects. **Davka Corp.** specializes in Jewish bibles and other resources.

Resources

Comptons Interactive Bible—New International Version
The Learning Company
617-494-1200
www.comptons.com

Davka Corp.
800-621-8227
www.davka.com

New Unger's Talking Bible
Parsons Technology
800-957-3111
www.parsonstech.com

Congratulations. You're not a computer novice anymore. In record time, you've learned everything you need to know to work confidently with your PC.

Have a great journey—and lots of fun along the way.

Glossary

A

Active Desktop In *Windows 98*, a feature that allows live Web content to be displayed on the *desktop.*

active matrix screen A high-quality *LCD* screen used on *notebook PCs.*

AGP Advanced Graphics Port, a high-speed video port available in new PCs.

adapter See *expansion board.*

application program A piece of software that does a particular task, such as word processing, database management, or accounting.

ASCII Pronounced "as-key," it stands for American Standard Code for Information Interchange. It's another term for *plain text*, a file format that includes only alphabetic characters and no format information.

B

backing up Creating copies of program and data files, in case the original is damaged.

baud A term used to describe data-transmission speeds, especially for *modems.* Baud is often used to mean *bits per second* (bps).

beta version A prerelease version of software, sometimes made available to the public so that the software's publishers can get feedback on its features.

bit The smallest unit of measurement for electronic data, a bit is one on or off signal. Eight bits make one *byte.*

bit depth The number of *bits* used to save a piece of graphic information. Generally, the higher the bit depth, the better the quality of the graphic.

bit-mapped graphics Graphics that are made up of an arrangement of tiny dots.

board See *expansion board.*

boot To start up the computer. The word is derived from the expression "to pull up by the bootstraps," because the computer uses information stored in its own chips to start itself up.

boot files System files used to *boot* the PC.

bug An error in a computer program or system. It got its name when a moth was found on a tube in one of the first computers.

bus A pathway for moving data inside a computer. It's important to know what bus standard your computer uses so that you can buy compatible *peripherals*.

browser Software used to navigate the *World Wide Web*.

byte Eight *bits*. A byte is enough information to convey a single alphabetic character in a file.

C

C prompt See *DOS prompt*.

cable modem An *adapter* designed to link a PC to a coaxial cable, offering high-speed *Internet* access.

cache memory A portion of memory set aside for temporary storage, generally used to speed up processing.

CAD Stands for "*computer-aided design*": using a computer for product design.

card See *expansion board*.

Carpal Tunnel Syndrome A wrist and hand problem caused by repetitive actions such as typing.

cascading A method of arranging windows on the *desktop* in which the windows are stacked one on top of another, with only the *title bars* and left-hand borders of the bottom windows showing.

cascading menus A set of *menus* and *submenus*.

CD-R Stands for "compact disc, recordable," a type of CD and CD drive that allows you to record data (once) onto CDs, a well as play back data stored on them.

CD-ROM Stands for "compact disc, read-only memory." CD-ROM discs hold about 650 *megabytes* of data and are used for distributing lots of information, such as software, multimedia entertainment titles, graphics libraries, or online reference works. The data on a CD-ROM is permanently etched on the disc and cannot be changed.

Celeron A *processor,* made by Intel, based on the *Pentium II* but less powerful.

central processing unit The *chip* on a computer's *system board* that does the main processing. For PCs, these chips are based on Intel's *Pentium* chip technology. (Older PCs may use Intel-compatible 386 or 486 chips.) Abbreviated CPU.

channel A special type of *World Wide Web* site designed to be downloaded to your computer on a regular schedule.

check box In Windows, a program control that allows you to pick an option by clicking in a box next to the option name.

child window A *window* within a window. *Program windows* may contain several child windows, containing separate files.

chip See *processor.*

click To press and release the left *mouse button* once to select something on screen.

client In networking, a computer or piece of software meant to retrieve files from a central computer called a *server.*

clip art Files containing ready-made, copyright-free images that you can buy on disk or download from the *Internet* and use in your own work.

Clipboard In *Windows,* a temporary holding place for information you cut or copy from a document. Data from the last cut or copy operation is kept on the Clipboard so that you can paste it to a new location.

clock speed The number of cycles per second (*megahertz*) at which a *processor* runs. For any given type of processor, the faster the clock speed, the faster the processor.

close button In *Windows,* the icon at the top right of a window that you can click on to close the window.

COM The designation for your computer's *serial ports.* The first serial port is referred to as COM1, the second as COM2, and so on. You use the name to tell setup programs where they can find a *peripheral*, such as a *modem* or a *mouse*, that is connected to the computer via a serial port.

command An instruction for the computer. In Windows, commands can be given in many ways: by choosing them from on-screen *menus*, by using the *keyboard*, or by clicking on buttons and *toolbars*.

command button A Windows program control. You activate a command by clicking on its button.

communication protocol A set of rules followed by the software at both ends of a *modem* connection, creating a common language for online communication.

computer-aided design Using a computer for product design. Abbreviated *CAD*.

contact management software A type of *personal information manager* designed for salespeople and others whose business relies on client contact. The software keeps a record of telephone contacts as well as names and addresses.

context menu In *Windows*, a *menu* that appears when you *right-click* on an object.

context-sensitive help Online help that gives you information for the task you are in the middle of. For example, if you are using a particular dialog box in an application and call up help, a program that offers context-sensitive help would automatically bring up a help window pertaining to that dialog box.

CPU See *central processing unit*.

CRT Stands for "cathode ray tube." See *monitor*.

cursor keys On a *keyboard*, the keys, labeled with arrows, that move the Windows *insertion point* (or "cursor") around the screen.

D

database Any collection of information, from a phone book to a company's inventory data. On a computer, you use a *database management program* to create and control databases.

database management program Software designed to handle large amounts of information on a computer.

desktop In Windows, the main interface, which you see when you first start your PC and that holds the tools and files you use to do your work.

desktop publishing Using a personal computer to lay out and produce complex documents.

dialog box In *Windows*, a box from which you choose command options.

digital flat panel interface A special graphics port that sends digital graphics data, suitable for use by *flat-panel displays*, instead of the analog data designed for *CRTs*. Abbreviated DFP interface.

DIMM Stands for "Double in-line memory module," a device, designed to plug into your computer's *system board*, that holds *memory* chips. Also see *SIMM*.

directory 1. In *DOS*, a section on a disk, like the file folders in Windows, in which you keep a related set of files. 2. A list of the files on a disk.

disc An alternate spelling for *disk*, usually used to refer to *CD-ROMs* and *DVDs*.

disk A magnetic surface on which information is written for permanent storage. Most PC users use internal *hard disks* to save the bulk of their data. *Floppy disks* and other removable disks are used to distribute files to others and to *back up* hard disk data.

disk cache An area in *memory* used to temporarily store information from the disk drive. Its use speeds up operations because the computer can access memory faster than it can access the *disk*.

disk drive The mechanism that reads information from a *disk*.

display See *monitor*.

display adapter A set of chips, often on an *expansion board*, that translates data into video information for a monitor.

docking station A hardware base that adds extra ports and other features to *subnotebook PCs*.

document A file created with an *application program*.

domain name The name used to identify the computers at a particular location on the *Internet*. Companies and other entities can register domain names with a central Internet authority so that computers all over the world can access their *servers* by using the domain name.

domain name service Software run by *ISPs* that routes Internet messages to known *domain names*.

DOS See *MS-DOS*.

DOS command line See *DOS prompt*.

DOS prompt The line *MS-DOS* displays when it's waiting for a command. On most computers it will be some variation of C:\>. (The letter, in this case C, names the current *disk drive*.)

dot matrix printer A type of *printer* used for special-purpose industrial printing.

dot pitch A measure of the closeness of the tiny red, green, and blue dots that make up each *pixel* on a color *monitor*.

double-click To press and release the a *mouse button* twice in quick succession. Double-clicking generally opens the object (program or file) whose *icon* you *double-click* on.

dragging Moving the mouse with the *mouse button* pressed down, usually in order to move an object or select a string of text on screen.

DRAM Stands for "dynamic random access memory." DRAM is what people usually mean when they just say "RAM" or "memory."

drawing program A program that creates *object-based graphics*, that is, pictures from collections of individual geometric shapes.

drive A: A PC's first *floppy disk* drive.

drive B: A PC's second *floppy disk* drive.

drive bay A space in a PC designed for adding extra *disk drives*.

drive C: A PC's *hard disk*.

driver A small program that runs *peripheral hardware*, such as a *printer* or *scanner*.

drop-down list In Windows, a list showing options for a *field* that appears when you click on an arrow next to the field.

DSL Stands for "digital subscriber line," a technology for sending digital messages at high speeds over phone wires.

DVD Stands for "digital versatile disc," a *storage* technology that looks like a *CD-ROM* but holds much more information—4.7 to 17 *gigabytes*.

E

EDO RAM Stands for "extended data output random access memory," a type of high-speed *memory*.

e-mail A method of posting messages over a *network* such as the *Internet*. The addressee receives the message almost instantaneously. Short for "electronic mail."

ergonomic keyboard A type of *keyboard* designed to reduce the risk of repetitive-stress disorders, such as *Carpal Tunnel Syndrome*, that can result from too much typing.

error message A message displayed by a piece of software to inform you that something has gone wrong.

Ethernet A technology designed to link computers over high-speed *local area networks*.

expansion board Boards that add processors to your *system board* to add extra functions to your computer. You add expansion boards via your computer's *expansion slots*.

expansion slot A place set aside on your computer's *system board* where you can attach *expansion boards* to add extra functions to your computer.

F

field 1. A place in a *dialog box* into which you add information. 2. One category of information in a *database*.

file A collection of data with a name attached, saved on a computer's *disk*.

file extension Three characters following a period at the end of a file name. The file extension usually indicates the *file format* or the program used to create or modify the file.

file format The kind of data a file holds. Any *application program* can read and save only certain file formats. The file format is usually indicated by the *file extension*.

Firewire A technology designed to link *PCs* and *peripherals*, such as *disk drives*, that require high-speed connections.

Flash card A storage technology designed to be used with digital cameras and other portable devices.

flat-panel display A monitor, usually based on *LCD* technology, that has a flat case, rather than the deep, TV-like form used for a *CRT*.

floppy disk A portable disk consisting of a floppy mylar disk enclosed in a hard shell.

folder In Windows, a method of grouping files saved on a disk. You can create a new folder whenever you need one. See also *directory*.

folder window A *window* that displays the file system of the PC. Compare *program window*.

font A collection of characters in a certain type style. On PCs, fonts are files, in either *TrueType* or *PostScript* format, that supply outlines for the shapes of the letters.

format 1. To prepare a disk to hold information. 2. The kind of information saved in a file. 3. To add design information to a document.

forum See *newsgroup*.

freeware See *public domain software*.

function keys A set of keys on a PC *keyboard*, usually labeled F1, F2, and so on, that can be programmed to carry out special commands.

G

gigabyte About a billion *bytes* or a thousand *megabytes* of data (1,073,741,824 bytes). Abbreviated GB.

graphical user interface An *interface*, such as that used by *Windows*, that lets the user give commands by manipulating graphical representations of the objects, such as files and programs, that the user interacts with. Sometimes abbreviated "*GUI*."

GUI Pronounced "gooey." See *graphical user interface*.

graphics adapter See *display adapter*.

H

hand-held computer An extremely small computer made to be carried in a pocket or briefcase. Also called a *palmtop PC*.

hard disk A storage device, either internal or external to a computer's *system unit*, that holds large amounts of data.

hardware The physical components of a computer system. Compare *software*.

hardware interface The technology used to connect *peripherals* to a PC. Some examples are *Firewire, USB,* and *PCI.*

hyperlink A method for navigating through documents on the *World Wide Web.* The creator of a Web site can make any graphic or piece of text a hyperlink, so that clicking on it calls up a related Web page.

I

icon In *Windows,* a small picture that represents a file, a program, or a command.

IDE Stands for "integrated drive electronics," the most common *interface* for connecting external *hard disk* to a PC. See also *SCSI.*

ink jet printer A type of printer that creates images on the page with controlled spurts of ink. See also *laser printer* and *dot matrix printer.*

insertion point In *Windows,* an *I*-shaped indicator that shows where any text you type will be inserted. You place the insertion point by pointing to the desired location with the *mouse* and clicking the left *mouse button.*

integrated program A program that combines features of several application programs in one, usually word processing, spreadsheet, database, graphics, and communications.

interface 1. The rules by which a piece of software communicates with you and you with it. Each piece of software has its own interface, although *Windows* programs generally have similar interfaces. 2. The method used to connect external devices to a PC. See *PCI* and *USB.*

interlacing For *monitors,* a method of drawing an image on screen in which only every other line of information is drawn in each pass. Compare *noninterlaced.*

Internet A "network of networks" through which computer users can communicate with others around the world, through *e-mail,* the *World Wide Web,* and other services.

Internet filter A piece of software that controls what *Internet* sites can be accessed from the PC that uses it.

Internet Service Provider A service that connects individual PC users to the *Internet.* Abbreviated *ISP.*

ISDN Stands for "integrated services data network," a technology used to send digital information at high speeds over phone wires.

ISP See *Internet service provider.*

J

joystick A *pointing device* designed for use with games.

K

keyboard The typewriterlike mechanism you use to input text and give commands.

keyboard shortcut A method of giving *menu* commands using the *keyboard* instead of a *mouse.*

kilobyte 1024 *bytes.* Abbreviated K or KB.

L

LAN See *local area network.*

laptop PC See *notebook PC.*

laser printer A type of *printer* that writes images onto paper using a laser beam, similar to the mechanism used for a copy machine. Generally, laser printers provide the highest-quality black-and-white images available from a desktop printer.

LCD Stands for "liquid crystal display," a technology used to create *flat-panel displays.*

Linux A type of *operating system* software.

local area network A setup by which a group of personal computers is connected, via cables and special networking software, so that the computers' users can share *files, e-mail, printers,* and other services.

LPT The PC's designation for *parallel ports.* The first parallel port is LPT1, the second is LPT2, and so on. You use the name to tell setup programs where they can find *printers* and other *peripherals* that are connected to the computer via those ports.

M

Macintosh A type of personal computer made by Apple Computer. Macintoshes use a different operating system and run different application software than do Windows PCs.

math coprocessor A *processor*, specially designed for speedy math calculations, that is added to the *system board* of some computers. The *Pentium* CPUs have a math coprocessor built in.

maximize/restore button In *Windows*, a button at the top right corner of every window that, when clicked on, enlarges the window to fill the screen. If the Window is already full size, clicking the button restores the window to its former size.

megabyte About a million *bytes* (1,048,576, to be exact). Abbreviated MB.

megahertz The number of cycles per second at which a *processor* works. Abbreviated MHz.

memory The place where a computer keeps programs and data when they are in use. Also called *random access memory* (*RAM*). Compare *storage*.

menu A list of commands displayed by a program from which you choose the command you want to give next.

menu bar In *Windows* programs, the list of *menu* names that ranges across the top of a window.

Microsoft Windows The operating system used by most PCs.

minimize button In Windows, a button at the top right corner of every window that, when clicked on, reduces the window to a *Program button* on the *taskbar*.

MMX A technology added to *Pentium* processors to speed up multimedia processing. MMX technology is included in *Pentium II* chips.

modem A device that *mo*dulates computer data into signals that can be carried over phone lines, and *dem*odulates data it receives from other modems over phone lines into a form readable by the computer.

monitor The screen on which programs display information. Also called *display*.

motherboard See *system board*.

mouse A *pointing device* that allows you to give commands and select items on screen in a *graphical user interface.*

mouse buttons Buttons on the top of a *mouse* that you click in order to activate a command. Generally, PC mice have two mouse buttons.

mouse pad A pad used under a *mouse* to make its movements smooth.

mouse port A socket on the back of some computers designed specifically for attaching a *mouse.*

MS-DOS Stands for "Microsoft disk operating system." Until the arrival of *Windows,* it was the standard *operating system* for PCs.

multiscan monitor A monitor designed to work with a variety of *display adapters,* at different *resolutions.*

N

network An arrangement by which personal computers are connected so that users of each one can share *files, e-mail,* and other services. See also *local area network* and *Internet.*

network interface card An adapter that connects a PC to a *local area network,* cable service, or other *network.*

newsgroup An *Internet* service that provides a location for users to post messages on a given topic. Also called a *forum.*

noninterlaced In *monitors,* a method of drawing the onscreen image that uses a single pass to draw the entire image. Compare *interlacing.*

notebook PC A relatively small, battery-operated PC, with a built-in *monitor* and *pointing device,* typically weighing between four and seven pounds. Also called *laptop PC.* Also see *subnotebook PC.*

O

object-based graphics Graphics created from collections of individual geometric shapes that can be manipulated separately.

OCR Stands for "optical character recognition." OCR software translates the shapes of letters from a scanned file into a file readable by *word processing software.*

online service A service, available by subscription, that offers such features as *e-mail*, libraries containing all types of information, *shareware* and *public domain software*, and online *forums* on which you can chat via your keyboard with other subscribers, in addition to *Internet* access.

operating system The software that takes care of basic system activities, such as reading from and saving to disk, so that *application software* can focus on doing its own particular tasks. The main operating system for PCs is *Microsoft Windows*.

option buttons In *Windows*, a set of buttons in a *dialog box* in which only one of the options can be picked.

P

paint program Graphics software that creates *bit-mapped graphics*, which create a picture by assembling tiny black-and-white or color dots.

palmtop PC See *hand-held PC*.

parallel port A connector used to attach *printers* and other devices to the computer.

passive matrix screen A type of *LCD* screen.

path A string of directory names that tells *Windows* where to locate to a particular *file* or *directory*. A path has three parts: the *disk drive* name, the list of *directories* that leads to the designated file or directory, and finally, the file name. The directory names are separated by backslash characters (\).

pathname See *path*.

PC Stands for *personal computer*, but usually refers more specifically to a *Windows*-based personal computer.

PC card A credit-card sized *expansion board* for *notebook PCs*.

PC-compatible 1. A *Windows*-based PC. 2. As an adjective, software or hardware that works with a Windows PC.

PCI A type of *hardware interface* for PCs.

PCL A page-description language used by *PC-compatible laser printers*. Stands for Printer Control Language.

PCMCIA card See *PC card*.

Pentium A type of *processor* created by Intel.

Pentium II A type of *processor* created by Intel, the second generation of the Pentium line of processors.

peripheral *Hardware*, such as a *modem* or *printer*, that you use with a computer.

personal computer Any computer made to be used by a single person.

personal information manager A kind of *database* program designed to track names, addresses, and scheduling information. Abbreviated *PIM*.

PIM See *personal information manager*.

piracy Illegally copying or distributing someone else's software, rather than buying your own copy.

pixel Short for "picture element." On a *monitor*, one pixel is a single dot of light out of all the dots that make up an image.

plain text See *ASCII*.

pointer An on-screen indicator, controlled by a *mouse* or other *pointing device*, you use to select an object on the desktop you want to work with.

pointing device A *hardware* device, such as a *mouse, trackball, joystick*, or *touchpad*, that you use to move the *pointer* on screen.

port A connector used to attach *peripheral* devices to the computer. See also *parallel port* and *serial port*.

portal site On the *World Wide Web*, a site designed to serve as a launch pad for your explorations. Portal sites provide links to Web pages in a variety of categories plus a *search engine* for finding sites that cover specific topics.

PostScript A language created by Adobe Systems, commonly used in *desktop publishing* applications and high-end *laser printers*. Like *TrueType*, PostScript is also a *font* format.

PowerPC The *processor* used for late-model *Macintosh* computers.

printer A device that puts text or pictures on paper.

processor A circuit in a computer that processes information. Processors are attached to the *system board* or to add-on *expansion boards*. See also *central processing unit*.

program Data that is interpreted by a computer's processor to instruct the computer how to behave. See also *application program, utility,* and *operating system.*

Program button In *Windows,* a button that appears on the *taskbar* for each open *program* and *folder window.*

program window In *Windows,* a *window* that displays the *interface* for an *application program.*

public domain software Software that its creators give out freely, without asking for payment. Also called *freeware.* Public domain software is available from *online services, user groups,* via the *Internet,* and from companies that sell compendiums of programs. See also *shareware.*

Q R

RAM See *memory.*

random access memory See *memory.*

reboot To turn off your computer and start it again, or to press the Ctrl, Alt, and Del keys, or the Reset key, to restart it. It's what you do when a computer freezes up. Many computers also provide a reset button that reboots the computer without turning off the power.

Recycle Bin In *Windows,* a storage area that holds deleted files. The Recycle Bin is an icon on the Windows *desktop* that, like other icons, can be opened so that its contents can be viewed. Emptying the Recycle Bin deletes its contents once and for all.

registry A part of the *Windows operating system* that stores information about every piece of installed software.

removable storage A *storage* system, such as that used for *floppy disks, CD-ROMs,* and Zip drives, in which the *disk* is separate from the disk drive.

resolution A measure of how many pieces of information are in a particular area in a visual representation. For *printers* and *scanners,* resolution is measured in dots per inch; on *monitors,* it is measured by the number of pixels on the screen. The higher the number, the sharper the image.

right-click To quickly press and then release the right *mouse button.* In Windows, right-clicking generally calls up a *menu* that lets you act on the item you clicked on.

S

save To record work onto a disk for permanent storage. Until work is saved, it exists only in *memory* and will be lost if the computer is turned off or its power is otherwise interrupted.

scanner A device that translates a graphic image into a computer-readable file.

screen shield A detachable plate that can be added to a *monitor* to reduce glare and, in some cases, radiation from the monitor.

scroll bar In *Windows*, a control that appears whenever a window contains more than it can show at one time. You can scroll the window's contents by clicking in the scroll bar.

SCSI Stands for "small computer systems interface," a method of connecting external hard drives and other *peripherals* to a PC. Pronounced "scuzzy."

SDRAM Stands for "synchronous dynamic random access memory," a type of high-speed *memory*.

search engine Software that searches through a file system—on your computer or on the *Internet*—to find files related to subjects you name.

select To choose the object you want to act on with the next command, usually by *clicking* on it.

serial port A connector used to attach *peripherals* to the computer. Usually the serial ports are used for a *mouse* or a *modem*.

server On a *network*, a computer or a piece of software that provides files or software services to other computers, called *clients*, on the network.

shareware Software that is distributed for free but that you are asked to pay for if you keep using it after an initial trial period. Shareware is usually distributed over the *Internet* and can be freely copied among friends and co-workers. See also *public domain software*.

shortcut In *Windows*, an icon that acts like a copy of another icon, but takes up much less room on disk. Shortcuts for *printers, files, folders*, or any other object can be kept on the Windows *desktop*, allowing easy access to that object without removing the original file from its original location on the disk.

SIMM Stands for "single in-line memory module." A device, designed to plug into your computer's *system board*, that holds *memory* chips.

slot See *expansion slot.*

software Computer programs. Compare *hardware.*

sound card An *expansion board* that increases the sound capabilities of your computer. Used with games, educational software, multimedia CDs, and music applications.

spreadsheet A type of *application program* designed for working with numbers. A spreadsheet's *interface* is patterned after an accountant's worksheet, with the data arranged in rows and columns.

Start button In *Windows,* a button on the left side of the *taskbar* that when clicked on, opens the *Start menu.*

Start menu In *Windows,* a menu on the *taskbar* that lets you start programs, open files, get help, and carry out other useful tasks.

startup disk A floppy disk that holds the DOS or Windows *boot files* so that it can be used to start the computer if the *hard disk* isn't functioning properly.

Startup menu A menu that appears during the PC's startup process if there is a problem loading *Windows.*

status bar A section of a *window* that includes information about its contents.

storage Where you keep files not currently in use. It usually refers to a computer's *hard disk.* Compare *memory.*

submenu In *cascading menus,* a *menu* that appears when you click on a main menu command.

subnotebook PC A particularly small *notebook PC,* usually weighing four pounds or less.

suite A set of several software applications sold as a unit.

surge protector A device that protects a computer from electrical surges. (The computer plugs into the surge protector, which plugs into an electrical wall outlet.)

SVGA Stands for "Super VGA." A graphics standard that supplies *resolutions* from 640-by-480 pixels to 1,024-by-768 pixels to a *monitor.*

system board The main board in the computer's *system unit* that holds the *central processing unit, memory,* and other circuitry. Also known as a *motherboard.*

system icon An *icon* at the top left corner of every window that, when clicked, displays the *system menu.*

system menu A *menu* that appears when you click on the *system icon* in any window, letting you close, resize, or move the window.

system requirements The *hardware* configuration required to run a piece of software. You should always check an application's system requirements before you buy it to make sure your computer can run it.

system unit The box on a desktop PC that holds the computer's workings, including the *system board* and *disk drives.*

T

tab In dialog boxes within *Windows* and Windows applications, a label that marks a "page" of options in the *dialog box.*

taskbar A bar that extends across the bottom of the *Windows desktop*, providing access to the *Start menu*, the system clock, and *program buttons.*

TCP/IP The *communication protocol* used for the *Internet.*

terabyte A trillion *bytes.*

text box In *Windows*, a box into which you type information.

text editor A simple word processor that creates files in *ASCII format.*

TFT Stands for "thin film transistor," another term used to describe an *active matrix screen.*

thread In a *newsgroup*, a group of messages responding to the same original posting.

tiling A method of arranging windows on your *desktop* in which the windows are placed border-to-border so that no part of any window is hidden.

title bar The bar that extends across the top of every window, holding the window's name plus the minimize, maximize, and close icons.

toggle A control that is either "on" or "off." In *menus*, toggle commands usually have a checkmark or bullet next to them if they are "on," and none if they are "off."

toolbar In *Windows* and Windows programs, a bar of buttons that extends across the top of a window. Each button on the toolbar activates a common command.

ToolTip A box that sometimes appears when you hold the *pointer* over an onscreen object, such as a button in a *toolbar,* that names the object you're pointing at.

top-level domain The part of a *domain name* that describes the type of organization the domain name belongs to. Common top-level domains are .com for commercial, .edu for educational, and .gov for government.

touchpad A *pointing device* used on many *notebook PCs.* You move the *pointer* onscreen by moving your finger over the touchpad.

trackball A device, consisting of a rotating ball embedded in a base, that can be used instead of a *mouse.*

TrueType A *font* format used by *Windows.* See also *PostScript.*

U

Unix A type of *operating system.*

URL Stands for "universal resource locator," a string of characters that identifies a file on the *Internet.*

USB Stands for "universal serial bus," a *hardware interface* used to connect *peripherals* to a PC.

user group A group of computer users who band together to offer each other help with computer problems and other computer-related services.

utility A piece of software designed to manage the computer itself, providing functions such as checking for *viruses* or backing up a *hard disk.*

V

vector graphics See *object-based graphics.*

V.90 A *communication protocol* used to control communications between 56K *modems.*

vertical refresh rate The number of times per second that a *monitor's* screen is redrawn from top to bottom, measured in Hertz (Hz). The higher the number, the less flicker on screen.

VGA Stands for "Virtual Graphics Array." A graphics standard that offers 640-by-480-pixel color resolution.

virus Software designed to cause damage to computers or files. Viruses generally enter your computer system via files you receive on floppy disks or over networks.

VRAM Stands for "video random access memory," a bank of memory on a *display adapter* that provides a place for the board to process graphics information.

W X Y Z

Web See *World Wide Web.*

Web browser See browser.

window A frame on the computer's screen that contains a file, an application, or a group of icons.

Windows See *Microsoft Windows.*

Windows 3.1 The first widely adopted version of *Microsoft Windows.*

Windows 95 A version of *Microsoft Windows* released in 1995.

Windows 98 A version of *Microsoft Windows* released in 1998.

Windows CE A version of *Microsoft Windows* designed for *hand-held PCs.*

Windows NT A version of *Microsoft Windows* designed for networked PCs.

Wintel A short form of "Windows" and "Intel," the two technologies that define PC-compatible computers.

Wizard A software tool, used in Windows, that leads you through a complicated process.

word processing software A type of *application program* that enables users to write, edit, and format text and, often, incorporate graphics.

workstation Another word for *personal computer.* Usually it refers to especially powerful PCs.

World Wide Web An *Internet* service that lets publishers post multimedia content. Users view the content and navigate through the Web using a *browser.*

wrist rest A soft pad that sits in front of a *keyboard* to support your wrists as you type to guard against wrist injuries associated with extensive keyboard use.

write-protecting Using a device on a floppy disk to ensure that nothing can be saved to the disk.

WYSIWYG Pronounced "wizzy-wig." Stands for "what you see is what you get." Used to refer to programs that can display a document on screen exactly as it will be printed.

Index

Nascar Racing 2 (Sierra/Cendant Software), 308
NEC, 42
   technical support number, 19
NetNanny (NetNanny Software), 318–19
Netscape
   Communicator, 212
   Navigator, 212
   Netcenter, 216
Network Associates
   First Aid, 195, 302
   ViruScan, 303
networking, 12
networking cards, 62, 82
Network Neighborhood icon, 116
New command, 150, 166
newsgroups, 230–35
   etiquette, 234–35
   finding, 232
   names, 233
   reading, 234
   replying to, 234
   threads, 234
newsletters, 22, 267
New Unger's Talking Bible (Parsons
      Technology), 334
Norton Anti-Virus (Symantec), 301, 303
Norton Uninstall (Symantec), 301
Norton Utilities (Symantec), 195, 301, 302
notebook PCs, 30
   batteries for, 39
   buying, 36–40
   keyboards, 37, 38
   vs. desktop PCs, 36–38
Notepad, 265
numeric keypad, 71, 72
NumLock (Number Lock) key, 71

O

Office (Microsoft), 257–59
Oil Change (CyberMedia), 304
Olympus, 93
online services, 205
   See also specific services; Internet
Online Services icon, 117
Open command, 124, 125
opening,
   files, 150–51, 152–53
   folders, 128
   programs, 147–49
   Recycle Bin, 186
operating systems, 11–15
   vs. application software, 245
   See also specific operating systems; Microsoft Windows
option buttons, 125
Organizer (Lotus Development), 275
Origin Systems/Electronic Arts, 305
   Ultima Online, 309
   Wing Commander series, 308
OS/2, 15
Outlook Express (Microsoft)
   address book, 229

as personal information manager, 274
for e-mail, 222–29
for newsgroups, 230–35
icon, 116
Inbox, 226
New Message window, 225–27
starting, 223
Outlook (Microsoft), 257, 259, 274–75

P

Packard Bell, 42
   technical support number, 19
page layout software, 267
PageMaker (Adobe), 267
Page Plus (SPC/Serif Software), 267
Paint, 289
painting programs, 289–91
   features to look for, 290
   scorecard, 289
   See also specific programs
Paint Shop Pro (Jasc), 289
Pajama Sam 2: Thunder and Lightning Aren't
      So Frightening (Humongous), 324
palmtop computers, See hand-held computers
Panasonic, 88
PaperPort Strobe (Visioneer), 90
parallel ports, 61, 100
Parsons Technology, 254
   New Unger's Talking Bible, 334
passive matrix screens, 38
pasting. See cutting and pasting
paths, 129, 131
Pause/Break key, 71
PC Brand, 33
PC cards, 39
PC Connection, 254
PCI slots, 62
PCL (Printer Control Language), 80
PC Magazine, 22
PC slots, 39
PC Warehouse, 254
PC Zone, 254
Pentium processor, 9, 45–47, 48
Pentium II processor, 45–46
peripherals, 61
   connecting, 61–63, 98, 100, 102–3
   See also specific types
personal information managers (PIMs)
   contact management software, 276
   features to look for, 277
   scorecard, 274
   structured, 274–75
   unstructured, 276–77
Persuasion (Adobe), 282
PhotoDeluxe (Adobe), 289, 291
photographs
   editing, 92
   printing, 85
   scanning, 89
   taking, with digital cameras, 92
Photoshop (Adobe), 289, 291

StreetFinder Deluxe (Rand McNally), 334
subnotebook PCs, 39
subscribing
    to channels, 237–38
    to newsgroups, 235
    to websites, 221
Sun Microsystems, 9
SurfWatch (SurfWatch Software), 318–19
surge protectors, 94–95, 101
SVGAs, 65–66
Symantec
    ACT, 274, 276
    Norton Anti-Virus, 301, 303
    Norton Uninstall, 301
    Norton Utilities, 195, 301, 302
    technical support number, 19
Syquest SparQ drive, 60
system board, 45, 62
system clock, 188
system date/time, changing, 188–89
system icon, 137
system menu, 137
system requirements, 17, 252
System Tools program group, 301
System Tray, 143, 165

T

tape drives, 60
taskbar, 141–43
    Auto Hide, 180
    moving, 181
    Program buttons, 139, 142–43, 147
    resizing, 181
    speaker icon, 143, 165
    Task Scheduler, 143
    See also Start menu
TaxCut (Block Financial Software), 281
tax preparation software, 280–81
    See also specific programs
technical support, 18–20
    numbers, 19
    PC purchase and, 33, 41, 44
text boxes, 125
text files, 153
TFT screens, 38
Thinkin' Things Sky Island Mysteries (Edmark), 322
time
    changing, 188
    daylight savings, 188
    zones, 188
title bar, 137, 138–39
.TMP files, 194
toolbars, 126–27, 137
    in taskbar, 179–80
    Quick Launch, 141–42
    showing/hiding, 127
ToolTips, 126, 127, 145
Toshiba America, 39, 42
    technical support number, 19
    website, 33

Total Annihilation (Cavedog), 311
touchpads, 40
trackballs, 67
TripMaker (Rand McNally), 333–34
troubleshooting, 192–95
    beeping, 112, 126, 192
    disk problems, 189
    file mess ups, 193–94
    frozen computer, 192, 196
    no disk space, 194
    nothing happens, 111
    sluggishness, 194–95
    startup, 111–12
TrueType fonts, 265
TurboTax (Intuit), 281
TV tuner, 161, 162

U

Ultima Online (Origin/Electronic Arts), 309
Undo command, 158, 193
uninstalling programs, 187, 261–62
Unix, 15
update utilities, 304
updating Windows, 190–91
URLs, 219, 220
USA Flex website, 33
USB ports, 63, 93, 100, 101
used computers, 34–35
user groups, 20–21
Users Control Panel, 179
utility software, 300–4
    antivirus software, 300
    backup utilities, 300
    categories of, 300
    general utilities, 300
    in Windows, 301–2
    scorecard, 301
    uninstall utilities, 300, 302–3
    update utilities, 304
    See also specific programs

V

V.90 protocol, 78
Ventura (Corel), 267
versions
    software, 256
    Windows, 11–14
vertical refresh rate, 67
VGA monitors, 65
video
    cards, 61
    formats, 163
    viewing, 162–63
viewing
    disk drive contents, 129
    DVDs, 161–62
    file extensions, 153
    lists of folders/files, 134–35
    toolbars, 127
    video clips, 162–63

View menu
    As Web Page command, 129
    Folder Options command, 140, 153
    Large Icons command, 129
    Toolbar command, 127
ViruScan (Network Associates), 303
viruses, 300, 303–4
Visioneer PaperPort Strobe, 90
Visio Technical (Visio Technologies), 286
Visio Technologies
    Visio, 286
    Visio Technical, 286
Visio (Visio Technologies), 286
volume control, 143, 165
VRAM, 65
    See also memory

W
wallpaper, 177
.WAV files, 162–63
Web TV for Windows, 162
Where Is Carmen Sandiego series
    (Broderbund), 326–27
Windows. See Microsoft Windows
windows, 136–40
    arranging, 138
    cascading, 138
    child, 151
    closing, 126, 137
    controls, 137
    folder, 136, 137
    maximizing, 137
    minimizing, 137
    moving, 138
    sizing, 137
    switching between, 138–39, 143
    tiling, 138
Windows 3.1, 12
    See also Microsoft Windows
Windows 95, 12
    Plus Pack, 176
    See also Microsoft Windows
Windows 98, 11, 12
    default settings, 140
    differences from Windows 95, 14
    Internet features, 14
    upgrading to, 14
    See also Microsoft Windows
Windows CE, 14
    See also Microsoft Windows
Windows Draw (Micrografx), 286
Windows for Workgroups, 13
    See also Microsoft Windows
Windows installation CD, 247
Windows key, 70
Windows magazine, 22
Windows Maintenance Wizard, 195, 301
Windows menu, 151
Windows NT, 12
    See also Microsoft Windows

Windows registry, 261
Windows Startup Menu, 112
Windows Tour, 115
Windows Update, 190–91
Wing Commander series (Origin/Electronic
    Arts), 308
Wizards, 146
    Backup, 172
    Internet Connection, 224, 231
    Multiuser Settings, 179
    Windows Maintenance, 195, 301
Wofenstein (id Software), 314
Word (Microsoft), 257, 258, 259, 264, 265–66
WordPad, 264–65
WordPerfect for Windows (Corel), 264, 266, 267
WordPerfect Suite (Corel), 258
Word Pro (Lotus Development), 264, 266, 267
word processing software, 263–66
    features to look for, 268–69
    scorecard, 264
    See also specific applications
workplace setup, 104–5
Works (Microsoft), 259, 264, 265–66, 270,
    272, 299
workstations, 9
World Wide Web, 209–22
    addresses (URLs), 219, 220
    browser software, 209
    buying hardware on, 32–34
    buying software on, 254–55
    hyperlinks, 212–13
    sampler, 214–15
    See also Internet
wrist rests, 73, 95

X
X2 protocol, 78
Xerox printers, 88

Y
Yahoo, 216, 217
Yahooligans, 216
You Don't Know Jack (Berkeley Systems), 313

Z
Zap (Edmark), 322
Zip drive (Iomega), 59–60, 129
    for backups, 172